J. PETER BRUZZESE
RONALD BARRETT
WAYNE DIPCHAN

SO-BEH-743

# Windows Server® 2008

## HOW-TO

SAMS | 800 East 96th Street, Indianapolis, Indiana 46240 USA

**Windows Server® 2008 How-To**

Copyright © 2010 by Pearson Education, Inc.

ISBN-13: 978-0-672-33075-9

ISBN-10: 0-672-33075-X

Library of Congress Cataloging-in-Publication Data

Bruzzese, J. Peter.
  Windows server 2008 how-to / J. Peter Bruzzese, Ronald Barrett, Wayne Dipchan.
     p. cm.
  ISBN 978-0-672-33075-9
  1. Microsoft Windows server. 2. Operating systems (Computers) I. Barrett, Ronald. II. Dipchan, Wayne. III. Title.
  QA76.76.063B786 2009
  005.4'476—dc22

                                    2009018967

Printed in the United States of America

First Printing July 2009

**Trademarks**

**Warning and Disclaimer**

**Bulk Sales**

Sams Publishing offers excellent discounts on this book when ordered in quantity for bulk purchases or special sales. For more information, please contact

　**U.S. Corporate and Government Sales**

　**1-800-382-3419**

　corpsales@pearsontechgroup.com

For sales outside of the U.S., please contact

　**International Sales**

　international@pearson.com

**Editor-in-Chief**
Karen Gettman

**Executive Editor**
Neil Rowe

**Development Editor**
Mark Renfrow

**Managing Editor**
Kristy Hart

**Project Editor**
Betsy Harris

**Copy Editor**
Kitty Wilson

**Indexer**
Lisa Stumpf

**Proofreader**
Kathy Ruiz

**Technical Editor**
Diane McSorley

**Publishing Coordinator**
Cindy Teeters

**Book Designer**
Gary Adair

**Compositor**
Nonie Ratcliff

# Contents at a Glance

# Table of Contents

# About the Authors

**J. Peter Bruzzese** is an independent consultant and trainer for a variety of clients, including CBT Nuggets (the Exchange 2007 Video Series) and New Horizons. Over the past decade, Peter has worked with Goldman Sachs, CommVault Systems, and Microsoft, to name a few. His focus has been, and continues to be, corporate support and training. For the past 10 years he has specialized in Active Directory and Exchange support and education, as well as certification training, and he holds the following certifications: MCSA 2000/2003, MCSE NT/2000/2003, MCITP: Messaging with Exchange 2007, and MCT from Microsoft; can from Novell; CCNA from Cisco; CIW Master and CIW Certified Instructor from CIW; and A+, Network+, and iNET+ from CompTIA.

Peter enjoys taking complex technical topics, like Server 2008, and breaking them down so they're easy to understand and enjoyable to learn. This has led to the formation of his company ClipTraining; at the company website, www.cliptraining.com, you can watch a variety of mini-training clips designed to assist others in learning. Peter believes that short training sessions in a familiar environment yield great results.

Peter is also a contributor to *Redmond* magazine, *Windows IT Pro* magazine, and several tech sites. He is a speaker for the TechMentor conferences, Microsoft TechEd conferences, the IT360 tech conferences in Canada, and the TEC conference, offering sessions that revolve mostly around Exchange. Last but certainly not least, he writes the Enterprise Windows blog for InfoWorld.

You can catch up with Peter at jpb@cliptraining.com.

**Ron Barrett** is the founder of RARE-TECH, an IT training and consulting company. He has been a technology professional for more than a decade, working for several major financial firms and dot-coms. Ron is a specialist in network infrastructure, security, and IT management. He is coauthor of *The Administrator's Guide to Microsoft Office 2007 Servers* and *How to Cheat at Administering Office Communications Server 2007,* and he has contributed to several other books on Windows administration. Along with book writing, Ron has contributed to several industry magazines, such as *Redmond* and *Windows IT Pro*, and he was featured in the book *Tricks of the Windows Vista Masters*. He has worked for Microsoft, writing research and analysis papers on Windows Server 2008, Windows HPC, and PerformancePoint Server 2007. In addition to writing, Ron has spoken at several technology conferences for CPAmerica and the AICPA, as well as TechMentor.

Be sure to catch Ron's daily blog on *Network World*'s Microsoft subnet, at www.networkworld.com/community/barrett.

**Wayne Dipchan** has been working with IT for the past 12 years and holds MCSE, MCDBA, and MCT certifications. His experience has allowed him to work in diverse business sectors. Starting out his career as an IT trainer, Wayne has had opportunity to work with New Horizons and Alpha Technologies, as well as coauthor an exam prep book on directory service design. He has also had opportunity to engineer, deploy, and support IT infrastructures for multiple small to medium-size businesses, ranging from construction to catering to manufacturing. In addition, Wayne has worked with health care systems such as Staten Island University Hospital and with financial companies such as Barclays Capital. He is the owner of AriLex Technologies LLC, a company focused on IT support and training. Wayne is currently employed with St. Peters University Hospital and involved with the design and deployment of multiple health information solutions.

You can reach Wayne at wdipchan@arilextech.com.

# Dedication

*For my father, Jerry Joseph Bruzzese. The one to whom I owe my love for life, music, travel, and people...along with a great many other things both physical and spiritual.*

*—J. Peter Bruzzese*


*To my wife, Alicia, and my children, Ronald and Emma. As the song goes, "Dream on, Dreamer, nothing comes easy...." But you certainly make it easier. All my love and thanks for your patience and support.*

*—Ronald Barrett*


*I would like to dedicate this book to my loving family, my wife, Davora, whose support in my career and every other part of my life has enabled me to accomplish my goals. And to my two daughters, Ariana and Alexandria, who keep me focused on my future goals so that I will be able to support them in all their endeavors.*

*—Wayne Dipchan*

# Acknowledgments

First and foremost, I'd like to thank Loretta Yates and Neil Rowe. They have shown a tremendous amount of confidence in me as a technical author. This has led to the creation of many different educational products, including the book you are holding, and I appreciate very much the trust they place in my hands each time they give me a green light to go forth and create.

I'd like to thank my coauthors Ron Barrett and Wayne Dipchan. I've had the privilege of working with each of you separately over the years. I'm pleased we had the chance to combine our efforts together on this book. The diversity of skill and experience will no doubt make this book of a higher quality, and for that I thank you both.

I would also like to thank those I work with, including Galen Gruman and Ted Samson at InfoWorld; Stonna Edelman and Laurie Wells at Realtime; Doug Barney and Lee Pender at *Redmond* magazine; and Amy Eisenberg, Sheila Molnar, and Brian Winstead at *Windows IT Pro* magazine.

Others I work with in the technical field and conference circuit who have been good friends and coworkers include David Solomon, Alan Wright, Greg Shields, Don Jones, Mark Minasi, Rhonda Layfield, Derek Melber, James Conrad, and last but not least Jeremy Moskowitz.

I would like to thank Alienware and especially Kathryn Diana for assisting me with a multitude of Alienware systems over the past few years, for both conference and writing engagements. Thanks to the M17 Alienware laptop (which miraculously runs Hyper-V), we were able to fully explore every aspect of Windows Server 2008. Alienware, I feel, makes the finest laptops I've ever worked on.

On a personal level, I want to thank my wife, Jennette, who knows when to pull me out of my office to remember what real life is all about. And my son, Lucas, who adds new facets to that real life each and every day. I would also like to thank my family and friends for their continued love and support. Thanks also to my business partner and friend, Tim Duggan. Thanks also to our sales manager, John. And to our dear friends at FlightSafety, Ram Singh, Marty Vitkovsky, and Moe Hoskins, who have been early adapters of our ClipTraining Library, as well as enthusiastic supporters.

**—J. Peter Bruzzese**

I would like to thank my coauthors. J. Peter Bruzzese has been a great friend and mentor in my writing career, gave me my first shot, and has been there along the way; thanks, Pete. I would also like to thank Wayne Dipchan, who is also a good friend and respected colleague. It has been a long time coming, and I am glad to have been able to collaborate with both of these talented gentlemen on this book. I would also like to thank Neil and everyone else at Sams for their support on this project. To my mom, thanks for all the talent; as you say, "It did not come from my father's side." Finally, thanks to Julie, my editor at *Network World*, for supporting me and being incredibly patient while waiting for me to complete this book.

**—Ronald Barrett**


I would first like to acknowledge Peter and Ron, the coauthors of this book. They have made this project a very positive experience. The collaboration between us has helped motivate me to keep trying to improve. I would also like to thank the team at St. Peters University Hospital, specifically Ramon Collante, Dave Draghi, Fernando Navarro, William Rears, and Frank Disanzo, for the support they gave me during this project. I could not end without mentioning some of the individuals who have contributed to my experience and knowledge as an IT professional, such as Anthony Dipchan, Jason Eberly, Anthony Galletta, Karol Kosiec, Greg Mazza, Tom Kelly, Micheal Wittig, Micheal Botticelli, Sudar Alagiya, and Ujjval Vyas; all of them have in some way contributed to the knowledge found in this book.

**—Wayne Dipchan**


As a collective group, the three authors would like to thank the following persons for their work on the book: our executive editor, Neil Rowe; project editor, Betsy Harris; development editor, Mark Renfrow; technical editor, Diane McSorley; copy editor, Kitty Wilson; proofreader, Kathy Ruiz; indexer, Lisa Stumpf; compositor, Nonie Ratcliff; and cover designer, Gary Adair.

# We Want to Hear from You!

As the reader of this book, *you* are our most important critic and commentator. We value your opinion and want to know what we're doing right, what we could do better, what areas you'd like to see us publish in, and any other words of wisdom you're willing to pass our way.

You can email or write me directly to let me know what you did or didn't like about this book—as well as what we can do to make our books stronger.

*Please note that I cannot help you with technical problems related to the topic of this book, and that due to the high volume of mail I receive, I might not be able to reply to every message.*

When you write, please be sure to include this book's title and author as well as your name and phone or email address. I will carefully review your comments and share them with the author and editors who worked on the book.

E-mail:     feedback@samspublishing.com

Mail:       Neil Rowe
            Executive Editor
            Sams Publishing
            800 East 96th Street
            Indianapolis, IN 46240 USA

# Reader Services

Visit our website and register this book at informit.com/register for convenient access to any updates, downloads, or errata that might be available for this book.

# Introduction: Using *Windows Server 2008 How-To*

# How to Educate Yourself About Windows Server 2008

Whenever you pick up a book that catches your eye, flip to an article that draws your interest, or research and locate a site or blog that strikes you, you are attempting to educate yourself in some way. Perhaps it is a subject you already know and, due to your preexisting knowledge, maybe you can extract the information you need much faster and easier than could a novice.

The motivation behind education varies from person to person. Some simply love to learn, to enhance their own knowledge of a subject even if they never intend to employ that knowledge in the working world. Some, on the other hand, are required to learn in order to perform their job. For example, a messaging engineer, much like a physician, must keep up with the latest practices and techniques in order to stay on top of his or her profession.

You might note that many books on the subject of Windows Server 2008 range up to 800, 900, or even 1,500 pages! And for some, that is just the kind of book needed to accomplish their messaging goals. However, this how-to book is designed to give an administrator what is needed to understand the concepts involved in managing an environment utilizing Windows Server 2008 and perform the tasks needed.

There are many ways to educate yourself about Windows Server 2008—through books, articles, websites, and so on—but for on-the-job, in-the-trenches, step-by-step information, look no further!

# How to Benefit from This Book

We've designed this book to be easy to read from cover to cover, in case your goal is to gain a full understanding of Windows Server 2008, while breaking down the subject matter into 12 easy-to-use chapters:

- ▶ Chapter 1, "Perform the Installation"
- ▶ Chapter 2, "Configure and Manage Server Core"
- ▶ Chapter 3, "Work with Server Manager"
- ▶ Chapter 4, "Manage Windows Server 2008"
- ▶ Chapter 5, "Install and Configure Specific Server Roles"
- ▶ Chapter 6, "Work with IIS 7.0"
- ▶ Chapter 7, "Implement and Utilize Hyper-V"
- ▶ Chapter 8, "Install and Configure Terminal Services"
- ▶ Chapter 9, "Understand and Manage Active Directory"

▶ Chapter 10, "Utilize Group Policy"

▶ Chapter 11, "Configure Security"

▶ Chapter 12, "Monitor Performance and Troubleshoot"

Within each of these chapters are sections that focus on the primary elements required to deploy Windows Server 2008 in a number of different scenarios. Perhaps you need a Server Core system that reduces attack surface or can be used for a Hyper-V solution. Maybe you want to work with Terminal Services to allow multiple clients access to an easy-to-manage location. Maybe you need a web server for your company or an entire Active Directory domain to handle logins and permissions combined with Group Policy. Whatever your needs, we will walk you through it.

Beneath each major heading in a chapter is a "Scenario/Problem" introduction. Each one serves as a starting point to consider. At times, the information provided helps you deal with a specific problem that you may be facing. However, typically a scenario is described that allows you to determine whether this is the direction needed for your particular situation or organization.

The "Solution" portion that follows "Scenario/Problem" may include additional information regarding a particular technology or design elements to consider. The text then provides more information, such as step-by-step instructions, so that you have more than just commands: You have the underlying reasons for the instructions given.

When additional information is needed regarding a subject and it doesn't fit neatly within the subject matter itself, or when it is essential that the message stand out a bit to catch your notice, we use a note.

**NOTE** This is an example of a note.

When lines of code are too long for the printed page, a code-continuation arrow (➡) has been used to indicate a manual break. For example:

```
start /w pkgmgr /iu:IIS-WebServerRole;WAS-WindowsActivationService;
➡WAS-ProcessModel;WAS-NetFxEnvironment;WAS-ConfigurationAPI
```

Perhaps the most important aspect of this book is that it provides step-by-step instructions that walk you through each and every step of the wizards and dialog boxes provided by Windows Server 2008. Along with clear instructions on managing and configuring your Windows Server 2008 environment, we provide clear figures and screenshots of only the most important elements you face visually while working with your servers.

## How to Continue Expanding Your Knowledge

Certainly there are more books, articles, and sites you can and should consider in expanding your knowledge of Windows Server 2008, especially as the software will no doubt continue to evolve and change as Microsoft adds more and more features, fixes, and enhancements. How do you stay on top of the flood of information regarding a subject as big as Windows Server 2008?

Several sites are invaluable and should be added to your Favorites at work. They include the following:

▶ **Microsoft TechNet, the Windows Server 2008 TechCenter:** http://technet. microsoft.com/en-us/windowsserver/2008/default.aspx. This continuously updated site is the official location of all things Windows Server 2008.

In addition, you might want to monitor the following blogs written by the Microsoft folks:

▶ **Windows Server Team:** http://blogs.technet.com/WindowsServer/

▶ **Terminal Services Team:** http://blogs.msdn.com/rds/

▶ **Windows Virtualization Team:** http://blogs.technet.com/virtualization/ default.aspx

▶ **System Center Team:** http://blogs.technet.com/systemcenter/

▶ **IIS Team:** www.iis.net

In addition to these Microsoft blogs, there are a couple other sites that we enjoy:

▶ **Greg Shields's coverage of the Microsoft Server world:** www.realtime-windowsserver.com

▶ **J. Peter Bruzzese's InfoWorld column:** http://www.infoworld.com/blogs/ j-peter-bruzzese

▶ **Ron Barrett's column for Network World:** www.networkworld.com/ community/barrett

These are just a handful of the sites we personally enjoy, and you will easily find many more. Choose the ones you feel are most helpful to you.

# CHAPTER 1

# Perform the Installation

# Determine Your Hardware Requirements for Windows Server 2008

**Scenario/Problem:** For any operating system (OS), hardware must meet minimum requirements in order to run the OS, and in a production environment, your hardware needs to meet at least the optimal requirements. You need to assess whether the hardware your organization owns will meet or—better yet— exceed the minimum requirements for the Windows Server 2008 OS.

**Solution:** Determine what the minimum, recommended, and optimal requirements are for Windows Server 2008 and compare your findings with your hardware.

When determining whether you have the hardware requirements needed to install and run an OS, you need to focus on three hardware resources:

▶ Memory:

**Minimum:** 512MB

**Recommended:** 1GB

**Optimal:** 2GB

▶ Processor:

**Minimum:** 1Ghz

**Recommended:** 2Ghz

**Optimal:** 3Ghz

▶ Disk space needed for system partition:

**Minimum:** 10GB

**Recommended:** 40GB

**Optimal:** 80GB

**NOTE** The recommendations take into consideration only what is needed to run the OS. You need to also determine whether any applications are going to run on the server and include any resources requirements for those applications.

**NOTE** Keep in mind that if you increase your memory above 16GB, you will need to increase your disk space requirements to accommodate for the pagefile (if kept on a system partition), hibernation, and the dump file.

**NOTE** You can use a tool called the Microsoft Assessment and Planning Toolkit (MAP) to inventory your servers and generate a report to help determine which servers will work for your Windows Server 2008 installations. At the time of this writing, the tool is located at http://technet.microsoft.com/en-us/library/bb977556.aspx.

# Perform Other Pre-Installation Tasks

**Scenario/Problem:** When you know that your server memory, processor, and disk space meet the requirements for Windows Server 2008, you need to perform some other recommended tasks before you actually install the Windows Server 2008 OS. What are these other tasks?

**Solution:** The following is a list of the tasks that should be performed before the actual installation.

- ▶ Check application compatibility
- ▶ Disconnect the uninterruptible power supply (UPS)
- ▶ Run the Windows Memory Diagnostic tool
- ▶ Identify mass storage device drivers
- ▶ Back up servers
- ▶ Disable virus protection software
- ▶ Prepare Active Directory

Some or all of these tasks are recommended, depending on the path of installation and whether this is a new installation or an upgrade from an existing OS; in addition, you need to perform the Active Directory prep only if you are going to promote your Windows Server 2008 machine to a domain controller and add it to an existing Windows 2000/2003 domain.

Now let's take a closer look at each of these tasks.

## Check Application Compatibility

Before you install Windows Server 2008, you must be sure that any third-party applications you plan to run on the server will be supported. One way you can do this is to contact the application vendor and get documentation on whether the application will run on Windows Server 2008. In a real-world environment, the documentation is very important because if things do not work as expected, you *may* be able to save your job by providing the documentation. (Obviously, you would have tested the application on a development server first.)

Another tool that you can use is the Microsoft Application Compatibility Toolkit 5.0 (ACT 5.0). This tool can be used to collect compatibility data about your environment into a centralized data store. Having this information can be essential when evaluating the risk involved with an OS upgrade.

**NOTE** ACT 5.0 can also be used for lower-impact changes to your platform, such as a browser upgrade or a Windows Update release. Check the following site for more details: http://technet.microsoft.com/en-us/library/cc507852.aspx.

## Disconnect the UPS

During the installation process, Windows Server 2008 attempts to detect devices attached to serial ports. If you have a UPS connected to a serial port, you may run into issues with the installation, so be sure to disconnect it until the installation is complete.

## Run the Windows Memory Diagnostic Tool

You can use the Windows Memory Diagnostic tool to test the random access memory (RAM) on your server. At the time of this writing, you can download this tool and a guide from http://oca.microsoft.com/en/windiag.asp. After you download the tool, you can perform the following steps:

1. Run the downloaded file `mtinst.exe` to start the setup for the Windows Memory Diagnostic tool.

2. Choose Create Startup Disk to install Windows Memory Diagnostic onto a floppy disk or choose Save CD Image to Disk to use a CD-ROM to which you can boot the server.

3. Reboot the server to the disk you just created.

4. The server will boot to the Windows Memory Diagnostic tool interface and automatically start the first test. It will continue to run tests with the same settings until you exit or pause.

**NOTE** To run a more thorough test on the memory, you can choose to run the extended test suite by pressing T while the Windows Memory Diagnostic tool is running. If you do this, it would be best to leave the tool to run overnight.

## Identify Mass Storage Device Drivers

If a vendor has supplied a driver file for your storage device, now would be a good time to have that file stored on a floppy, a CD, a DVD, or a flash drive. You should store files either in the root directory or in a folder named according to the processor architecture. During the installation, you will have the opportunity to load this driver.

## Back Up Servers

Backing up servers is standard procedure when making any platform changes. Make sure you have a good backup of any critical data. When performing an OS upgrade, it is a good idea to make sure you have a backup of the boot and system partitions as well as the system state data. An alternative way to back up this configuration data is to create a backup set for Automated System Recovery (ASR).

> **NOTE** You should consider this recommendation if you are planning to upgrade an existing OS.

## Disable Virus Protection Software

Virus protection software can affect the speed of your upgrade. Every file that is copied to your server will need to be scanned.

> **NOTE** You should consider this recommendation if you are planning to upgrade an existing OS.

## Prepare Active Directory

There are two steps in preparing the Active Directory service for a new Windows Server 2008 domain controller:

- ▶ Prepare the forest.
- ▶ Prepare the domain.

> **NOTE** You need to prepare Active Directory only if you are going to build a Windows Server 2008 domain controller that will be joined to an existing Windows 2000/2003 domain.

Let's first go through the steps to prepare the forest:

1. Log on to the Schema Master of your existing domain with an account that is a member of either the Enterprise Administrators, Schema Administrators, or Domain Administrators group.

2. Copy the adprep directory from the sources\adprep on the Windows Server 2008 installation CD to the schema master.

3. From a command prompt, navigate to the adprep folder you just copied. Then run adprep/forestprep.

4. For a read-only domain controller (RODC), run adprep/rodcprep.

5. Wait for the task to complete and replicate prior to running the second portion of the ADS preparation.

When you have waited for the changes to replicate, you can follow these steps to prepare the domain:

1. Log on to the infrastructure master of your existing domain with an account that is a member of the Domain Administrators group.

2. Copy the adprep directory from sources\adprep on the Windows Server 2008 installation CD to the infrastructure master.

3. From a command prompt, navigate to the adprep folder you just copied and then run adprep\domainprep\gpprep.

4. Wait for the task to complete and replicate.

Now that you have completed some or all of the pre-installation tasks, you can start with the installation of Windows Server 2008. But first you must decide which edition of Windows Server 2008 you need for your environment.

# Decide What Edition of Windows Server 2008 to Install

**Scenario/Problem:** Many different editions of Windows Server 2008 are available. The various editions allow support on x86, x64, and Itanium processors and also allow for native high availability, load balancing, and virtualization. You need to review all the various editions and decide which one best fits your organization's needs.

**Solution:** You need to take a close look at each of the available editions of Windows Server 2008 and evaluate them in terms of your organization's infrastructure goals.

The available editions are as follows:

▶ Windows Web Server 2008

▶ Windows Server 2008 Standard

▶ Windows Server 2008 Standard without Hyper-V

▶ Windows Server 2008 Enterprise

▶ Windows Server 2008 Enterprise without Hyper-V

▶ Windows Server 2008 Datacenter

▶ Windows Server 2008 Datacenter without Hyper-V

▶ Windows HPC Server 2008

▶ Windows Server 2008 for Itanium-Based Systems

> **NOTE** This chapter does not include descriptions of Windows Server 2008 Standard, Enterprise, and Datacenter without Hyper-V as these are identical to their corresponding counterparts with Hyper-V. However, editions without the Hyper-V role are available.

## Windows Web Server 2008

The title really speaks for itself: This edition is built for a single purpose, as a web server. Windows Web Server 2008 comes with architectural enhancements included within IIS 7.0, ASP.NET, and Microsoft .NET Framework. This edition is used to deploy web pages, web sites, web applications, and web services.

Windows Web Server 2008 supports the following:

- 32GB RAM on 64-bit (4GB on 32-bit)
- Four multicore processors

## Windows Server 2008 Standard

Windows Server 2008 Standard is a robust server OS that includes the following features to improve functionality, security, management, and reduce infrastructure costs:

- Web services
- Hyper-V (hypervisor-based virtualization)
- Terminal Services
- Presentation virtualization
- Application virtualization
- Network Access Protection (NAP)
- BitLocker
- RODCs
- Windows Service Hardening
- Bidirectional Windows Firewall
- Next-generation cryptography support
- Server Manager
- Windows Deployment Services
- Windows PowerShell
- Next-generation TCP/IP
- Server Core

Windows Server 2008 Standard supports the following:

- 32GB RAM on 64-bit (4GB on 32-bit)
- Four multicore processors
- 250 network access service connections (RRAS)
- 50 network policy server connections
- 250 terminal server connections
- Hyper-V virtualization with one free instance

## Windows Server 2008 Enterprise

Windows Server 2008 Enterprise adds high availability, the latest in security, and scalability to the Standard edition. The following are some of its features:

- Failover clustering (up to 16 nodes)
- Fault-tolerant memory synchronization
- Cross-file replication
- Licensing for up to four additional virtual server instances
- Active Directory Federation Services (ADFS)
- Advanced certificate services
- Active Directory Domain Services (ADDS)

Windows Server 2008 Enterprise supports the following:

- Eight processors
- 2TB RAM on 64-bit (64GB RAM on 32-bit)
- Unlimited number of virtual private network (VPN) connections
- Unlimited Network Access Service connections
- Unlimited Network Policy Server connections

## Windows Server 2008 Datacenter

This edition can be used for large-scale virtualization needs and added scalability for mission-critical applications in a large IT infrastructure. The following are some of the features of this edition:

- Large-scale virtualization (Licensing allows you to add an unlimited number of virtual instances.)
- Failover clustering
- Dynamic hardware partitioning
- Windows Server High Availability Program

Windows Server 2008 Datacenter supports the following:

- 2TB RAM on 64-bit(64GB on 32-bit)
- 64 x64 64-bit processors and 32 x86 32-bit processors
- Unlimited virtual image use rights
- Hyper-V based unlimited virtualization use
- 16-node failover clustering
- Hot add/replace memory and processors on supported hardware
- Fault-tolerant memory synchronization
- Cross-file replication (DFS-R)
- Unlimited Network Access Services connections (RRAS)
- Unlimited Network Policy Server connections
- 65,535 terminal server connections
- Advanced identity management

## Windows HPC Server 2008

Used specifically for high-performance computing (HPC), this edition enables you to scale to thousands of processing cores. This is advantageous when you're load balancing heavy workloads across multiple processors and need to manage and monitor your HPC environment for stability and health.

## Windows Server 2008 for Itanium-Based Systems

Windows Server 2008 for Itanium-Based Systems allows you to run Windows Server 2008 on Itanium-based systems. Itanium-based processors have the ability to handle intensive computing needs of business-critical applications in an enterprise-level environment. An Itanium processor uses a whole new architecture, not just extending the 32-bit architecture to 64-bit, and it can thus be called a native 64-bit processor. Another feature of this processor is the Intel Explicitly Parallel Instruction Computing (EPIC) architecture, which improves performance of the processor through instruction-level parallelism, maximizing opportunities to execute instructions in parallel. Up to six instructions can be processed in parallel.

Windows Server 2008 for Itanium-Based Systems supports the following:

- Dynamic hardware partitioning
- Use of Itanium RAS (Reliability, Availability, and Scalability)
- 2TB RAM
- 64 Itanium processors or 64 cores
- Hot add/replace of memory and processors

- ▶ Eight-node failover clustering
- ▶ Fault-tolerant memory synchronization
- ▶ Licensing for unlimited virtual instances with a third-party virtualization product

Now you know what each edition of Windows Server 2008 has to offer. Say that you decide that you need to install the Standard edition. Let's get started with the installation and see what your options are.

# Install Windows Server 2008

**Scenario/Problem:** You have decided to install Windows Server 2008 Standard edition. You need to decide whether you are going to perform a manual installation or an unattended installation. There may be some servers that will need to be upgraded also.

**Solution:** The following sections look at the procedures for doing both a manual installation and an unattended installation. We will also consider what is involved in upgrading to Windows Server 2008 from an existing operating system.

## Manual Installation

The Windows Server 2008 installation procedure has been streamlined. If you are familiar with the Windows 2003 Server installation, you may remember that during the installation, you were prompted to answer configuration questions. With Windows Server 2008, these prompts have been moved to the Initial Configuration Task Wizard, which appears when the installation is complete. The following is the only information you need to provide during the actual installation:

- ▶ Language, currency, and keyboard layout information
- ▶ A valid product key
- ▶ Installation location
- ▶ Which version of the operating system you are going to install (if no product key is entered)
- ▶ Whether you are performing an upgrade or fresh installation

The complete setup for Windows Server 2008 requires only three stages:

- ▶ Operating system setup, including key validation
- ▶ Initial configuration tasks
- ▶ Server Manager setup

## Operating System Setup

Follow these steps to set up the OS:

1. Insert the installation CD and boot the server to the CD.

2. When you are prompted for language, time and currency, and keyboard format information, as shown in Figure 1.1, make the appropriate selections and click Next.

FIGURE 1.1
Configuring language, time and currency, and keyboard information.

3. The Install Now option appears. If you are unsure of what hardware requirements are needed, you can click the link What to Know Before Installing Windows. You can also click the link to perform and repair the OS rather than perform a full installation.

4. Input your product key and check the box Automatically Activate Windows When I'm Online (see Figure 1.2). Click Next.

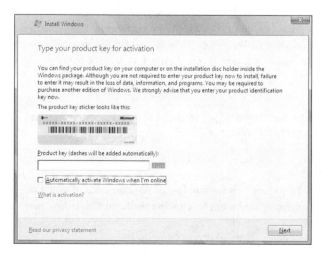

FIGURE 1.2
Providing a valid product key.

5. If you did not enter a product key in the previous window, you now have to choose which edition of Windows Server 2008 you will install and check the box I Have Selected an Edition of Windows That I Purchased (see Figure 1.3). If you did enter a product key, the installation program will be able to identify which edition of Windows Server 2008 you are going to install. Then click Next.

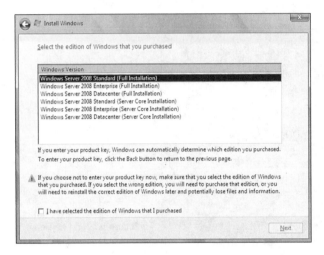

FIGURE 1.3
Selecting the edition of Windows Server 2008 to install.

> **NOTE** Chapter 2, "Configure and Manage Server Core," discusses in detail the installation of Windows Server 2008 Server Core.

6. Read the license terms and accept them by checking the box. Then click Next.

7. In the screen that now appears, you decide whether to perform and upgrade or a custom (advanced) installation of Windows. Because you booted from the installation CD, the Upgrade option is disabled (see Figure 1.4). Click Custom (Advanced).

> **NOTE** If you wanted to perform an upgrade, you would need to execute the installation procedure from within the original Windows OS.

8. On the next screen, decide where you want to install Windows and, if you have any third-party storage drivers, load them by clicking the Load Driver link (see Figure 1.5).

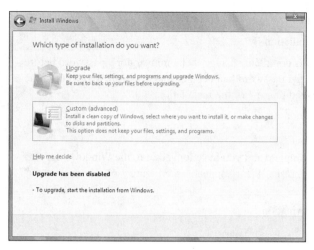

FIGURE 1.4
The Upgrade option is disabled when you boot from the installation CD.

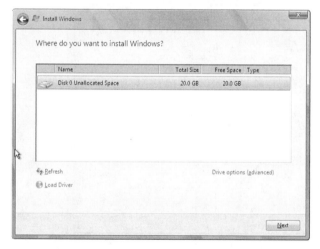

FIGURE 1.5
Loading third-party storage drivers and choosing where to install them.

Now the actual Windows installation takes place. You will see the progress of each step as it completes, by percentage. During the installation, the server will reboot multiple times. The installation will complete the following tasks:

- ▶ Copying files
- ▶ Expanding files
- ▶ Installing features

> Installing updates

> Completing installation

9. When the installation is complete, change the administrator's password before the first logon. When the password had been changed you are logged in to the OS. You have completed phase 1 of the installation.

## Initial Configuration Tasks

Now that the OS install is complete and you have logged in to the Windows Server OS, the Initial Configuration Tasks Wizard appears (see Figure 1.6). There are three sections in this wizard:

> Provide computer information

> Update this server

> Customize this server

FIGURE 1.6
The Initial Configuration Tasks Wizard.

So what configuration changes can you make in these different sections?

In the Provide Computer Information section, you can do the following:

> Change the time zone.

> Configure the network settings on your network interface card (NIC) interfaces. You can also assign static IP addresses, subnet masks, default gateways, and DNS/WINS server. In many environments, you will probably be teaming two

NICs for a production data LAN (using third-party software) and have a separate NIC dedicated for backup data connected to a backup LAN. Alternatively, you can leave the setting to be automatically assigned by a DHCP server, assuming that you have a DHCP server configured.

> **NOTE** In a real-world environment, you will usually assign static IP addresses to infrastructure servers. If this is the case, you will need to have gathered this information along with valid IP addresses for the default gateway and for DNS and WINS servers prior to the installation, along with the new server name if you are held to a strict naming convention in your organization.

 ▶ Supply a computer name for the server, along with domain or workgroup information.

You need to reboot the server for these changes to take effect.

In the Update This Server section, you can do the following:

 ▶ Enable automatic updates and feedback.

 ▶ Configure the download and installation of OS updates.

In the Customize This Server section, you can do the following:

 ▶ Add the server role or multiple roles. When you select a role, a wizard takes you through the complete installation of that role. You can choose from the following roles:

  ▶ Active Directory Certificate Services

  ▶ Active Directory Domain Services

  ▶ Active Directory Federation Services

  ▶ Active Directory Lightweight Directory Services

  ▶ Active Directory Rights Management Services

  ▶ Application Server

  ▶ DHCP Server

  ▶ DNS Server

  ▶ Fax Server

  ▶ File Services

  ▶ Network Policy and Access Services

  ▶ Print Services

  ▶ Terminal Services

  ▶ UDDI Services

> ▶ Web Server (IIS)

> ▶ Windows Deployment Services

▶ Add features. As with roles, when you select a feature, a wizard takes you through the installation of that feature. There are many features to choose from, as shown in Figure 1.7.

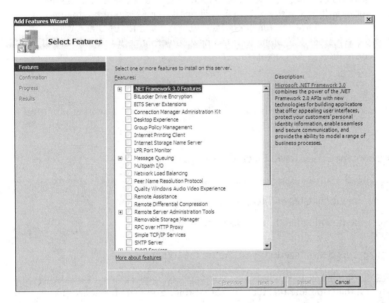

FIGURE 1.7
Selecting features you would like to install.

> **NOTE** With both the roles and features lists, if you highlight a role or feature, you see a description of each role or feature on the right side of the list. When you are selecting roles and features, keep in mind that you should install as few as possible or only items you are currently planning to use. If you install unnecessary roles and/or features, you will also install services and possibly open up ports that will not be used in production but will render the server less secure. Chapter 5, "Install and Configure Specific Server Roles," provides a more detailed discussion of installing and configuring roles and features.

▶ Enable Remote Desktop connections to the server.

▶ Configure the OS firewall settings. By default, the firewall is enabled.

Now let's move on to phase 3 of the installation.

## Server Manager Setup

Server Manager (shown in Figure 1.8) gives you a complete overview of your server. When looking at the default details pane, you can see computer information, security information, and a summary of the roles and features installed. And at the bottom of the page, you see a resources and support section. On the left side of the window are many tools to help you add/remove and configure roles and features. You can also see options for diagnostics, configurations, and disk management. When you have completed your changes in Server Manager, your manual installation is complete.

FIGURE 1.8
Server Manager.

> **NOTE** We will take a closer look at Server Manager in Chapter 3, "Work with Server Manager."

## Unattended Installation

Now that you have completed the manual installation, let's take a look at how you would go about performing an unattended installation. With Windows Server 2008, you use a unattend.xml file rather than an unattend.txt file; in fact, the unnattend.xml file also replaces the Sysprep.inf, Winbom.ini, and Cmdlines.txt files. The XML format has been adopted because it makes it easier to describe nested values, add new elements, and validate the answer file. You can open the unattend.xml file in Internet Explorer 5.5 and later to parse the .xml file and see if it is well formed. If the file is not formed correctly, Internet Explorer shows you where the errors are.

To run an unattended installation, you execute the setup.exe file with the unattend switch:

```
C:>setup.exe /unattend:<path>\unattend.xml
```

The unattend.xml file contains the responses needed while running the setup.exe file. This file contains such information as computer name, acceptance of the End User License Agreement (EULA), installation disk information, and so on. You can also show or hide the user interface (UI) for each value that is set by using ShowUI flag = Yes/No. Let's take a look at how the installation reacts when you use the ShowUI flag:

▶ **ShowUI flag = Yes and setting is specified in the unattend.xml file:** Setup uses the setting specified in the unattend.xml file and shows the UI with this setting.

▶ **ShowUI flag = No and setting is specified in the unattend.xml file:** Setup uses the setting specified in the unattend.xml file and does not show the UI.

▶ **ShowUI flag = Yes and the setting is not specified in the unattend.xml file:** Setup shows the UI, with the default value, and the user can change this setting, if needed.

▶ **ShowUI flag = No and the setting is not specified in the unattend.xml file:** Setup uses the default value and does not show the UI.

While performing an unattended installation over a network, the system installer must have access to the unattend.xml file. When the setup is started from removable media (CD or DVD), the setup program looks for the unattend.xml file in the following locations:

▶ The current working directory

▶ The root of the removable media where setup.exe was initiated

▶ Other removable media, such as floppy disks, USB devices, or another CD or DVD

The syntax for the unattend.xml file is broken up into elements, and each element needs to be opened and then closed in the proper order (when nested). When this is achieved, it is a well-formed .xml file. There is only one root element, <unattend>. Figure 1.9 shows a portion of an unattend.xml file, with some syntax explanation, so that you can get the feel for the syntax.

The running of the unattend.xml file stops with an error message if any of the following is true:

▶ The EULA has not been accepted

▶ The product key is invalid

▶ The install disk cannot be written to

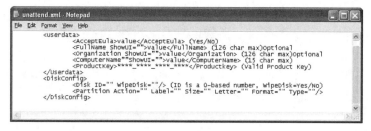

FIGURE 1.9

An unattend.xml file with some syntax information.

Creating an unattend.xml file can be tricky, but when you have this file created, it can make your job much easier. There are some tools available on the web that can help you create these files. You can also get very creative by adding some scripting to your installations to automatically generate computer names that adhere to your naming convention as well as many other configuration options.

# CHAPTER 2

# Configure and Manage Server Core

# Determine Your Need for Server Core

**Scenario/Problem:** During the process of installing Windows Server 2008, perhaps you noticed the Server Core option. What exactly is Server Core, and does your particular company have a need to implement it?

**Solution:** Server Core is a new feature in the Windows Server world. It installs a command-line administration-only version of Windows Server 2008 that helps reduce the attack surface of the server. Traditionally, there are many attack options on a Microsoft server, and you, the administrator, need to be aware of that and take action to ensure security. However, with Server Core, less code is installed (that is, there is a smaller footprint), and with that reduction in code comes a reduction in the number of places an attacker can hit. Fewer moving parts equals fewer vulnerabilities.

**NOTE** What is the *attack surface area* of an operating system? Keep in mind that each application added to a system provides a corresponding opportunity for attack and so poses a risk. In addition, certain services may leave your system open to infiltration. This is all considered the attack surface, and the goal in securing a system is to reduce that surface, typically by turning off or removing features that are unnecessary.

Until you see a Server Core system for yourself, you may not believe that you are really going to be working from a command prompt again. But that is truly what you have at your disposal. In fact, the Explorer shell is not even installed. You may be surprised to learn that you aren't working with the new PowerShell command prompt.

**PS NOTE** At the time of this writing, PowerShell was not functional in Server Core because it requires the .NET Framework, which cannot be installed on a Server Core system at this time. The .NET team has worked on providing a modularized version for Server Core admins to be able to work with PowerShell, and this will be available in R2. See the section "Incorporate Server Core Changes in Server 2008 R2," later in this chapter.

Now, keep in mind that Server Core isn't able to provide all the server roles that a typical server would have. The supported roles in Server Core include the following:

- ▶ Active Directory Domain Services (ADDS)
- ▶ Active Directory Lightweight Directory Services (AD LDS)
- ▶ DHCP Server

> ▶ DNS Server

> ▶ File Services

> ▶ Internet Information Services (IIS)

> ▶ Print Services

> ▶ Streaming Media Services

> ▶ Windows Virtualization (Hyper-V)

And, as you will soon see, you cannot use the Server Manager tool to install these roles. Instead, you need to install them through the command line, using a tool called ocsetup.exe.

Keep in mind that third-party application software cannot typically be installed and managed on a Server Core server, so this server isn't going to be used for things like your antivirus management or even some of the management solutions that Microsoft provides that must be installed on top of the server and require certain underlying services to be running. What this is a good fit for in an environment, however, is in areas like DNS or DHCP services or even file services.

> **NOTE** Although IIS is installable on Server Core, Server Core doesn't currently support ASP.NET. Due to the lack of support for managed code, there are many reasons you might not be able to use Server Core for your particular web server (for example, no IIS-ASPNET, IIS-NetFxExtensibility, IIS-ManagementConsole, IIS-ManagementService, IIS-LegacySnapIn, IIS-FTPManagement, WAS-NetFxEnvironment, and WAS-ConfigurationAPI).

# Install Server Core

> **Scenario/Problem:** You have decided that Server Core is exactly what you need in your environment. What is involved in installing Server Core?

**Solution:** Installing Server Core is simple. The real work is what comes after you perform the installation and have to configure the server to function through the command-prompt interfaces rather than the typical GUI interfaces that you have become so used to. Before we address those concerns, let's get Server Core up and running.

The minimum requirements are your initial concern. You want to ensure that you hardware meets the following requirements:

> ▶ **RAM:** 512MB RAM (which is the same minimum for the full installation of Windows Server 2008), although 1GB or more is always appreciated, especially if Hyper-V will be utilized.

▶ **Processor:** 1GHz for an x86 processor or 1.4GHz for an x64 processor

▶ **Disk space:** 10GB

You certainly want to be prepared with your Windows Server 2008 installation media and with a valid product key, although you can evaluate a server for quite some time by extending the grace period (see the section "Extend the Evaluation," later in this chapter).

> **NOTE** You may be wondering whether your existing servers can run Windows Server 2008 or whether you need to purchase new systems. Each server in your environment may be a little different, depending on when you purchased those servers and what they are. There is a tool called the Microsoft Assessment and Planning Toolkit (MAP) that you can use to inventory your servers and generate a report to help determine which servers will work for your Windows Server 2008 installations. At the time of this writing, the tool is located at http://technet.microsoft.com/en-us/library/bb977556.aspx.

## Server Core Installation Options

When you are confident that you have a system capable of running Windows Server 2008 Server Core, perform the following steps:

1. Insert the disc, and when the auto-run Install Windows dialog appears, confirm the language, time and currency format, and keyboard or input method. Then click Next.

2. When you see the Install Now screen, click the blue and white arrow button.

3. In the Select the Operating System You Want to Install screen (shown in Figure 2.1), note that there are three Full Installation choices and three Server Core Installation choices. Select one of the Server Core options and click Next.

> **NOTE** Server Core comes in Standard, Enterprise, and Datacenter editions for i386 and x64 platforms. You will probably opt for the Standard edition because most of the differences found in the Enterprise and Datacenter editions are not especially relevant in Server Core. The Enterprise Server Core does, however, get you more processor and memory support, as well as clustering. Datacenter provides the hardware program and 99.999% reliability, but you may not require these guarantees.

4. When you see the license terms, read or scan the terms and then select the I Accept the License Terms checkbox and then press Next.

5. When asked Which Type of Installation Do You Want? select Custom (Advanced).

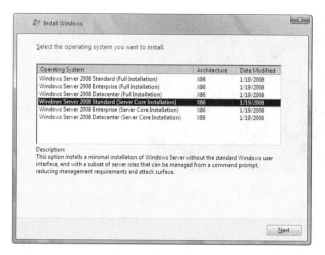

FIGURE 2.1
Choosing the flavor of Server Core that you require.

**NOTE**  Server Core requires a clean installation. You cannot upgrade from an earlier version or convert from a full installation to a Server Core installation. There is no upgrade to or from Server Core. So, if you install an incomplete version of Server Core, you cannot later upgrade to the full version. You have to start with a clean installation of the full version of Windows Server 2008.

6.  On the next screen, which asks, Where Do You Want to Install Windows? either choose some advanced options such as Load Driver or Drive Options (Advanced) or select the disk you want to use for the installation files. Click Next. The Installing Windows screen will appear, indicating that the system is copying files, expanding files, installing features, installing updates, and, finally, completing installation. Your system may reboot several times.

7.  When you see the login screen, type Administrator for the username and leave the password blank. Click OK.

8.  Provide and confirm a new password and then click OK. The system says Preparing Your Desktop, and you eventually see a simple command prompt, as shown in Figure 2.2.

Server Core is not much to look at to begin with. At this point, you have installed a server with very little happening on the desktop.

FIGURE 2.2
The Server Core cmd.exe desktop.

## Extend the Evaluation

Evaluating Windows Server 2008 software does not require product activation or entry of a product key. Any edition of Windows Server 2008 can be installed without activation and evaluated for an initial 60 days. If you need more time to evaluate Windows Server 2008, you can reset (or re-arm) the 60-day evaluation period three times, extending the original 60-day evaluation period by up to 180 days, for a total possible evaluation time of 240 days. After this time, you need to uninstall the software or upgrade to a fully licensed version of Windows Server 2008.

There is a support article from Microsoft, located at the time of this writing at http://support.microsoft.com/kb/948472, that should put your mind at ease that this isn't a trick that will get you in any kind of trouble with the Microsoft policy. Microsoft gives you a tool, called slmgr.vbs, to extend the evaluation.

To start with, as your initial 60-day evaluation period comes to an end, you are going to want to check the number of days you have left. From the command prompt, type slmgr.vbs -dli to see the current status of the evaluation period. To reset, or re-arm, the period for another 60 days, you type slmgr.vbs -rearm. Remember that you can do this three times.

# Configure Server Core Postinstallation

> **Scenario/Problem:** Server Core is installed, and the command prompt is up, but where do you go from here? How do you make the necessary configuration changes to the system?

**Solution:** First, it may be comforting to know that there are *some* GUI tools you might be able to use. For example, type taskmgr, and you see the familiar Task Manager, which tells you how your server is doing. You can also use Notepad, although you might prefer to use one of the two Control Panel applets that are still available to you in GUI format. Type `timedate.cpl` (for the Date and Time applet) or `intl.cpl` (for the Regional and Language Options applet). These were allowed to stay in Server Core because they do not interfere with security, and they make configuring certain aspects of the OS easier.

> **NOTE** If you accidentally close your command prompt, you can retrieve it by pressing Ctrl+Alt+Delete, choosing Task Manager, and then clicking File, Run and typing `cmd.exe`.

## Configuration Commands

Now, what would you normally need to do to configure a traditional server? Most likely, the following would come to mind:

- ▶ Changing the computer name
- ▶ Configuring network interfaces
- ▶ Joining the domain
- ▶ Installing (and activating) the license key
- ▶ Enabling the firewall
- ▶ Installing roles and/or features
- ▶ Adding hardware
- ▶ Configuring Windows Update

To perform these tasks, you need to become familiar (or refamiliarize yourself) with the following commands:

- ▶ **Netsh:** For many IP configuration settings. See http://support.microsoft.com/kb/242468.
- ▶ **Net User:** To change the administrative password. See http://support.microsoft.com/kb/251394.
- ▶ **Netdom:** To change the server name and/or join a domain. See http://technet.microsoft.com/en-us/library/cc776879.aspx.
- ▶ **Shutdown:** For after a configuration change, when you need to restart your system. See http://support.microsoft.com/kb/317371.
- ▶ **Slmgr:** The Software License Management tool, for installing and activating the license for the system. See http://support.microsoft.com/kb/555965/en-us.
- ▶ **Pnputil:** To help you install device drivers that aren't automatically included with Windows Server 2008. See http://support.microsoft.com/kb/937793.
- ▶ **SCRegEdit.wsf:** Enable Remote Desktop, automatic updates, terminal server client connections, and more. See http://support.microsoft.com/kb/555964/en-us.

> **NOTE** For some of these commands to work, you might have to change your direc-
> tory to `c:\Windows\System32i`.

Let's look at how you might use these commands to make changes in Server Core.

To change the computer name, you would perform the following steps:

1. Locate the current name of the server by typing `hostname` or `ipconfig`.

2. Type `netdom renamecomputer <ComputerName> /NewName <NewComputerName>`.

3. Restart the computer, which you can do by using the `shutdown` command.

To make changes to the static IP settings on the server, you first need to identify your network interfaces. The `netsh` command is your friend in this case:

```
netsh interface ipv4 show interfaces
```

Make a note of the number in the `Idx` column for your network adapter(s). Then type the following:

```
Netsh interface ipv4 set address name="<Id>" source=static address=<the
➥static IP you are setting> mask=<the subnet mask for that
➥address> gateway=<the default gateway for that address>
```

If you want to use DHCP, you can type `source=dhcp`.

To configure your DNS settings, you need to perform an additional step with `Netsh` and type the following:

```
Netsh interface ipv4 add dnsserver name=<interface
➥name> address=<DNS Server IP Address> index=1
```

where `index` is the interface number.

To join your domain you would type this:

```
Netdom join <Name of Your Computer> /domain:<Name of Your
➥Domain> /userd:<UserName> /passwordd:*
```

Make sure to use a domain account that has permission in the domain to join computers to the domain. You can enter a password when you're prompted for one.

Before you activate, you are going to want to make sure you put in a license key. You may have done this during the installation process, but if you didn't, you need to now type the following:

```
Slmgr.vbs -ipk <License Key>
```

If you want to activate the server, you type the following:

```
Slmgr.vbs -ato
```

To configure the firewall, you use the `netsh advfirewall` command, although this takes a bit of work. A better method may be to take the Firewall snap-in from a system running Windows Vista or Windows Server 2008 and configure the settings remotely. However, you first need to enable remote management of the firewall by typing the following:

```
Netsh advfirewall set currentprofile settings remotemanagement enable
```

Moving on to the installation of hardware, you may find that simply plugging it in will work because the driver may be included with Windows Server 2008. If that is the case, you can install the hardware, and you are all set. If that is not the case, perform the following:

1. Copy the driver files to the Server Core system. To do this, from the command prompt type the following:

   ```
   pnputil -i -a <Name of the INF file for the driver>
   ```

> **NOTE** If your old DOS skills are a little rusty, it's time to start shaking the dust off some of those DOS books in your library...or just do a quick search online for basic DOS commands, such as copy.

2. If you want to see a list of drivers on the system, type the following:

   ```
   sc query type=driver
   ```

3. While there are many other configuration commands you might want to investigate and use, for now, use the following to enable automatic updates:

   ```
   cscript scregedit.wsf /AU /4
   ```

> **NOTE** The 4 in this command is to automatically download and install updates. There are other options in the GUI portion, and they are represented at the command prompt by other numbers; however, they don't work with a Server Core server.

> **NOTE** If configuring Server Core through the command line is not your cup of tea, you might consider searching for GUI alternatives. Several of them have been developed to make your life easier. One such tool, the Windows 2008 Server Core Configurator, is a collection of scripts that allows you to do all the tasks just discussed. You can locate this tool at www.codeplex.com/CoreConfig.

## Install Roles and Features

While you may initially think of using Server Manager to install roles and features in Windows Server 2008, this console is not provided under Server Core. You therefore need to use the `ocsetup.exe` command.

The first thing you might want to do is see a list of the roles and features that are currently installed. To do this, simply type `oclist.exe` at the command prompt. Figure 2.3 shows the list that is returned.

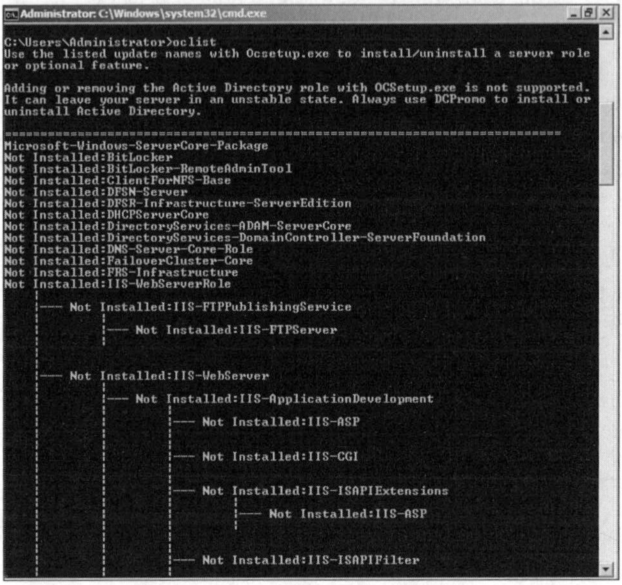

FIGURE 2.3
Viewing a list of installed roles and features.

Using this list, you can now use the `ocsetup.exe` command to install roles and/or features by typing the following:

```
Start /w ocsetup "role/feature name"
```

**NOTE** The role/feature name is case-sensitive. See the list you pull up with `ocsetup.exe` for the correct role/feature name capitalization.

For example, if you want to install the DNS Server role, you type the following:

```
Start /w ocsetup DNS-Server-Core-Role
```

**NOTE** The /w prevents you from seeing the command prompt until the operation is complete. Therefore, if you see the command prompt, you know that the installation succeeded.

**NOTE** Installing Active Directory is a little different in Server Core than in Windows Server 2008. Much as in the full installation version of Windows Server 2008, you would still use dcpromo to install Active Directory. However, you cannot use the wizards as you would ordinarily do. Instead, you need to use an unattend file. Microsoft recommends that you run dcpromo on another server running Windows Server 2008 and create the unattend file for the installation. To install the role, you then type dcpromo /unattend:<filename>.

When you install Server Core, the Server service is installed by default, but there are additional file service features you might want to add, such as the following:

- ▶ File Replication Service (FRS-Infrastructure)
- ▶ Distributed File System service (DFSN-Server)
- ▶ Distributed File System Replication (DFSR-Infrastructure-ServerEdition)
- ▶ Services for Network File System (both ServerforNFS-Base and ClientForNFS-Base)

In addition to the roles you can install, Server Core supports the following optional features:

- ▶ Failover clustering (FailoverCluster-Core)
- ▶ Network load balancing (NetworkLoadBalancingHeadlessServer)
- ▶ Subsystem for UNIX-based applications (SUACore)
- ▶ Backup (WindowsServerBackup)
- ▶ Multipath I/O (MultipathIo)
- ▶ Removable storage (Microsoft-Windows-RemovableStorageManagementCore)
- ▶ BitLocker drive encryption (BitLocker)
- ▶ Simple Network Management Protocol (SNMP) (SNMP-SC)
- ▶ Windows Internet Name Service (WINS) (WINS-SC)
- ▶ Telnet client (TelnetClient)

Installing features is very similar to installing roles. In this case, you type Start /w ocsetup <feature> (remembering that the feature name is case-sensitive).

# Manage Server Core

**Scenario/Problem:** Server Core is installed, and you have it configured with the roles you want to utilize. At this point, you are concerned about the management side of a command-prompt-only server. How do you manage Server Core?

**Solution:** There are many ways to work with Server Core and manage the roles and features you have installed. One of them is to use a command prompt (either locally or through a remote connection), but that probably isn't what you want to here. You are hoping for a GUI method.

Well, in addition to using the command-prompt directly, you can also connect through Terminal Services or through Windows Remote Shell, but again, this probably isn't what you are looking for. You can also use remote Microsoft Management Console (MMC) snap-ins to manage Server Core systems in the same way you would use them to remotely administer other systems.

At this point, it should be obvious how to work with Server Core locally, so let's consider some of the remote options.

## Manage Server Core with Terminal Services

To connect to a Server Core system from a Terminal Services client, you have to enable Remote Desktop for Administration mode. You can do this on a Server Core system by typing the following at the command prompt:

```
Cscript c:\windows\system32\scregedit.wsf /ar 0
```

When this is complete (the screen says "Registry has been updated"), you can go to another system and open the Remote Desktop Connection program. (A quick way to do this if you are using Windows Vista is to run the `mstsc.exe` app from the Start menu's instant search bar.) You can use the IP address or the name of the server running Server Core, make the connection, and log in. Ultimately, you will still be working with a command prompt, however (which is why we don't have a figure here —it would simply be another command prompt).

Type `logoff` at the command prompt when you are finished.

## Manage with TS RemoteApp

Now, something a little more modern than managing via Terminal Services, although ultimately with the same end result, is the use of TS RemoteApp to publish the `cmd.exe` application. With Windows Server 2008, you have the ability to publish a specific application without having users connect to the entire desktop. In the case of Server Core, this becomes logical because there is nothing happening on the desktop.

To enable this feature on your Server Core system, you need to perform the following steps:

1. On another Windows Server 2008 system, add the Terminal Services role through Server Manager.

2. Open the MMC and add the TS RemoteApp MMC snap-in.

3. Connect to the Server Core system.

4. From the Results pane, select RemoteApp Programs and locate the `cmd.exe` application (located at `\\<ServerName>\c$\windows\system32\cmd.exe`).

5. From the Allow list, click Remote cmd.exe and then Create RDP Package.

6. Use the RDP package to connect to the server that is running Server Core.

## Manage with Windows Remote Shell

Using Windows Remote Shell to connect to a Server Core system requires you to know command-line syntax. You must first enable Windows Remote Shell on the Server Core system by performing the following steps:

1. Type `WinRM quickconfig` at the command prompt.

2. On another system, open a command prompt.

3. Use `WinRS.exe` to initiate all your commands to the remote Server Core system. For example, type `winrs -r:<Server Core System Name> dir c:\windows` to see the `c:\windows` directory information on your Server Core system.

At this point, you can perform any of the command-line tasks you normally would locally at the Server Core system but through the Remote Shell.

## Manage Server Core with MMC Snap-ins

This is what you may have been waiting for throughout this chapter: the ability to manage Server Core through familiar GUI snap-ins for your MMC snap-ins.

To get started, make sure the Windows Firewall (if it is configured on the Server Core system) will allow an MMC connection. You can allow all snap-ins to connect or allow only specific ones.

To allow all snap-ins to connect, type the following:

```
Netsh advfirewall firewall set rule group="remote administration"
➥new enable=yes
```

Allowing only specific snap-ins requires a bit more work. You type the following:

```
Netsh advfirewall firewall set rule group="<rulegroup>" new enable=yes
```

**NOTE** The reason this second method may require a bit more work is because the rule groups are outlined for some, but not all, snap-ins. Some snap-ins simply do not have a rule group, in which case enabling the groups for Event Viewer, Services, or Shared Folders will often be enough to allow other snap-ins to work. For this reason, unless you have a major security concern, it would be easier to simply enable all snap-ins.

Some of the MMC snap-ins and corresponding rule group names are listed here:

- ▶ **Event Viewer:** Remote Event Log Management
- ▶ **Services:** Remote Services Management
- ▶ **Shared Folders:** File and Printer Sharing
- ▶ **Task Scheduler:** Remote Scheduled Tasks Management
- ▶ **Reliability and Performance Monitor:** Performance Logs and Alerts (and File Printer and Sharing)
- ▶ **Disk Management:** Remote Volume Management
- ▶ **Windows Firewall with Advanced Security:** Windows Firewall Remote Management

When you have the MMC configured on your Server Core system, you can begin managing with it, if you have the right credentials to do so. Another concern is whether the Server Core system is a domain member. If it isn't, you have a little more work to do in order to connect.

So, to begin with, if you are managing a Server Core system that is part of the domain, you perform the following steps:

1. Open an MMC snap-in. (Choose an easy one to work with and a familiar one, such as Computer Management. Or you can type mmc at the Start instant search bar and open a blank console.)

2. Right-click the top-left part of the hierarchy and select Connect to Another Computer.

3. Type the computer name of the Server Core system.

Now you should be able to use the snap-in the same way you would any other remote system you work on.

If, however, the Server Core system is *not* a part of the domain, you have to create a connection credentially to the Server Core system from your client machine. To do that, type the following:

```
Open a command prompt on the client machine and type: cmdkey /add:<Server
➡Core System Name> /user:<Administrator Account User Name>
➡/pass:<Administrator Password>
```

You can now manage the Server Core machine as you would any other system in the domain.

# Incorporate Server Core Changes in Windows Server 2008 R2

**Scenario/Problem:** Windows Server 2008 R2 comes with revisions to Server Core. Do those revisions affect your environment and your use of Server Core on a system running Windows Server 2008 R2?

**Solution:** Depending on what you use Server Core for in your environment, the following changes may or may not affect you:

- ▶ Active Directory Certificate Services has been added in R2.
- ▶ WoW64 support for 32-bit applications is now an optional feature and not installed by default.
- ▶ New optional features include a subset of the .NET Framework 2.0, a subset of the .NET Framework 3.0 and 3.5 (including Windows Communication Framework [WCF], Windows Workflow Framework [WF], and LINQ, but not including Windows Presentation Framework [WPF]).
- ▶ Windows PowerShell (woohoo!!!) will be functional in the R2 version of Server Core.
- ▶ ASP.NET and additional IIS support have been added. And although you cannot use the IIS GUI console in Server Core, you can use it remotely to manage IIS in R2 if the web management service is enabled and configured.
- ▶ FSRM (File Server Resource Manager) will provide new functionality designed to simplify storage management for all storage architectures.

**NOTE** When the word *subset* is used above for the .NET portions that have been added, the idea is that the Server Core team didn't seek to add to the footprint of the system with items that aren't necessary to Server Core. So, only those aspects that would make sense are implemented.

To install .NET 2.0, you run the following:

```
Start /w ocsetup NetFx2-ServerCore
```

To install .NET 3.0 and 3.5 functionality, you run the following:

```
Start /w ocsetup NetFx3-ServerCore
```

# Make Progress in Server Core Administration

**Scenario/Problem:** You have the basics down. The server is installed and configured, and you know how to manage the system. There must be more. Where do you go next?

**Solution:** There are many Server Core books currently on the market that you might want to consider, and two are especially interesting:

- *Administering Windows Server 2008 Server Core* by John Paul Mueller
- *Windows Server 2008 Server Core Administrator's Pocket Consultant* by Mitch Tulloch

However, the Internet may be a better option for locating quick, need-to-know information regarding your Server Core server.

Here are a few sites you might appreciate:

- **From the MSDN Microsoft Developer site:** http://msdn.microsoft.com/en-us/library/ms723891(VS.85).aspx
- **From the Microsoft TechNet Online Magazine:** http://technet.microsoft.com/en-us/magazine/2009.02.geekofalltrades.aspx?pr=blog
- **The Server Core Microsoft blog site:** http://blogs.technet.com/server_core/

# CHAPTER 3

# Work with Server Manager

# Use Initial Configuration Tasks

**Scenario/Problem:** The installation of your server is complete, and now you are looking at the Initial Configuration Tasks window. What should you configure initially?

**Solution:** The Initial Configuration Tasks Wizard appears immediately after your first login after your installation. This wizard was designed to assist administrators in configuring servers postinstallation. In fact, many of the questions that you might typically answer during a server installation are handled in Windows Server 2008 in this wizard, after the server OS has been installed.

The Initial Configuration Tasks Wizard replaces the Post-Setup Security Updates feature that was introduced in Windows Server 2003, Service Pack 1 and goes beyond security and into the full configuration for a new server.

**NOTE** If you closed the Initial Configuration Tasks Wizard or selected the checkbox Do Not Show This Window at Logon, you can reopen the wizard by typing oobe in the Start menu's instant search bar.

The Initial Configuration Tasks Wizard has three sections, as shown in Figure 3.1:

- ▶ **Provide Computer Information:** In this section, you can set the time zone, configure networking and provide a computer name (the default is a random name you do not want to keep), and join a domain.

- ▶ **Update This Server:** This section is for enabling automatic updates and feedback settings, and for quickly downloading and installing updates.

- ▶ **Customize This Server:** This section allows you to add roles and features, enable Remote Desktop, and configure Windows Firewall.

When you close the Initial Configuration Tasks Wizard, Server Manager opens to assist you.

FIGURE 3.1
Working with the Initial Configuration Tasks Wizard.

# Navigate Settings with Server Manager

**Scenario/Problem:** The new role-based computing model is a bit overwhelming at first. How does the new Server Manager help you manage Server 2008? And how do you work with it?

**Solution:** Server Manager is a single-console replacement for a variety of tools under Windows Server 2003. Within this console, you can view and manage just about every aspect of your server, as shown in Figure 3.2.

Through the Server Manager, you can view and make changes to the server roles and features you want to include on your server. You can also perform management operations in regard to those roles or in relation to storage, configuration, and diagnostics (including performance)—all under a single MMC-based interface.

In addition to opening Server Manager after the Initial Configuration Tasks Wizard closes, you see the Server Manager console when you perform any of the following tasks:

▷ Log in to Windows Server 2008 as an administrator

▷ Open Server Manager by selecting its icon on the Quick Launch toolbar

▶  Click Server Manager in Administrative Tools

▶  Right-click Computer and choose Manage

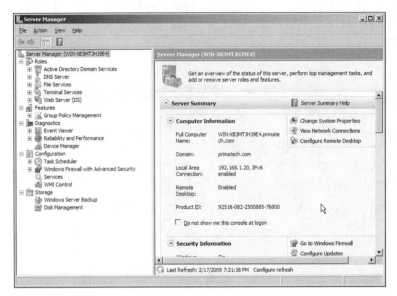

FIGURE 3.2
A look into the one-stop administration of Server Manager.

Once Server Manager is running, you can see the Server Summary section by selecting your server at the top of the hierarchy. Then you see the following sections:

▶  Computer Information

▶  Security Information

▶  Roles Summary

▶  Features Summary

▶  Resources and Support

**NOTE**  The Server Summary is an excellent place to start if you are working on a server you haven't configured personally. Typically, consultants move around, and you may at some point be required to perform a task on a server that is unfamiliar to you. The Server Summary should be your first stop.

While the Server Manager is filled with tools that are discussed in detail in different sections of this book, it is Role Management where Server Manager shines. In fact, you might find that this is the reason you return to the Server Manager because you may prefer to use the specific tools for a job. For example, you can use the Server Manager to handle your Active Directory Users and Computers configuration, but as an administrator, you might prefer to simply access that tool under Administrative Tools directly.

# Perform Role and Feature Management

**Scenario/Problem:** You have several different servers you want to configure, each with a different set of services. You need to determine the roles and features to install and then perform the installation of those options.

**Solution:** Before performing the steps of role and feature installation, it's a good idea to get a better grasp of the many different options you actually have at your disposal. Unlike the roles that are allowed through Server Core (which you learned about in Chapter 2, "Configure and Manage Server Core"), there is a great deal more you can do with a fully functional Windows Server 2008 system.

> **NOTE** A simple question you might be asking is "What is the difference between a server role and a server feature?" A role, according to Microsoft, "describes the primary function of the server." So, for example, configuring your server to act as a DNS server involves installing that role. On the other hand, a feature might "provide auxiliary or supporting functions" within a system. An example of a feature is the .NET Framework.

## Know Your Server Roles

Table 3.1 lists the Server Roles shown in Figure 3.3 (in the Add Roles Wizard) and their descriptions.

TABLE 3.1    **Server Roles**

| Role | Description* |
| --- | --- |
| Active Directory Certificate Services (AD CS) | Used to create certification authorities and related role services that allow you to issue and manage certificates used in a variety of applications. |
| Active Directory Domain Services (AD DS) | Stores information about objects on the network and makes this information available to users and network administrators. Uses domain controllers to give network users access to permitted resources anywhere on the network through a single logon process. |
| Active Directory Federation Services (AD FS) | Provides simplified, secure identity federation and Web single sign-on (SSO) capabilities. Includes the Federation Service, which enables browser-based Web SSO, a Federation Service proxy to customize the client access experience and protect internal resources, and Web agents to provide federated users with access to internally hosted applications. |

continues

TABLE 3.1    **Server Roles** (continued)

| Role | Description* |
|------|-------------|
| Active Directory Lightweight Directory Services (AD LDS) | Provides a store for application-specific data, for directory-enabled applications that do not require the infrastructure of AD DS. Multiple instances of AD LDS can exist on a single server, and each can have its own schema. |
| Active Directory Rights Management Services (AD RMS) | Helps you protect information from unauthorized use. AD RMS establishes the identity of users and provides authorized users with licenses for protected information. |
| Application Server | Provides central management and hosting of high-performance distributed business applications, such as those built with Enterprise Services and .NET Framework 3.0. |
| DHCP Server | Enables you to centrally configure, manage, and provide temporary IP addresses and related information for client computers. |
| DNS Server | Provides name resolution for TCP/IP networks. DNS Server is easier to manage when installed on the same server as AD DS. Installing AD DS allows you to install and configure DNS Server to work together with AD DS. |
| Fax Server | Sends and receives faxes and allows you to manage fax resources, such as jobs, settings, reports, and fax devices, on this computer or the network. |
| File Services | Provides technologies that help you manage storage, enable file replication, manage shared folders, ensure fast file searching, and enable access for UNIX client computers. |
| Hyper-V | Provides the services you need to create and manage virtual machines and corresponding resources. |
| Network Policy and Access Services | Provides Network Policy Server (NPS), Routing and Remote Access Services (RRAS), Health Registration Authority (HRA), and Host Credential Authorization Protocol (HCAP), which help safeguard the health and security of your network. |
| Print Services | Enables you to share printers on a network, as well as to centralize print server and network printer management tasks. It also enables you to migrate print servers and deploy printer connections, using Group Policy. |
| Terminal Services | Enables users to access Windows-based programs that are installed on a terminal server or to access the full Windows desktop. With Terminal Services, users can access a terminal server from within your corporate network or from the Internet. |

TABLE 3.1    **Server Roles** (continued)

| Role | Description* |
|------|-------------|
| UDDI Services | Provides Universal Description, Discovery, and Integration (UDDI) capabilities for sharing information about web services within an organization's intranet or between business partners on an extranet. |
| Web Server (IIS) | Provides a reliable, manageable, and scalable web application infrastructure. |
| Windows Deployment Services | Provides a simplified, secure means of rapidly and remotely deploying Windows operating systems to computers over the network. |

\* Descriptions adapted from the Windows Server 2008 Wizard Descriptions.

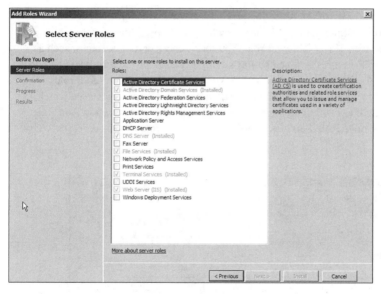

FIGURE 3.3
The Add Roles Wizard.

Within a role, role services may be involved as sub-elements. In addition, some roles require that specific features also be installed. For example, the Application Server role notifies you that the .NET Framework 3.0 feature is required in order for the role to function.

When attempting to install a role that requires additional necessary services and features, you are greeted with the option Add Required Role Services, as shown in Figure 3.4.

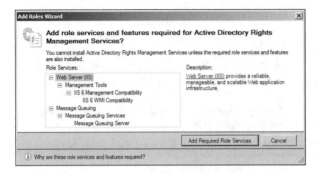

FIGURE 3.4
A request for permission to install necessary services and/or features for a role to function.

However, the majority of the time, you can install a role with selected services and return later to configure additional ones. Nowhere, perhaps, is this better seen than with regard to your IIS Web Server role. You may choose certain services, such as ASP.NET, HTTP Redirection, and so forth, but you can always return later and add role services. As you can see in Figure 3.5, you can view the health of all roles installed by selecting Roles from the navigation pane and then you can see which services are included within a particular role. You can choose the option Add Role Services or Remove Role Services to make changes to a role (in this case, the Web Server role).

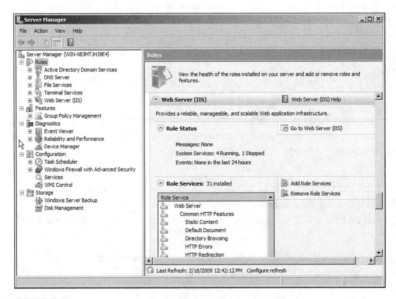

FIGURE 3.5
A look at services installed from within Server Manager.

## Know Your Server Features

As mentioned earlier, server features (shown in Figure 3.6) provide supporting functionality to a role (as in the case of .NET Framework 3.0) or may stand alone (for example, PowerShell). Table 3.2 describes the features you can install on a server.

TABLE 3.2    **Server Features**

| Feature | Description* |
| --- | --- |
| .NET Framework 3.0 Features | Combines the power of the .NET Framework 2.0 APIs with new technologies for building applications that offer appealing user interfaces, protect your customers' personal identity information, enable seamless and secure communication, and provide the ability to model a range of business processes. |
| BitLocker Drive Encryption | Helps to protect data on lost, stolen, or inappropriately decommissioned computers by encrypting the entire volume and checking the integrity of early boot components. Data is decrypted only if those components are successfully verified and the encrypted drive is located in the original computer. Integrity checking requires a compatible trusted platform module (TPM). |
| BITS Server Extensions | Allows a server to receive files uploaded by clients using BITS. BITS allows client computers to transfer files in the foreground or background asynchronously, preserve the responsiveness of other network applications, and resume file transfer after network failures and computer restarts. |
| Connection Manager Administration Kit | Generates Connection Manager profiles. |
| Desktop Experience | Includes features of Windows Vista, such as Windows Media Player, desktop themes, and photo management. Desktop Experience does not enable any of the Windows Vista features by default; you must manually enable them. |
| Failover Clustering | Allows multiple servers to work together to provide high availability of services and applications. Failover Clustering is often used for file and print services, database, and mail applications. |
| Group Policy Management | A scriptable MMC snap-in that provides a single administrative tool for managing Group Policy across an enterprise. Group Policy Management is the standard tool for managing Group Policy. |
| Internet Printing Client | Enables clients to use Internet Printing Protocol (IPP) to connect and print to printers on the network or Internet. |
| Internet Storage Name Server (iSNS) | Provides discovery services for Internet Small Computer System Interface (iSCSI) storage area networks. iSNS processes registration requests, deregistration requests, and queries from iSNS clients. |

*continues*

TABLE 3.2    **Server Features** (continued)

| Feature | Description* |
|---|---|
| LPR Port Monitor | Enables the computer to print to printers that are shared, using any Line Printer Daemon (LPD) service. (LPD service is commonly used by UNIX-based computers and printer-sharing devices.) |
| Message Queuing | Provides guaranteed message delivery, efficient routing, security, and priority-based messaging between applications. Message Queuing also accommodates message delivery between applications that run on different operating systems, use dissimilar network infrastructures, are temporarily offline, or are running at different times. |
| Multipath I/O | Along with the Microsoft Device Specific Module (DSM) or a third-party DSM, provides support for using multiple data paths to a storage device on Windows. |
| Network Load Balancing (NLB) | Distributes traffic across several servers, using the TCP/IP networking protocol. NLB is particularly useful for ensuring that stateless applications, such as a web server running IIS, are scalable by adding additional servers as the load increases. |
| Peer Name Resolution Protocol (PNRP) | Allows applications to register on and resolve names from your computer, so other computers can communicate with these applications. |
| Quality Windows Audio Video Experience (qWave) | Acts as a networking platform for audio and video (AV) streaming applications on IP home networks. qWave enhances AV streaming performance and reliability by ensuring network quality-of-service for AV applications. It provides admission control, runtime monitoring and enforcement, application feedback, and traffic prioritization. On Windows Server platforms, qWave provides only rate-of-flow and prioritization services. |
| Remote Assistance | Enables you (or a support person) to offer assistance to users who have computer issues or questions. Remote Assistance allows you to view and share control of the user's desktop in order to troubleshoot and fix issues. Users can also ask for help from friends or coworkers through Remote Assistance. |
| Remote Differential Compression | Computes and transfers the differences between two objects over a network, using minimal bandwidth. |
| Remote Server Administration Tool | Includes snap-ins and command-line tools for remotely managing roles and features. Note that there is a collection of tools to choose from; you have to expand the list and select what you like unless you enable all of them. |
| Removable Storage Manager (RSM) | Manages and catalogs removable media and operates automated removable media devices. |
| RPC over HTTP Proxy | Relays RPC traffic from client applications over HTTP to the server as an alternative to clients accessing the server over a VPN connection. |

TABLE 3.2   **Server Features** (continued)

| Feature | Description* |
|---|---|
| Simple TCP/IP Services | Supports the following TCP/IP services: Character Generator, Daytime, Discard, Echo, and Quote of the Day. Simple TCP/IP Services is provided for backward compatibility and should not be installed unless it is required. |
| SMTP Server | Supports the transfer of e-mail messages between e-mail systems. |
| SNMP Services | Includes the SNMP Service and SNMP WMI Provider. |
| Storage Manager for SANs | Helps you create and manage logical unit numbers (LUNs) on Fibre Channel and iSCSI disk drive subsystems that support Virtual Disk Service (VDS). |
| Subsystem for UNIX-based Applications | Along with a package of support utilities available for download from the Microsoft website, enables you to run UNIX-based programs and compile and run custom UNIX-based applications in the Windows environment. |
| Telnet Client | Uses the Telnet protocol to connect to a remote telnet server and run applications on that server. |
| Telnet Server | Allows remote users to perform command-line administration and run programs using a Telnet client, including UNIX-based clients. |
| TFTP Client | Is used to read files from, or write files to, a remote TFTP server. TFTP is primarily used by embedded devices or systems that retrieve firmware or configuration information or a system image during the boot process from a TFTP server. |
| Windows Internal Database | Acts as a relational data store that can be used only by Windows roles and features, such as UDDI Services, Active Directory Rights Management Services, Windows Server Update Services, and Windows System Resource Manager. |
| Windows PowerShell | Is a command-line shell and scripting language that helps IT professionals achieve greater productivity. It provides a new administrator-focused scripting language and more than 130 standard command-line tools to enable easier system administration and accelerated automation. |
| Windows Process Activation Service | Generalizes the IIS process model, removing the dependency on HTTP. All the features of IIS that were previously available only to HTTP applications are now available to applications hosting Windows Communication Foundation (WCF) services, using non-HTTP protocols. IIS 7.0 also uses Windows Process Application Service for message-based activation over HTTP. |
| Windows Server Backup Features | Allow you to back up and recover your operating system, applications, and data. You can schedule backups to run once a day or more often, and you can protect the entire server or specific volumes. |

continues

TABLE 3.2    **Server Features** (continued)

| Feature | Description* |
| --- | --- |
| Windows System Resource Manager | Can control how CPU and memory resources are allocated. Managing resource allocation improves system performance and reduces the risk that applications, services, or processes will interfere with each other to reduce server efficiency and system response. |
| WINS Server | Provides a distributed database for registering and querying dynamic mappings of NetBIOS names for computers and groups used on the network. WINS maps NetBIOS names to IP addresses and solves the problems arising from NetBIOS name resolution in routed environments. |
| Wireless LAN Service | Configures and starts the WLAN AutoConfig service, regardless of whether the computer has any wireless adapters. WLAN AutoConfig enumerates wireless adapters and manages both wireless connections and the wireless profiles that contain the settings required to configure a wireless client to connect to a wireless network. |

* Descriptions adapted from the Windows Server 2008 Wizard Descriptions.

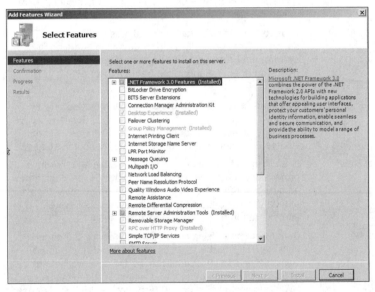

FIGURE 3.6
The Add Features Wizard.

## Install Roles

The process of installing a role or feature varies, depending on exactly what you are installing. In addition, the wizards allow you to select multiple roles/features.

The number of variables involved in installing roles is too great to use to provide a step-by-step solution. Therefore, let's look at installing one role and one feature to show the basic process and provide a basis for other possibilities.

To install roles perform the following:

1.  Open Server Manager.

2.  Select the Roles link from the navigation pane.

3.  Under the Roles Summary portion in the work console, select the link Add Roles.

4.  The first time you add a role, you are greeted with a Before You Begin dialog. Select the checkbox Skip This Page by Default now, or you will continue to see this page every time you add a role. Click Next.

5.  On the Select Server Roles Page, select one or more roles to install on this server. In this scenario, select Application Server. Click Next.

**NOTE** When you select a role, you may see the pattern on the left change to include the role and role services.

6.  On the Application Server page, read the Introduction to Application Server. Note other aspects of the installation of this particular role under the Things to Note section and/or view Additional Information by selecting one of the links provided, as shown in Figure 3.7. Click Next.

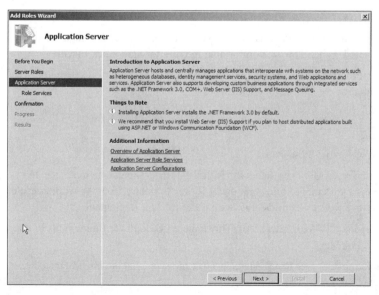

FIGURE 3.7
The Application Server introduction.

7.  On the Select Role Services page, choose additional services that relate to the installation of the role. In this case, as you can see in Figure 3.8, there are many services you can add that are not necessarily required. Choose the ones you want and click Next.

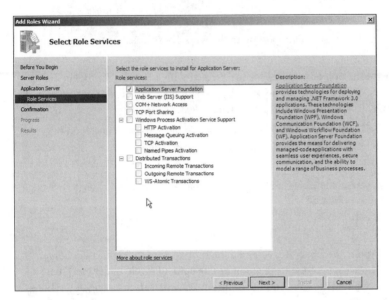

FIGURE 3.8
Selecting role services.

8.  On the Confirmation page, review the roles, role services, and/or features you have selected. When you are comfortable moving forward, click Install.

9.  Note the Progress of the installation on the Installation Progress. When you see the Installation Results page, click Close.

## Remove Roles

To remove a role, follow these steps:

1.  Return to Server Manager, select the Roles link from the navigation pane, and then select the Remove Roles link under Roles Summary from the work console. The Remove Roles Wizard begins, with a Before You Begin page.

2.  Either read this page or select Skip This Page by Default for future visits to this wizard. Click Next.

3.  On the Remove Server Roles page, deselect the roles that are already installed. Click Next.

4.  On the Confirm Removal Selections page, make sure this is truly what you want to do and click Remove.

5. Note the progress of the removal, and on the Results page, look for confirmation of the removal of that role. Click Close.

## Administer Roles Through Server Manager

The Server Manager may (or may not) be the perfect place to administer your installed role. Some like to use the individual tools from Administrative Tools, whereas others may like a single console for administering all roles at once.

To administer roles through Server Manager, you expand the Roles section in the navigation pane and look for the role you want to manage. From the hierarchy, you can select the expansion link for the role to see the corresponding tools.

> **NOTE** When you select a particular role, you see a summary of that role, including events that relate to that role. You might find this more helpful than going to Event Viewer directly because it narrows down the result to match the role you are looking into. You can also quickly see the system services that relate to your role and see if they are running (or you can stop/restart those services) directly from the Roles Summary.

## Install Features

To add features to your Windows Server 2008 system, perform the following steps:

1. Open Server Manager.

2. Select the Features link in the navigation pane.

3. Under the Features Summary portion in the work console, click the link Add Features.

4. From the Select Features page, choose any of the many available features. (You might note that some are already installed and perhaps you don't remember installing them, but remember that certain roles may install features as well.) When you're done choosing features, click Next.

5. On the Confirm Installation Selections page, confirm your selection and then click Install.

6. Note the progress of your installation. When the Results screen appears, click Close.

> **NOTE** To remove a feature, you can select the Remove Features option from the Features Summary and follow the wizard.

Not all features can be managed through the Server Manager console because they do not all come with additional tools for management. For example, PowerShell and the

.NET Framework do not have management consoles that you can work within Server Manager.

# Use the Command-Line Server Manager (`ServerManagerCmd.exe`)

**Scenario/Problem:** You want to automate certain aspects of your environment. How does the new command-line Server Manager (`servermanagercmd.exe`) tool help?

**Solution:** There is quite a bit you can do with the new `ServerManagerCmd.exe` command, including the following:

▶ Automatically install or remove roles, role services, and features.

▶ View logs and run queries regarding roles, role services, and features.

▶ Run with an XML file to expedite automated installations that are repetitive through the use of an XML answer file.

**NOTE** To learn more about creating an answer file to work with `ServerManagerCmd.exe`, see http://technet.microsoft.com/en-us/library/cc766357.aspx.

To get started, you need to be a member of the Administrators group on the server and be running a command prompt with elevated privileges. From the command prompt, you can type `ServerManagerCmd.exe -help` to get started. Note that the response provides syntax and parameter information. For greater detail on the use of `ServerManagerCmd.exe`, see http://technet.microsoft.com/en-us/library/cc748918.aspx. Let's look at several examples that make it a bit easier to see how this tool may come in handy.

For starters, enter `ServerManagerCmd.exe -query` to see the various roles and features you have installed as well as roles and features you could install (see Figure 3.9).

**NOTE** If you want to push the result of the query out to an XML file, you can type `ServerManagerCmd.exe -query c:\`*filename*`.xml`.

FIGURE 3.9
ServerManagerCmd.exe -query.

For each role, a role identifier must be used. For example, to install the Print Server role, you use Print-Services as the role identifier. You can install roles by typing the following (making sure to use the correct syntax, as shown in the results from -query):

ServerManagerCmd -install <role identifier>

**NOTE** If you want the system to reboot after the role is installed, you type -restart at the end of the command.

To remove a role, you type the following:

ServerManagerCmd -remove <role identifier>

Remember that features can be installed just as easily as roles, through the use of the ServerManagerCmd command. For example, to quickly install PowerShell from the command prompt, you type the following:

ServerManagerCmd -i PowerShell

Sometimes adding or removing a role will cause other items—role services and/or features—to be added or removed. You might want to see what will be done by the installation and/or removal of a certain role, and this is where the WhatIf command can be helpful. You can type the following:

```
ServerManagerCmd -install <Role/Feature Name> -whatif
```

You now see the possible results before you execute the command. (You can include -logpath c:\filename.txt at the end of this command to port the response to a .txt file.)

> **NOTE**  For an overview of Server Manager commands, see http://technet.microsoft.com/en-us/library/cc748918.aspx.

## Know What R2 Will Bring to Server Manager

**Scenario/Problem:** What should you expect to see change with Server Manager with Windows Server 2008 R2?

**Solution:** Learning a new server OS can be somewhat overwhelming at first, and you might not notice deficiencies or areas for improvement. Thankfully, the Microsoft Development Team knows those areas and has certainly made changes for R2 that will make sense once you see them. These changes include the following:

▶ You will be able to manage remote servers through Server Manager through PowerShell remoting. Server roles and features will be manageable through local and remote PowerShell 2.0 scripts. (Look for more than 240 new cmdlets to work with, too!)

▶ The Best Practices Analyzer tool will be added to Server Manager. This is a tool that has been quite handy for Exchange, SQL, and other servers for a while now, and we welcome its use in Server 2008.

# CHAPTER 4

# Manage Windows Server 2008

# Use the Microsoft Management Console (MMC)

**Scenario/Problem:** You have been given the task of identifying any configuration issues and correcting them in your organization's Windows Server 2008 infrastructure. What tool will you use to review, configure, and identify issues in your environment?

**Solution:** The Microsoft Management Console (MMC) can be used to review, configure, and identify issues within the environment. MMC is nothing new to the Windows OS. You may have used it extensively while working with Windows 2000/2003 Server. In fact, you may have seen version 1.0 in the Windows NT 4.0 Option Pack. If this is the case, you can safely move on to the next section or browse through this section for a review. If you are new to Windows Server configuration and management, you will find that the MMC will become the tool that is used most extensively but at the same time is not really recognized as being used at all because it is just the platform used to add snap-ins.

Let's take a look at how to launch a new MMC and then add snap-ins:

1. Select Start, Run.

2. Type mmc and click OK. Windows Server 2008 launches a new MMC, as shown in Figure 4.1. Notice that you can't really do much with this tool at the moment.

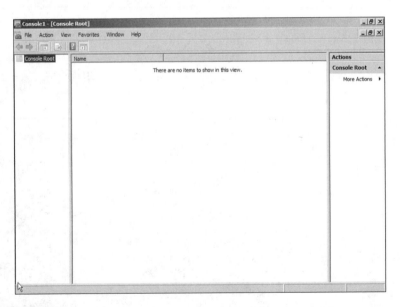

FIGURE 4.1
A new MMC.

For the MMC to be of any use to you, you need to add one or more snap-ins. A snap-in is a program that allows you to perform a specified administrative task. Next, you'll add a snap-in that will allow you to manage your disks.

3. On the MMC menu bar, select File, Add/Remove Snap-in (or press Ctrl+M). The Add or Remove Snap-ins dialog box appears, as shown in Figure 4.2. On the left side of the Add or Remove Snap-ins dialog box you see listed all the available snap-ins you can use.

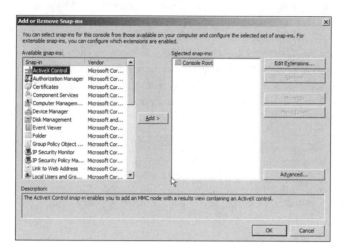

FIGURE 4.2
The Add or Remove Snap-in dialog box.

4. You want to be able to manage your disks, so select Disk Management and click the Add button. Now for this and many of the other snap-ins, you are asked if you would like to manage this server or another remote server, as shown in Figure 4.3. You are going to manage the local server.

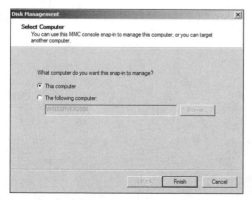

FIGURE 4.3
Choose whether to manage this server or a remote server.

**NOTE** The available snap-ins list may change as you add applications to your server.

5. Leave This Computer selected and click Finish. You will notice that Disk
Management has been added to the Selected Snap-ins area on the right side of
the Add or Remove Snap-ins dialog box. At this point, you could add more
snap-ins, depending on what you want to manage. If you accidentally add a
snap-in, you can easily remove it by highlighting the snap-in and clicking the
Remove button. You can further customize snap-ins by editing the extensions
available for a snap-in. For example, if you were to select the Group Policy
Editor snap-in from the Selected Snap-ins side of the dialog box, you could then
click Edit Extensions to bring up the Extensions for Group Policy Object Editor.
By selecting the Enable Only Selected Extensions button, you can remove (or, if
previously removed, add) extensions for the Group Policy Editor snap-in (see
Figure 4.4).

**NOTE** You might see different wizard options, depending on what snap-in you select.
For example, select ActiveX Controls and Certificates and you will need to answer
more configuration prompts. With other snap-ins, such as Authorization Manager,
there will be no further configuration prompts; the snap-in will just appear in the
Selected Snap-ins list.

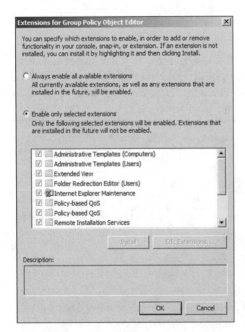

FIGURE 4.4
Removing snap-in extensions.

6. Now that you have selected the Disk Management snap-in, click OK to add it to your MMC. The Disk Management snap-in appears under Console Root in the left pane of your MMC. Also notice the word *Local* in parentheses next to the snap-in. This indicates that you will manage the local server with this snap-in.

7. If you are planning to use this MMC again, save it. Saving a custom MMC is as easy as saving a Word document: Just select File, Save. You need to provide a name for your new MMC and then choose where you want to save it.

You have now successfully configured your own custom MMC. Although you added only one snap-in, you can see how you will be able to gather the tools you use the most into one MMC and use it to easily manage Windows Server 2008. You can also manage remote servers from your custom MMC. This comes in handy if you have multiple servers to manage; you can create your custom MMC on your desktop and connect to remote servers to manage (assuming that you have the needed security permissions). Here's how you connect your custom MMC to a remote server:

1. Open the custom MMC you just configured.

2. Add the Computer Management snap-in, selecting the default Manage the Local Machine when prompted. (Disk Manager allows you to manage only the local server.)

3. After you add the Computer Management snap-in, locate it under Root Console in the left pane of your MMC, right-click it, and select Connect to Another Computer, as shown in Figure 4.5.

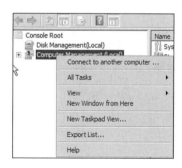

FIGURE 4.5
Selecting to connect to another computer.

4. In the Select Computer dialog box that appears (see Figure 4.6), insert the name or IP address of the remote server you would like to manage. Then click OK.

Now you see the remote server name in parentheses after the Computer Management snap-in. You are ready to manage your remote server.

There should be no doubt in your mind now about how the MMC can ease the task of administration in your Windows Server environment. Even if you are managing a global enterprise, you will be able to connect to each of your servers and manage them from one desktop. You may be thinking, however, there would be a lot of work in building all the custom MMCs. No need to worry: Microsoft has preconfigured many MMCs and grouped commonly used tools together. Let's take a look at some of these preconfigured MMCs.

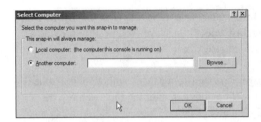

FIGURE 4.6
Inserting the name or IP address of the remote server.

# Work with Preconfigured MMCs

**Scenario/Problem:** You want to manage your Windows Server 2008 environment but do not want to create custom MMCs. What are some of the preconfigured MMCs you can use?

**Solution:** Although there are many preconfigured MMCs, in this section, we focus on just two MMCs that are directly associated with managing your Windows Server 2008 OS:

▶ Server Manager

▶ Computer Manger

**NOTE** There are preconfigured MMCs for just about all the Microsoft applications and roles, such as Exchange, SQL, and IIS, to name just a few. In addition to these, third-party vendors develop applications that also allow you to use an MMC.

## Server Manager

The Server Manager MMC contains the snap-ins that allow you to accomplish the following tasks:

▶ Add or remove server roles

▶ Add or remove server features

▶ Monitor system events

▶ Manage devices

▶ Schedule tasks

▶ Manage local users and groups

- ► Configure Windows Firewall
- ► Configure storage
- ► Perform backups

> **NOTE**  See Chapter 3, "Work with Server Manager," for more details on how to use the different snap-ins in the Server Manager MMC.

## Computer Manager

There is some overlap in terms of the tools in Server Manager and in Computer Manager. You may also remember Computer Manager from previous versions of Windows Server (2000/2003). A couple obvious items that you do not see in Computer Manager but do see in Server Manager are the roles and features snap-ins. But as you compare Server Manager and in Computer Manager, as shown in Figure 4.7, you also find many others missing. So when would you choose one over the other? Well, basically, where they overlap, it's up to you. In these cases, Microsoft has given you multiple ways to accomplish identical tasks. Two specific snap-ins are available in Computer Manager but not in Server Manager:

- ► Routing and Remote Access
- ► Shared Folders

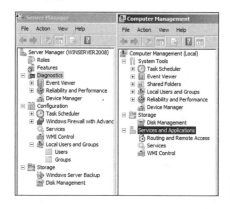

FIGURE 4.7
Comparison of Server Manager and Computer Manager.

### Routing and Remote Access

As the title of this snap-in suggests, you can configure two functions: routing and remote access. A router is used to separate network segments or subnets. With the routing portion of the Routing and Remote Access snap-in, you have the ability to configure your server to act as a software router. This would be okay for small subnets, with not too much traffic passing from one subnet to another (for example, in a test environment). When traffic increases (for example, in any production environment), you will use hardware routers to accomplish this task.

**NOTE**  It is strongly suggested that you use a hardware router even in a test or development environment. When developing or testing new technologies, you will want the testing done in an environment that is close, if not identical, to your production environment.

The remote access portion of the Routing and Remote Access snap-in allows you to configure the server to provide two types of remote connectivity: VPN and dial-up. Remote access allows users to connect to the organization's network as if they are local. For example, they can connect to drives using Windows Explorer and map to network printers, also Universal Naming Convention (UNC) paths are fully supported.

### Shared Folders

The Shared Folders snap-in allows you to see what folders are shared on the server, how many sessions (connections) there are to the shares, and what shared files are open. This snap-in is truly a useful tool when managing your server. Say that you needed to reboot the server and want to see if there are any active sessions to the shares. From the session view, you can easily see who is connected, from where they are connected, how long they have been connected, and even how long the session has been idle. In some cases, you may get a call that a file is in use and should not be— maybe someone has left a file open on his or her workstation and left for the day. You will be able to see whether the file is open and what user has it open. If needed, you can close that open file by using this tool. (It is usually a good idea to make sure the person asking you to close the file has seniority over the person who has the file open.)

Let's now take a look at some other tools that help you manager Windows Server 2008.

## Utilize Device Manager

**Scenario/Problem:** You recognize that there are many different hardware components to manage. Where can you go to get an overview of the hardware components installed on your Windows server and get a look at their status?

**Solution:** The Device Manager is a one-stop shop for hardware management of your server. As shown in Figure 4.8, the Device Manager (found in the Control Panel) lists all your hardware devices. From the Action menu, you can scan for new hardware or add legacy hardware. If there are any issues with a particular type of hardware on the server, you see a yellow triangle with an exclamation point. You can further diagnose the issue by opening the properties of the device to see more details. When you right-click any of the hardware installed, you have the option to update driver software, disable the device, and uninstall the driver. Many times, you will find that either reinstalling a driver or uninstalling and rescanning for hardware will fix issues with hardware drivers.

FIGURE 4.8
Manage hardware with Device Manager.

**NOTE** You have probably already noticed that the Device Manager is also accessible from the Server Manager MMC and the Computer Manager MMC.

**NOTE** Many server hardware vendors include a web interface that allows you to view the status of your hardware and identify any issues. You can interface such a component, as well as your event alerts, to your ticketing system in order to be proactive in your server management. This is covered in more detail in Chapter 12, "Monitor Performance and Troubleshoot."

# Work with the Task Scheduler

**Scenario Problem:** You want to be able to automate specific jobs or tasks on your Windows Server 2008 server. How can you configure your server to automate these tasks?

**Solution:** The Task Scheduler enables you to automate many different tasks on your server. You might be familiar with the Task Scheduler from previous Windows server operating systems. However, the Task Scheduler in Windows Server 2008 has much more functionality than those earlier versions.

You can get to the Task Scheduler in more than one way, and one of the easiest is to open Server Manager. From Server Manager, you navigate to Configuration and then Task Scheduler. When you highlight the Task Scheduler, you see the following:

▶ **An overview of Task Scheduler:** You see information on what you can do with Task Scheduler and some instructions on how to use it.

▶ **Task status:** Here you can see whether your scheduled tasks are running successfully. On the top right you can select how far back you want to check, with options of last 1 hour, last 24 hours, last 7 days, and last 30 days. Then, by expanding the tasks listed in the lower portion, you can confirm whether a scheduled task completed successfully.

▶ **Active tasks:** All tasks that are active (that is, scheduled tasks that are scheduled to be run and have not expired) are shown in this area.

If you select Task Scheduler, Task Scheduler Library, Microsoft, Windows, you see some preconfigured tasks, as shown in Figure 4.9. Also notice that you can organize your scheduled tasks in folders.

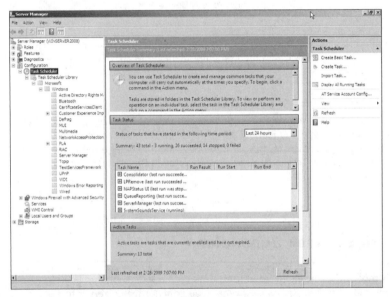

FIGURE 4.9
Task Scheduler overview and preconfigured tasks.

A big difference between older versions of Task Scheduler and the current one is the number of triggers available to kick off a scheduled task. A trigger is an event that causes a scheduled task to start. In previous versions of Windows server operating systems, you could only have a task scheduled to run at a specified time and reoccur at the same time, if needed. The time of day would be the trigger for the scheduled task. With Windows Server 2008, you can use the following triggers:

▶ On a schedule

▶ At logon

- At startup
- On idle
- On an event
- At task creation/modification
- On connection to a user session
- On disconnect from a user session
- On workstation lock
- On workstation unlock

We have certainly come a long way from the AT command prompt tool in the NT 4.0 days. The new Task Scheduler gives you a wide variety of options for scheduling tasks. We will take a look at the steps involved in creating a scheduled task that brings up a message when the server is unlocked. As you go through the steps, you'll learn about some of the other new features of Task Scheduler. Follow these steps:

1.  Open Server Manager (or Computer Manager).

2.  Navigate to Task Scheduler. In Server Manager, Task Scheduler is found under Configuration.

3.  In the Actions pane (right side) are two options to create a task:

    - **Create a Basic Task:** This takes you through a wizard to create a scheduled task.

    - **Create Task:** This option allows you to create a scheduled task manually.

    Click Create Task to open the Create Task dialog box (see Figure 4.10).

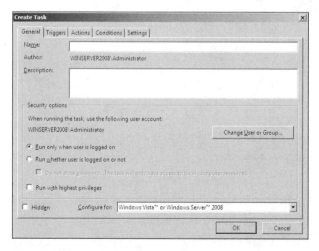

FIGURE 4.10
The Create Task dialog box.

4. In the General tab, enter the following:

   ▶ The task name

   ▶ A description of the task

   ▶ The account the task will run under

   ▶ Whether the task should run only when a user is logged on or if it can run whether a user is logged on or not

   ▶ The privilege level

   ▶ Whether you want the task to be hidden

5. Click the Triggers tab and then click New. The New Trigger dialog box appears (see Figure 4.11). Click on the Begin the Task drop-down box to display all the triggers available. The options in this dialog box change, depending on which trigger is selected. Select On Workstation Unlock.

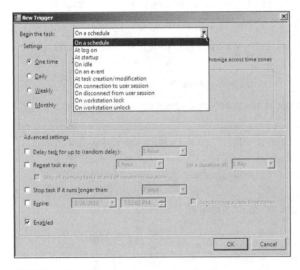

FIGURE 4.11
Selecting a trigger for a scheduled task.

6. With this trigger selected, do any of the following, as needed:

   ▶ Select any user or a specified user

   ▶ Delay the task

   ▶ Repeat the task

   ▶ Stop the task if it runs longer than a specified time

   ▶ Activate and expire the task on set dates

   ▶ Enable the task

Notice that you can have more than one trigger for each of your scheduled tasks.

**NOTE** Many of the selections in the New Trigger dialog box are the same for all the triggers, but some differ. Select each one to see the differences.

7. Click the Actions tab and then New. The New Action dialog box appears (see Figure 4.12). The action is the task that needs to be run. There are three actions to select from:

   ▶ Start a Program

   ▶ Send an E-mail

   ▶ Display a Message

   Select Display a Message. (Note that the dialog box options vary, depending on your selection.)

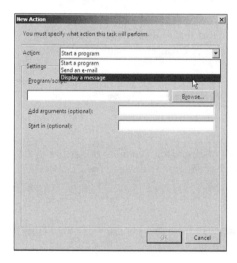

FIGURE 4.12
Selecting an action.

8. Give the message a title and add what you want to say in the message. For example, you might want the message to say "Please do not log off user" because when servers run applications in a console, it may be necessary for a user to be logged on to have the application run.

9. Click the Conditions tab and set the following:

   ▶ Start only if the computer is idle and specify how long to wait for idle. Also stop if the computer ceases to be idle.

   ▶ Start only if connected to AC power and stop if switched to battery power.

   ▶ Wake the computer to run the task.

   ▶ Run only if a specified network connection is available.

10. Click the Settings tab, and you see the following options for your scheduled task:

  ▶ Allow task to be run on demand

  ▶ Run task ASAP after the scheduled time is missed

  ▶ Restart the task if it fails on a certain interval and up to a specified number of times.

  ▶ Stop the task if it runs too long

  ▶ Force the task to stop if it does not end when requested

  ▶ Delete the task if it is not scheduled to run again after a specified amount of time

You can also specify how to manage a new instance of the task.

When you click OK, you have successfully configured a scheduled task. You can test your task by locking the server and then unlocking it to see if you get the message.

In this section, you created a simple scheduled task to show the functionality of the improved Task Scheduler. You can clearly see that this tool can be leveraged in many ways to successfully manage your Windows Server 2008 infrastructure.

# Manage Windows Server 2008 Using Remote Desktop

**Scenario/Problem:** You are given the task of managing hundreds of servers in multiple regions. What is one technology that you can use to remotely control your Windows Server 2008 machines?

**Solution:** Remote Desktop allows you to manage from one central location multiple Windows Server machines that may physically sit in different regional offices.

By default, remote access to your Windows Server 2008 server is disabled. You need to enable this feature to be able to access the server remotely. While this is an easy task, it does differ a little from the process in Windows 2000/2003 Server. Follow these steps to enable remote access:

1. Right-click Computer, in the Start menu, and select Properties. The Windows 2000/2003 Server Properties dialog box does not appear; instead, a System Control Panel appears (see Figure 4.13). The System Control Panel gives you a nice overview of your server that has the following sections:

  ▶ **Windows Edition:** This shows the edition of Server 2008 that you are running and what service pack level you have installed.

▶ **System:** This shows your processor, RAM, and system type (32 or 64-bit).

▶ **Computer Name, Domain, and Workgroup Settings:** If you click the Change Settings link in this area, you can change the server name and join or remove the server from a domain or workgroup.

▶ **Windows Activation:** If you are running an evaluation copy of Windows Server 2008, in this section you can see how long your evaluation period has before it expires. If you have purchased the same edition of Windows Server, you can add the product key here by clicking on the Change Product Key link.

FIGURE 4.13
The System Control Panel.

---

**NOTE** For information on how to extend your evaluation period, see Chapter 2, "Configure and Manage Server Core."

---

2. Click the Remote Settings link in the Tasks section at the top left of the System Control Panel. The other two links, Device Manager and Advanced System Settings, take you to the same dialog box but directly into their respective tabs.

3. When the Systems Properties dialog box appears, if needed, select a setting other than Don't Allow Connections to This Computer:

> ▶ **Allow Connection from Computer Running Any Version of Remote Desktop (less secure):** This option allows any Windows OS to connect to the server.

> ▶ **Allow Connection from Computers Running Remote Desktop with Network Level Authentication (more secure):** This option allows connections only from clients running at least Remote Desktop version 6 and supports the new Credential Security Support Provider (CredSSP). Windows Vista and Windows XP with Service Pack 3 meet these requirements. However, with Windows XP, Service Pack 3 you need to enable this functionality by updating the registry on the client. (See http://support.microsoft.com/kb/951608 for instructions.)

**NOTE** Network Level Authentication is a new authentication technology that allows a user's credentials to be authenticated prior to launching Remote Desktop and getting to the logon screen. This can help prevent malicious attacks on the server.

4. To allow users to connect to your server, give them permission. Click the Select Users button and then add local or domain users to the local Remote Desktop Users group. Notice that local administrators do not need to be added here because they already have the permissions needed to connect.

5. Click OK three times, and you have enabled users to connect to this server via Remote Desktop.

Not surprisingly, there are multiple ways to enable Remote Desktop connections. You can accomplish this with Group Policy and also while installing the Terminal Services role.

When you have enabled Windows Server 2008 to accept Remote Desktop connections, you connect from your client workstation as follows:

1. Select Start, Run and enter mstsc.

2. Provide your credentials.

3. Click OK, and you're connected. (Yep, it's as easy as 1, 2, 3.)

4. To disconnect, log off the Remote Desktop session.

The edition of Windows Server 2008 you have installed dictates how many concurrent connections are allowed. How can you tell how many connections are active at any given time? The Terminal Services Manager helps with that. You can get to this tool by selecting Administrative Tools, Terminal Services, Terminal Services Manager (see Figure 4.14). This tool enables you not only to view who is connected but also to log them off and disconnect their session or send them a message. You might wonder what the difference is between logging off and disconnecting. A user can close his or her connection to a server without logging off; this allows his or her applications to continue to run. Also, upon reconnecting, that person is put back where he or she left off. When logging off the session, you are no longer running any applications under that session. Another way to see who is connected is to use the User tab of the Task Manager, from which you can also disconnect, log off, or send a message to users.

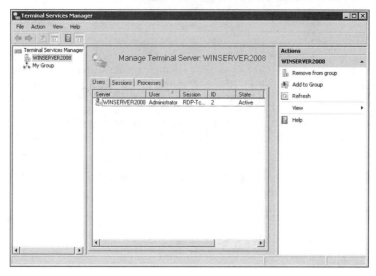

FIGURE 4.14
Terminal Services Manager.

From time to time, you will find that you are unable to connect because all the allowed connections are being used. How can you see who is connected? In this case, you can use the Terminal Services Manager to connect to a remote computer. There is, however, a command-line tool, Query User, you use while you are connected to another server. Here's how you use it:

1. Connect to another server on your domain.

2. Get to a command prompt by entering cmd in the Run box under the Start menu.

3. Enter Query User /server:<servername>. The output gives you the follow-ing information (see Figure 4.15):

   ▶ User name
   ▶ Session name
   ▶ ID
   ▶ State
   ▶ Idle time
   ▶ Logon time

FIGURE 4.15
Query User results.

Now you know who is connected to the server, but say that you are working on a critical issue and must connect to this server. How will you be able to log off one of the users? Follow these steps:

1.  At the command prompt type logoff /<server:servername> <ID>, where <ID> corresponds to the ID number associated with the user you want to log off, which you found when using the Query User command.

2.  Run the Query User command again to confirm that the user has been logged off. The user who was connected and then logged off receives a message that his or her connection has been terminated.

You can now connect to the server via a Remote Desktop connection.

> **NOTE**  You will want to make sure the user you are disconnecting is not currently working on any critical process; he or she may even be logged on to work on the issue you are responding to. If possible, try to communicate to the user that you are logging him or her off prior to doing so.

## Configure Backups and Perform Restores

> **Scenario/Problem:** As part of the Business Continuity Management Team, you have been given the responsibility of making sure your Windows Server 2008 operating systems and data are backed up. You also have the task of performing disaster recovery tests and restoring the servers from your backups. How will you configure backups and perform restores?

**Solution:** You need to understand the requirements for recovering your server and data in your organization, most likely dictated by service-level agreements (SLA). SLAs define the amounts of time allowed for the recovery of your servers and what data needs to be available. Another item they define is retention of data, or how long to keep your data. In some environments, you may need to retain data for up to seven years for auditing purposes. (And believe me: The auditors will show up and expect to have access to the data.)

The first step in managing your backups is to devise a backup policy. You need to consider the different types of backups needed, which depends on your organization's infrastructure. The following are some of the different backups to consider:

- System state backups (Automated System Recovery [ASR])
- File system data backups
- Database backups (full database backups and transaction log backups)
- Exchange Server backups

**NOTE** In this book we cover only Windows Server 2008 system state (ASR) and file system data backups and restores using the backup utility within Windows. In a real-world scenario, you would probably use a third-party tool, such as IBM's Tivoli Enterprise or Symantec's NetBackup. Usually these third-party tools also allow you to set the number of versions of a file you want to keep.

Say that you work with your business division and come up with the following SLAs for server and data recovery:

- Data files must be recoverable from at least the prior business day.
- Server recovery should be less than or no more than six hours.
- Data must be retained for at least five years.

Keeping these SLAs in mind, you need to make sure you have a daily backup of all data files and system state. You also need to have a plan that incorporates five-year retention of data, possibly on a monthly archive backup. And you need to consider your space requirements for this and also the media used, as some tape media may not have a good storage life.

If you think about this for a bit, you will realize that a daily backup of all data will cause you to duplicate quite a bit of data on your backups every day. This would waste storage and also require a large backup window (that is, time to run the backup). Ideally, you want to run the backups during a time when server utilization is at its lowest and finish prior to the start of the business day. Making incremental backups of data is the solution to this issue. You can perform full data backups on the weekend (usually when you can afford to have a larger backup window) and then perform incremental backups during the week. Incremental backups back up only the data that changes since the last backup. The drawback to this solution, in the past, was the time it would take to restore the data; you would first have to restore the last full backup and then restore the incremental backups. With Windows Server 2008, you no longer need to restore from multiple backups. Instead, you just choose the date of the backup you would like to restore.

**NOTE** Some third-party backup solutions use what is called "forever incremental" technology. This technology allows you to set your backups to back up only what has changed, and it also keeps active the data that has not changed. When the unchanged data remains active, the restore time will be shorter because you will need to perform only one restore—not restore the full backup and then all the differentials. Many backup solutions back up only what has changed on the block level of a file. Windows Server 2008 also backs up on the block level. Backing up on the block level only backs up identical data once, even if the data can be found on different files. An example of this would be a company letterhead. The letterhead is on many files but is only backed up once with pointers to each file that uses the letterhead. This technology improves space utilization.

Now let's look at how to configure Windows Server 2008 to back up your data files and system state on a schedule:

1. Select Start, Administrative Tools, Windows Server Backup. The Windows Server Backup window appears.

2. In the Actions pane, click on Backup Schedule to invoke the Backup Schedule Wizard. A scheduled backup automatically includes the system state.

3. Click Next on the Getting Started page.

4. Select one of two options:

   ▶ **Full Server:** Select this option to back up all the data, applications, and system state.

   ▶ **Custom:** Select this option to exclude some volumes from your scheduled backup.

5. On the Backup Configuration page, select Custom and click Next. On the page that appears next, you can exclude volumes. However, notice that you can't exclude a volume that contains the OS files.

**NOTE** If you had chosen to do a one-time backup, you would be given the option Enable System Recovery at this point to include the system state. If this box is unchecked, you are not forced to back up the volume that contains the OS.

6. Specify the time of day the backup should run. Or, if you like, you can back up the data multiple times in one day.

7. Select your destination type. Windows Server Backup looks for external disks to which to back up the data. You can select a local volume by clicking Show Available Disks; however, in this case, the backup utility reformats that disk and uses it solely for backup data, and you will no longer be able to see the disk via Windows Explorer. The backup disk selected needs to be at least 1.5 times the

size of the amount of data being backed up. If it isn't, you will not be able to complete the Backup Schedule Wizard.

If you choose to do a one-time backup, you have some additional options:

▶ You can select a local disk or provide a UNC path to a shared folder as a backup destination.

▶ You can allow all users who have permission to the share access to back up data or specify a user.

▶ You can decide whether to use VSS Copy backup or VSS Full backup. Use VSS Copy backup if you use third-party backup software to back up your data to ensure that the third-party software will still see the file as not backed up. (Remember that this is a one-time backup that you can run to make sure you back up some select files.)

---

**NOTE** When launching the Windows Server Backup utility, you may receive the notice "Windows Server Backup is not installed on this computer." You then need to install the feature from Server Manager. If the command-line feature is selected, you need to also install Windows PowerShell.

---

Here's how you recover a file that has been backed up:

1. From the Actions pane in the Windows Server Backup utility, click Recover to open the Recovery Wizard.

2. Select to recover files from the local computer rather than from a remote computer.

3. Choose the date you want to recover the file from.

4. Choose Files and Folders from the three recovery types:

   ▶ Files and Folders

   ▶ Application

   ▶ Volume

   You can now navigate to the file you intend to recover. Obviously, you needed to have backed up a file or folder to see it available for recovery here.

5. Select one of the three recovery options:

   ▶ Specify the location you would like to recover the file to.

   ▶ Indicate what to do if a duplicate file exists in that location.

   ▶ Restore the security settings.

6. Confirm your choices and perform the recovery.

**NOTE** For more information on Windows Server 2008 backup capabilities, see
http://technet.microsoft.com/en-us/library/cc770266.aspx.

In this chapter, we have really just touched the surface when it comes to managing the
Windows Server 2008 infrastructure. The information in this chapter provides a good
foundation, and as you become more involved with managing your environment, you
will find many other tools, both native Microsoft and third-party tools, that will help
you with managing Windows Server 2008.

# CHAPTER 5

# Install and Configure Specific Server Roles

# Install and Configure the DNS Server Role

**Scenario/Problem:** Before installing Active Directory, you need to install and configure the DNS (Domain Name System) Server role on your server. How do you install and configure the DNS Server role in Windows Server 2008?

**Solution:** There are two ways to install the DNS Server role in Windows Server 2008. The first is in the Initial Configuration Tasks window. This screen prompts you to perform several actions after the initial installation of Windows Server 2008, including adding roles and features to your server. Another way is to launch Server Manager (see Chapter 3, "Work with Server Manager") and choose Add roles.

**NOTE**  In this chapter, you will add the DNS Server role using the Initial Configuration Tasks window. In many cases, DNS needs to be installed and configured as an initial task before you add other roles, such as Active Directory Domain Services. You will add additional roles and features in this chapter by using the Server Manager.

To install the DNS Server role, perform the following steps:

1. In the Initial Configuration Tasks window, click Add Roles in the Customize This Server section. When the Add Roles Wizard appears, click Before You Begin, verify the items that appear, and click Next.

2. On the Select Server Roles screen, check the DNS Server role and click Next.

3. On the screen that appears next, which provides an overview of the DNS Server role and information about DNS and Active Directory (Things to Note), as well as links to additional information about DNS in Server 2008, click Next.

4. The confirmation screen provides an overview of the role(s) to be installed. This screen provides an informational message explaining that the server may need to be restarted after the DNS Server role is installed (see Figure 5.1). Click Install to begin the installation.

5. In the next screen, which informs you that the installation is successful and that DNS can now be configured in the DNS Manager, click Close.

6. Restart the server if you are prompted to complete the installation of the DNS Server role.

You have now installed the DNS Server role. The actual installation is straightforward and quite simple. The installation gives enough information for DNS to be operational. However, you will want to consider how to create and configure zones and look at other configuration tasks for the DNS Server role.

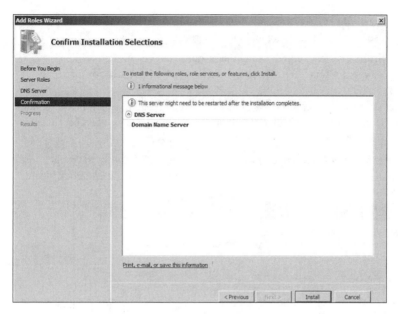

FIGURE 5.1
The confirmation screen for installing the DNS Server role.

## Create and Configure DNS Lookup Zones

The DNS Server role is installed, but there is still work to perform. The installation automatically created the forward lookup zone and the Start of Authority (SOA) for your DNS server. If you need a reverse lookup zone, you need to create one using the Configure a DNS Server Wizard. To round out our discussion, we will look at how to create and configure both forward and reverse lookup zones from start to finish.

You can use the Configure a DNS Server Wizard to work through the process:

1. Select Start, Server Manager or Administrative Tools, DNS Manager.

2. Highlight your DNS server, right-click, and choose Configure a DNS Server.

3. When the Configure a DNS Server Wizard launches, click Next.

4. Choose the lookup zone types for your network: forward lookup (small networks), forward and reverse lookup (large networks), or configure root hints only. In this case, you want to configure forward and reverse lookup zones. Choose the appropriate radio button and click Next.

5. On the next page, click Yes to create a forward lookup zone (recommended). Click No if you do not want to create a forward lookup zone. Click Next.

6. Choose the zone type for this DNS server. These are the options:

   ▶ **Primary:** Creates a copy of the zone that can be updated directly on this server.

> ▶ **Secondary:** Creates a copy of a zone on another server. These zones are used for load balancing and fault tolerance.

> ▶ **Stub:** Creates a copy of only the resource records needed to identify DNS servers for that zone. These servers are not authoritative for that zone.

Select the radio button Store the Zone in Active Directory (which is available to writable domain controllers). You will be setting up a primary zone because this is our first DNS server in our 2008 domain. Click Next.

7. Choose the replication scope of the zone data. Figure 5.2 shows the replication options. Choose to replicate to all DNS servers in this domain and click Next.

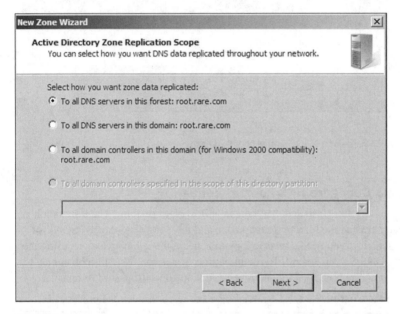

FIGURE 5.2
Replication scopes for DNS servers.

8. Choose a zone name. This can be the domain name (for example, rare-tech.com), or perhaps the zone name will reflect a specific area of your domain (for example, research.rare-tech.com) and click Next.

9. When you are asked to choose how the zone handles dynamic updates—the choices are Secure (recommended for Active Directory), both Secure and Non-secure, and Do Not Allow Dynamic Updates—choose Secure and click Next.

10. The wizard now prompts you to set up a reverse lookup zone. You want to create a reverse lookup zone, so choose Yes and click Next.

11. Choose the zone type for reverse lookups: Choose primary and click Next.

12. Choose a replication type for reverse lookups, just as you did for the forward lookups: Choose to replicate all DNS servers in this domain and click Next.

13. Choose whether to use an IPv4 or IPv6 reverse lookup zone. Your choice of IP version will determine this choice. Choose your type and click Next.

14. Choose the network ID (IPv4) or the IP address prefix (IPv6) for the reverse DNS zone. Enter the information for your reverse zone name and click Next.

15. Once again, choose how to handle dynamic updates. Pick your option and click Next.

16. You now have the option to add forwarders for DNS queries. You will not configure this DNS server to forward queries, so choose no and click Next.

> **NOTE** Forwarders forward queries that your DNS server cannot resolve. If you do not configure forwarders, the DNS server will simply use the built-in root hints servers to find out how to route the requests.

17. Finalize the DNS server role configuration by clicking Finish on the wizard. The zones are now created and ready for use. Figure 5.3 shows the DNS Manager with both IPv4 and IPv6 reverse lookup zones.

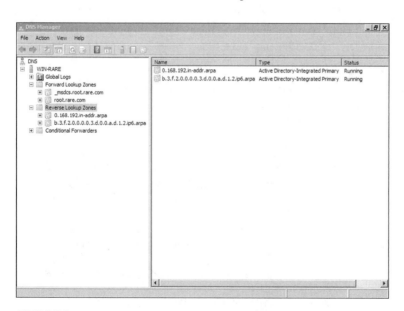

FIGURE 5.3
DNS Manager, showing IPv4 and IPv6 reverse lookup zones.

Now that you have your zones set up, let's look at some other configuration options that will allow you to optimize and better manage your DNS Server role.

## Manage a DNS Server

You now have a fully functioning DNS Server role installed, but you can still do more configuring. Let's will now take a look at monitoring, logging, management of zone records, and other tasks you can perform.

Begin by opening the DNS Manager and highlighting your DNS server. If you right-click, you can immediately see that there are a number of tasks you can perform at the DNS server level, including the following:

- ▶ **Configure a DNS Server:** You use this to set up lookup zones, dynamic updates, replication, and forwarding.

- ▶ **Create Default Application Directory Partitions:** You use this to create a partition to store and replicate DNS data outside Active Directory.

- ▶ **New Zone:** You use this to create additional forward or reverse lookup zones.

- ▶ **Set Aging/Scavenging for All Zones:** You use this to set a schedule (hours or days) to search for and delete stale records in the DNS database.

- ▶ **Scavenge Stale Resource Records:** You use this to delete stale records in the DNS database immediately.

- ▶ **Update Server Data Files:** You use this to update all data files in a zone for which the DNS server is the primary.

- ▶ **Clear Cache:** You use this to clear out records of resolved queries.

- ▶ **Launch nslookup:** You use this to launch the command-prompt tool for performing DNS troubleshooting and testing.

- ▶ **All Tasks:** You use this to stop, start, pause, and restart.

- ▶ **Properties:** You can use these eight tabs for configuring and managing your DNS server. Table 5.1 shows the tabs and the options that can be configured.

TABLE 5.1    **DNS Server Properties**

| Properties Tabs | Options/Settings |
| --- | --- |
| Interfaces | You can select the IP addresses that will handle DNS queries. You can use all IP addresses or designate which IP addresses will handle queries. |
| Forwarders | These are DNS servers used to resolve queries that this DNS server cannot resolve. If a forwarding server is not available, you can use root hints. |
| Advanced | On this tab, you can provide the server version number and options to configure, such as the following:<br>▶ Disable recursion (and forwarders)<br>▶ BIND secondaries<br>▶ Fail on load if bad zone data<br>▶ Enable round robin<br>▶ Enable netmask ordering<br>▶ Secure cache against pollution |

TABLE 5.1    **DNS Server Properties** (continued)

| Properties Tabs | Options/Settings |
| --- | --- |
| | You can also specify the type of name checking (multibyte UTF8 is the default), from where to load zone data (Active Directory, the registry, or both [the default]), and whether to enable automatic scavenging of stale records. |
| Root Hints | Root hints provides a method of resolving queries that do not exist on the local DNS server. Root hints can be used in lieu of forwarders. You can add, edit, remove, or even copy root hints from other servers. |
| Debug Logging | Debug logging assists in debugging DNS errors by capturing various DNS components, such as the following:<br>▶ Packet direction<br>▶ Packet contents<br>▶ Packet type<br>▶ Transport protocol<br>▶ Other options (details, address filtering)<br><br>You can also set the log's file path, name, and maximum size. |
| Event Logging | You can maintain a record of errors, warnings, and other events. You can log no events, errors only, errors and warnings, or all events (the default). |
| Monitoring | You can perform manual or automatic testing of your DNS server configuration. You can test a simple query, recursive query, or both. Automatic testing can be configured in intervals of seconds, minutes, or hours. |
| Security | You can add, remove, or change access and control permissions to this DNS server for users, groups, and built-in security principals within Active Directory. |

## Manage a DNS Zone

As you have seen so far, there are many parts involved in configuring and managing a DNS server. In fact, although the initial installation of the DNS Server role provides a functioning DNS server, it is hardly complete, and there are many ways to customize the DNS server for a particular environment.

It is at the zone level that you perform most of the management of DNS for your network. This is where you add and delete records, establish zone transfers, and establish a WINS server (if needed).

Let's begin by looking at the properties page for your DNS zones. To view it, right-click the server name in the DNS Manager. If you are using Server Manager, highlight the server and choose Properties from the Action menu to the right.

**NOTE** In the initial zone setup, you made many of these choices. Here you can manage and change the choices you initially made while creating the zone. You will also see many configuration settings that are similar to those of the DNS server. These setting, of course, reflect changes at only the zone level.

Forward and reverse lookup zones have many of the same properties to manage. Therefore, we will look at them from a forward lookup zone viewpoint and make reference to any dissimilarity between the two zones.

The properties page contains six tabs to manage DNS zones. They are the following:

- **General:** Here you can pause/restart, change the zone type (and Active Directory integration), change replication type, choose how to handle dynamic updates, and set aging/scavenging for this zone.

- **Start of Authority (SOA):** You use this tab to set the SOA for the zone. On this tab you specify the primary server, the zone administrator's e-mail address, refresh/retry/expiration intervals, and TTL settings.

- **Name Servers:** You use this tab to manage authoritative name servers for this zone.

- **WINS:** Here you can create a WINS lookup database for use with legacy clients or applications that rely on WINS for name resolution. For reverse lookup zones, we configure WINS-R.

- **Zone Transfers:** On this tab you enable zone data replication to specified servers.

- **Security:** You can add, remove, or change access and control permissions to this DNS server for users, groups, and built-in security principals within Active Directory.

Right-clicking the server name (or choosing the Action menu) in a zone reveals several other management functions:

- **Update Server Data File:** Sends a command to update the zone file.

- **Reload:** Sends a command to reload this zone.

- **New Host (A or AAAA):** Creates a new resource record for a host.

- **New Alias (CNAME):** Creates a new alias resource record.

- **New Mail Exchanger (MX):** Creates a new mail exchange record.

- **New Domain:** Creates a new DNS domain under the current domain.

- **New Delegation:** Creates a new delegated domain.

- **Other New Records:** Creates other records. See Table 5.2 for a list of other DNS records that can be created.

TABLE 5.2    **Other DNS Record Types**

| Other Records | Function Provided |
| --- | --- |
| Andrew File System Database (AFSDB) | Indicates the location of either of the following standard server subtypes: an AFS volume location (cell database) server or a Distributed Computing Environment (DCE) authenticated name server. |
| ATM Address (ATMA) | Maps a DNS domain name to an ATM address. |
| Host Information (HINFO) | Indicates RFC-1700 reserved character string values for CPU and operating system types for mapping to specific DNS host names. |
| ISDN (ISDN) | Maps a DNS domain name to an ISDN telephone number. |
| Mail group (MG) | Adds domain mailboxes, each specified by a mailbox (MB) record in the current zone, as members of a domain mailing group that is identified by name in this record. |
| Mailbox (MB) | Maps a specified domain mailbox name to a host that hosts this mailbox. |
| Mailbox or Mail List Information (MINFO) | Specifies a domain mailbox name to contact. Also, specifies a mailbox for receiving error messages for the mailing list or mailbox specified in the record. |
| Next (NXT) | Indicates the nonexistence of a name in a zone by creating a chain of all the literal owner names in that zone. NXT records also indicate what resource record types are present for an existing name. |
| Pointer (PTR) | Used in domains to perform reverse lookups of address-to-name mappings. Points to a location in the domain name space. |
| Public Key (KEY) | Stores a public key that is related to a DNS domain name. This public key can be of a zone, a user, or a host or another end entity. Authentication occurs via a SIG record. |
| Renamed Mailbox (MR) | Specifies a domain mailbox name, used as a forwarding entry for a user who has moved to a different mailbox. |
| Responsible Person (RP) | Specifies the domain mailbox name for a responsible person and maps this name to a domain name for which text (TXT) resource records exist. |
| Route Through (RT) | Provides an intermediate-route-through binding for internal hosts that do not have their own direct wide area network (WAN) address. |
| Service (SRV) | Allows administrators to use several servers for a single DNS domain. |
| Cryptographic Signature (SIG) | Authenticates a resource record set of a particular type, class, and name and binds it to a time interval and the signer's DNS domain name. |
| Text (TXT) | Serves as descriptive text to be associated with a specific DNS domain name. How this descriptive string of characters is used depends on the DNS domain. |

continues

TABLE 5.2    **Other DNS Record Types** (continued)

| Other Records | Function Provided |
|---|---|
| Well Known Service (WKS) | Describes the well-known TCP/IP services supported by a particular protocol and provides TCP and UDP availability information for TCP/IP servers. |
| X.25 (X25) | Maps a DNS domain name to a public switched data network (PSDN) address. |

Many of the other record types listing in Table 5.2 are unique to Windows Server 2008. So, as you have seen, you need to do more than just click Next to create a complete installed, configured, and managed DNS server.

> **NOTE** We looked at how to install and configure DNS as an individual role. If you were installing Active Directory Domain Services on this server, installing this role would automatically launch the installation of the DNS Server role.

Now that the DNS role is set up and configured, you can begin installing other roles, such as Active Directory Domain Services or DHCP, for your server. In fact, let's look now at installing and configuring the DHCP Server role in Windows Server 2008.

# Install and Configure the DHCP Server Role

**Scenario/Problem:** You need to manage IP addresses on your network, and you'd like to do so efficiently. Static IP addresses are not an option because you need to deal with expansion, contraction, and hardware changes in your environment. You also want to ensure that your internal network is secure from threats posed by public networks. Corporate policy calls for a separation of certain resources between business divisions within the same domain.

**Solution:** With technology budgets shrinking and more demand being put on IT staff to provide business solutions, there is a need to automate normal IT functions and make management easier. One of the often-overlooked but perhaps most efficient time-saving tool is the DHCP Server role. As with the DNS Server role, this role is not automatically installed and needs to be added to your Windows Server 2008 server in order to lease IP addresses to workstations. Let's look at installing the DHCP Server role and take a look at how to configure it on a network.

To install the DHCP Server role, perform the following steps:

1. Launch the Server Manager, scroll down to the roles summary, and click Add roles.

2. After the Add Roles Wizard launches, choose the DHCP Server role from the selections. You will notice immediately that the wizard populates with seven options on the left side of the screen:

   ▶ Network Connection Bindings

   ▶ IPv4 DNS Settings

   ▶ IPv4 WINS Settings

   ▶ DHCP Scopes

   ▶ DHCPv6 Stateless Mode

   ▶ IPv6 DNS Settings

   ▶ DHCP Server Authorization

   Click Next to begin the installation of DHCP.

3. On the next screen, which provides an overview of the DHCP Server role, information about DHCP and IP addressing (Things to Note), and links to additional information about DHCP in Windows Server 2008, click Next.

4. Check the bindings of DHCP to ensure that you have a static IP address for the server. Here you have the option of allowing different network cards to service DHCP clients on separate subnets. Check the IP addresses and type (IPv4 or IPv6) and recheck the details to ensure that you are binding the correct IP address to the correct adapter. Click Next.

5. Set the parent domain as well as the preferred and alternate DNS servers. Also validate that the preferred and alternate DNS servers are correct and online. Figure 5.4 shows a valid preferred DNS server and an invalid alternate DNS server. Click Next.

6. Choose whether to use WINS on the network and insert your preferred and alternate WINS server IP addresses. Most newer clients and applications do not require WINS, so accept the default, WINS Is Not Required and click Next.

7. Choose the DHCP scope(s). Click Add and then provide the following:

   ▶ Scope name (for example, rare-tech)

   ▶ Starting IP address

   ▶ Ending IP address

   ▶ Subnet mask

   ▶ Default gateway

   ▶ Subnet type: Wired (with a lease duration of 6 days) or Wireless (with a lease duration of 8 hours)

   Check the box to activate the scope (unchecking would not activate the scope) and click OK. Finally, add additional scopes, if needed, and click Next.

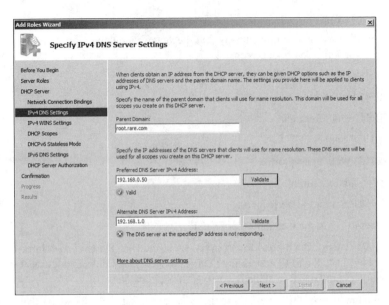

FIGURE 5.4
The Add Roles Wizard showings the IPv4 DNS server settings.

8. Set the option to enable or disable the IPv6 stateless mode for the DHCP server.
   Either DHCPv6 can assign IPv6 addresses or the clients can be configured automatically. When you're done making your selection, click Next.

> **NOTE** When choosing how to handle address leases with DHCPv6, keep in mind
> that whichever method you choose (stateful or stateless), if the router you are using
> supports IPv6, the settings in the router must match the settings in the DHCP server.

9. As with IPv4, set the parent domain as well as the preferred and alternate DNS
   servers. Then validate the DNS servers and click Next.

10. Choose the credentials that will be used to authorize with Active Directory
    Domain Services (AD DS): You can use the current credentials, choose alternate
    credentials, or choose to skip authorization with AD DS. Click Next.

11. When you see the confirmation page to review all your DHCP selections before
    installing the DHCP Server role, if everything matches with your specifications,
    click Install.

12. Finally, when you see that the installation is successful and that DHCP can now
    be configured in the DHCP Manager, click Close.

With the DHCP Server role installed, you are now ready to lease IP addresses to
clients connected to your Windows Server 2008 server.

## Configure Additional Settings in DHCP

Although the DHCP Server role is functional when installation is complete, there are still some configurations to make to the DHCP server. In fact, in some cases (perhaps when decommissioning an old DHCP server), you might not have activated a new DHCP server you installed on your server. So let's examine how to activate and finish the configuration of DHCP in Windows Server 2008. To configure the DHCP Server role, perform the following steps:

1. Select Start, Server Manager or Administrative Tools, DHCP Manager.

2. Highlight the DHCP server and select the Actions menu. Here you can configure some key items, including the following:

   ▶ **Add/Remove Bindings:** This is useful if network cards were added, removed, or configured after the initial installation.

   ▶ **Unauthorize:** You can remove the authorization of the DHCP server in this directory.

   ▶ **Backup:** You can back up the configuration and the database.

   ▶ **Restore:** You can restore the configuration and the database.

   ▶ **All Tasks:** You can start, stop, pause, resume, or restart the DHCP Server role service.

   ▶ **Properties:** You can view or change the location of the DHCP database and backup files.

We'll now move on to configuring the settings for IPv4 and IPv6. Because many of the options are the same, and IPv4 is still the dominant protocol, we will look at the settings from an IPv4 perspective. Throughout the section, we highlight where the differences exist, using notes titled "For IPv6."

## Configure IPv4 and IPv6 Settings

This section looks at the options you can configure for IPv4 in the DHCP Server role. Because these settings are unique to each network, this section serves as an overview of available options. To begin configuring IPv4, in the DHCP Manager, expand the DHCP server and highlight IPv4. Next click the Actions menu, and you see several options for configuring and managing IPv4:

▶ **Display Statistics:** Shows DHCP server statistics, including uptime, requests, declines, total scopes, total addresses, and percentages of addresses in use and available.

▶ **New Scope:** Sets up a scope for delivering IP addresses to clients.

▶ **New SuperScope:** Allows you to group several divergent scopes under a logical name.

▶ **New Multicast Scope:** Allows the sending of messages to select clients connected to the network without adding overhead and without disturbing clients that are not listening.

▶ **Define User Classes:** Adds a class for clients that need similar DHCP options.

▶ **Define Vendor Classes:** Adds a class for clients that have a specific vendor type (for example, Windows 98, Windows 2000).

▶ **Reconcile All Scopes:** Compares scope information with the registry. In addition, corrects and repairs any inconsistencies found within the scopes examined.

▶ **Set Predefined Options:** Verifies and sets options for IPv4 in the DHCP server, such as the router, time server, log server, IP layer forwarding, and so on.

▶ **Properties:** Specifies properties, in four tabs:

  ▶ **General:** In this tab you can configure when the statistics are updated, in hours and minutes, enable DHCP audit logging, and show the BOOTP table folder.

  ▶ **DNS:** Here you can enable DNS dynamic updates (always or only if requested), discard A and PTR records when a lease is deleted, and enable dynamic updates for legacy (Windows NT 4.0) clients.

  ▶ **Network Access Protection:** In this tab you can enable or disable NAP. You can also set the behavior of the DHCP server when NPS is unavailable.

  ▶ **Advanced:** On this tab you can configure the number of times DHCP should attempt conflict detection before leasing an IP address. You can also verify and change the audit log file path for DHCP. Again, you can change the connection bindings for network cards. Finally, you can configure the credentials for dynamic DNS updates to the DHCP server.

> **NOTE** **For IPv6:** In the IPv6 properties page, there is not a Network Access Protection tab because security is built in to the protocol. On the Advanced tab, there are no conflict detection settings because IPv6 by design does not experience conflict errors.

## Configuring Scope Options

After you have created scopes (superscopes or multiscopes), you still have some options you can configure in the DHCP Manager. Some options available are similar to the server-level configurations. At the scope level, you can view the statistics, reconcile the scope, and set properties. You can also activate or deactivate scopes. If you did not activate the scope during installation of the DHCP Server role, you should activate the scope here. Figure 5.5 shows a scope activation.

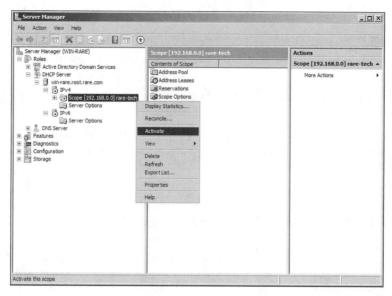

FIGURE 5.5
Activating the IPv4 scope in the DHCP manager.

The properties page is again broken down into four tabs:

▶ **General:** In this tab you can set the scope name, starting and ending IP addresses, lease duration, and whether the lease is limited (days, hours, minutes) or unlimited.

▶ **DNS:** In this tab you can enable DNS dynamic updates (always or only if requested), discard A and PTR records when a lease is deleted, and enable dynamic updates for legacy (Windows NT 4.0) clients.

▶ **Network Access Protection:** This tab allows you to enable or disable NAP and choose to use a default or custom profile.

▶ **Advanced:** This tab lets you configure options for leasing to DHCP, BOOTP clients, or both. You can also set the lease duration for BOOTP clients.

> **NOTE** For IPv6: At the scope level, there are a few differences on the properties page. On the DNS tab, there is no support for dynamic updates for legacy clients. Again, there is no Network Access Protection tab. The Advanced tab is replaced with the Lease tab, where you can configure settings for temporary and non-temporary addresses. In addition, you can configure both the preferred and valid lifetimes in days, hours, and minutes.

Besides the scope options, you can configure and manage the following options:

▶ **Address Pool:** You can add exclusion ranges for IP addresses.

▶ **Address Leases:** You can view active leases, the expiration date, and the status of NAP.

▶ **Reservations:** You can add reservations to clients that you want to ensure have the same IP address when DHCP renews its lease with the client machine.

▶ **Scope or Server Options:** You can assign options that apply to all scopes (server options) or clients within a scope (scope options). Some assigned options are DNS servers, routers, time servers, mail servers, and so on.

# Configure IPv6 in Windows Server 2008

**Scenario/Problem:** The new server roles you have added to Windows Server 2008 have added support for IPv6. You need to understand IPv6 addressing and how it is used in local networks and the Internet. You also need to understand why the new standard is necessary.

**Solution:** While IPv4 is still a widely used standard and most of our examples focus primarily on IPv4, in installing and configuring server roles, we do give attention to the IPv6 standard. Therefore, it is beneficial to be aware of what IPv6 is and how it will affect you today and going forward in the network.

IPv6 was introduced as a means of addressing the shortcomings of its predecessor, IPv4. The following are some of the advantages of IPv6:

▶ **Larger address space:** IPv6 uses a 128-bit address space ($3.4 \times 10^{38}$ available address combinations), making it expandable to virtually indefinite levels. This large address space also allows you to arrange address spaces into multilevel subnets.

▶ **Security:** The absence of NAT means IPv6 can implement end-to-end IPSec. IPSec support is not optional (as it is in IPv4); it is required, greatly improving security.

▶ **Better efficiency:** IPv6 involves reduced header information and better support for QOS. In addition, fragmentation is handled by the sending host.

Of course, the enhancements come with some changes. IPv6 addresses use 16-bit blocks that are represented by four-digit hexadecimal numbers. An IPv6 address is broken down into three parts: the site prefix (48 bits), the subnet ID (16 bits), and the interface ID (64 bits). Figure 5.6 shows an example of an IPv6 address.

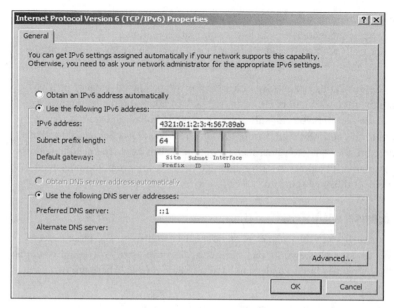

FIGURE 5.6
An IPv6 address, showing the site prefix, subnet ID, and interface ID.

This is a big change from the four-digit integers of IPv4, but it is not the only change. The structure of classes, public/private networks, stateful and stateless addressing, and header information have also changed.

IPv6 categorizes addresses by type and scope. IPv6 uses the following three address types:

▶ **Unicast:** A packet is delivered to a single interface.

▶ **Multicast:** A packet is delivered to multiple interfaces. Broadcasts are not used and have been replaced with multicast.

▶ **Anycast:** A packet is delivered to the nearest multiple interfaces.

IPv6 categorizes addresses by the following scopes:

▶ **Global:** This scope begins with a prefix of 2 or 3 (for example, 3FFE) that can be used over the Internet. It is assigned by an ISP or the registry.

▶ **Unique local:** This scope begins with a prefix of FC or FD (for example, FD00) and is used in internal (private) networks.

▶ **Link local:** This scope begins with the prefix FE80, is automatically assigned by the OS, is usable only within a subnet, and is not routable.

In addition to these three scopes, scopes exist for special addresses such as loopback addresses. One notable scope is the 6to4 address scope, which uses the 2002 prefix. This scope is designated for converting IPv4 addresses to IPv6 addresses.

Other features are neighbor discovery, which allows a client to announce its existence to its neighbor in a subnet. Stateless address configuration allows a client to automatically configure itself with an IP address (link-local), using prefix discovery from the router. IPv6 can easily be extended for new functions.

In Windows Server 2008, you can use either IPv4 or IPv6. The advantages of IPv6 make it a highly attractive option. However, the lack of adoption, the learning curve involved, and the fact that you can still use IPv4 make many administrators consider IPv6 more of future consideration. Going forward from Windows Server 2008, IPv6 will become more the standard rather than an option, as it is now. The need to address the lack of available IP addresses for the Internet makes it important to understand how to implement this new standard.

## Make Progress with IPv6

The discussion of IPv6 in this chapter is by no means exhaustive. The topic is deep enough to fill a book on its own. In fact, several books have been written and would be beneficial to anyone needing to understand and implement IPv6. These are two great titles to check out:

- ▶ *TCP/IP Unleashed*, 3rd edition, by Karanjit S. Siyan and Tim Parker
- ▶ *Migrating to IPv6: A Practical Guide to Implementing IPv6 in Mobile and Fixed Networks* by Mark Blanchet

The following are great websites that provide information on IPv6:

- ▶ **The IPv6 Information Page:** www.ipv6.org
- ▶ **IPv6.com, the source for all things IPv6:** www.ipv6.com
- ▶ **Microsoft's TechNet site, which provides information on IPv6 in Windows:** http://technet.microsoft.com/en-us/network/bb530961.aspx

# Install and Configure the File Services Role

**Scenario/Problem:** You need to share files and folders on your network. However, the files and folders exist on several servers, and a few of them are Windows 2003 servers. As well as providing a single logical file share, you want to add search capabilities, reporting, storage limits, and support for UNIX clients that need to access some of these files.

**Solution:** You can solve this problem by installing the File Services role in Server 2008. The File Services role is not a single application but a group of services that facilitate sharing files—distributing shares over several servers, managing resources (including reporting), providing search capability, and providing support for POSIX clients.

To install the File Services role, perform the following steps:

1. Launch the Server Manager, scroll down to the roles summary, and Click Add Roles.

2. When the Add Roles Wizard appears, choose the File Services role and click Next.

3. On the next page, which includes Introduction to Files services, Things to Note, and Additional Information sections, take note of the information and check out a few of the links. When you are ready to proceed, click Next.

4. Next, you see the role services you can install (see Figure 5.7), depending on what you want to accomplish with your file server. You can really pick and choose the components you would like to install. In this case, you will install all the file services components except the indexing service.

> **NOTE** As you may have noted in the Things to Note section of the wizard, Windows Search Service and Indexing Service cannot be installed on the same server. Microsoft recommends installing the Windows Search Service, unless there is a need to support older indexes.

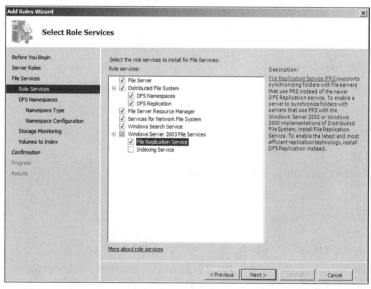

FIGURE 5.7
Installation choices for the File Services role.

5. Create a DFS namespace. You can choose to create this name now or later by using Server Manager, but in this case, create a DFS namespace now, choose the name, and click Next.

6. Choose the namespace type. Domain-based namespaces are stored on one or more namespace servers and within Active Directory Domain Services. If you choose a domain–based namespace, you then have the option of also enabling Windows Server 2008 mode. Stand-alone namespaces are stored on a single namespace server. After you choose your namespace type, click Next.

7. Configure your namespace by adding folders (see Figure 5.8) and folder targets, which serves as your virtual view of the namespace. After you have added folders, click Next.

FIGURE 5.8
Add folders to configure DFS namespaces.

8. At this point, configure your storage usage monitoring. Choose the NTFS volumes you want to monitor and choose the monitoring options. The first section is Specify the Usage Threshold of This Volume; this is a percentage of the volume drive space. The second section offers a choice of reports:

   ▶ Large File Report
   ▶ Least Recently Accessed Files
   ▶ Most Recently Accessed Files
   ▶ Quota Usage Report
   ▶ Duplicate File Report
   ▶ Files by Owner Group Report (default)
   ▶ Files by File Group Report (default)
   ▶ File Screen Audit Report

   Choose the reports and volume threshold and then click Next.

9. Choose the location of the reports that should be created when a volume threshold is reached. You can also choose to receive reports via e-mail. Click the Send Reports to the Following Administrators checkbox, enter an e-mail address and an SMTP server for e-mail delivery, and click Next.

10. Choose your Windows Search Service options by simply checking the options you want to index to be used with Windows Search Service.

11. When you see the confirmation page where you can review your installation choices, confirm that everything is correct and click Install.

12. When the installation is complete, you receive a results report that confirms that all services were installed correctly. If there are any errors, you can view what failed to install and why in this section of the wizard. If all is well and everything has installed correctly, click Close and restart the server.

After the server is restarted, you can go to Server Manager and look at some more options you have for the configuration of your file services.

At the file services level, you can add additional file services roles. Therefore, if you installed only the File Services role or just a few of the roles, you can now add more. The other two configurable/manageable roles are Share and Storage Management and DFS Management. Let's assume that you've installed all the roles you chose earlier, and you now need to manage the File Services role in Windows Server 2008. Let's take a look at what is involved in managing the remaining file services roles.

## Work with Share and Storage Management

The Share and Storage Management role is broken down into two sections: Share and Storage Manager and File Server Resource Manager. Choose the Share and Storage Manager, and you notice immediately that all your shares are visible and sorted by protocol (see Figure 5.9)

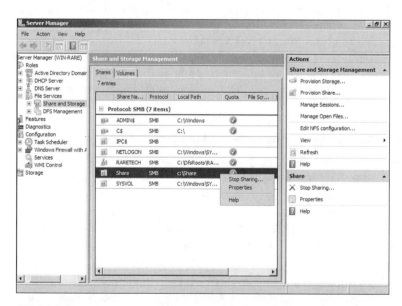

FIGURE 5.9

Managing your file shares by using the Share and Storage Manager.

The Actions pane shows the items you can manage:

▶ **Provision Storage:** You can create volumes from available disk space on the server or storage subsystems that support Virtual Disk Service (VDS). You can also use this wizard to provision LUNs in a storage array.

▶ **Provision Share:** You can create volumes and folders that can be shared. You can also manage access permissions, disk quotas, and file screens.

▶ **Manage Sessions:** You can view or disconnect one or more users from shared folders that reside on this server.

▶ **Manage Open Files:** You can view or close one or more directories or files that reside on this server.

▶ **Edit NFS Configuration:** This configuration guide provides assistance for setting up a file share that can be used with UNIX clients. It contains wizards for identity mapping and creating NFS folder shares. It provides guidance for setting up domain authorization, opening firewall ports, and using additional resources to allow NFS to work correctly.

If you highlight a share, you see more actions:

▶ **Stop Sharing:** Stops sharing a folder or volume that is on this server.

▶ **Properties:** Contains two tabs for configuration: Sharing and Permissions. The Sharing tab contains information about the share path and advanced setting. In the advanced settings, you can configure the user limit, access enumeration, and availability of offline files (caching). In the Permissions tab you can view and configure share permissions and NTFS permissions.

As you can see, there is not much to configure, but you have quite a bit of control over the Share and Storage Management role. Next let's look at the File Server Resource Manager.

## Work with the File Server Resource Manager

The File Server Resource Manager portion of the Share and Storage Management role contains three areas of management:

▶ **Quota Management:** You can create a quota to limit how much disk space a DFS folder can use. You can create a quota by using a quota template, or you can create a custom quota. The quota properties allow you to change the quota template or space limit, set a soft or hard quota or warning thresholds, and disable a quota.

▶ **File Screen Management:** You can create a file screen to block particular file types from being saved to a volume or folder. As with quota management, you can use predefined templates (audio/video files, executables), or you can create a custom filter. The screen filters can be active (not allow saving) or passive (allow saving and report). You can set up e-mail alerts, send warnings to the event log, run commands or scripts, and generate reports. You can also create new templates and add or edit existing file groups, as needed, to exclude or include file types.

**NOTE** Editing file groups using File Screen Management can be useful for organizations that need to save video files (for example, in .avi format) to their DFS file shares but perhaps want to block all other audio and video file formats from being saved in the folder. Editing the audio and video file group allows you to remove files with the .avi extension but leave the rest. Conversely, as new formats become used, you can add those file extensions here to be blocked.

▶ **Storage Reports Management:** You can configure and schedule reporting tasks for volumes or folders, choose volumes or folders to report on, select reports to generate, select the reporting format, choose the report delivery method (either e-mail or saved to a preset location on the server), and create a schedule for the reports to run. When a report is created, you have the option of running the report on demand from the Actions pane.

Now that you have considered how to manage your file shares and file server resources, let's look at managing the DFS Management role.

## Work with DFS Management

The DFS Management role is broken down into two parts: namespace and replication. The management snap-in begins with a Getting Started page that provides an overview of management tasks; you can also perform some tasks from the Action pane. The Action pane allows you to do the following:

▶ Create new namespaces

▶ Create new replication groups

▶ Add namespaces to display

▶ Add replication groups to display

The namespace and replication parts provide additional tasks. Let's look at each one individually and examine how to create and manage a namespace, set up replication, add additional servers to a namespace, delegate management permissions, and create reports. Let's begin by looking at managing namespaces.

### Manage Namespaces

To create a new namespace, you click the New Namespace choice to launch the New Namespace Wizard. Then you follow these steps:

1. Choose a server to host the namespace and click Next.

2. Enter a name for the namespace and edit the settings to change the shared folder permissions. Click Next.

3. Choose Domain-based (and Mode) or Stand-Alone and then click Next.

4. Review the settings and click Create.

You can now choose to display namespace that are not currently viewable in DFS Management. Here's what you do:

1. Click Add Namespaces to Display from the Actions pane.

2. Choose your domain and server and click Show Namespaces.

3. Choose the namespace to display and click OK.

Here's how you delegate management permissions:

1. Click Delegate Management Permissions from the Actions pane.

2. Select the domain and click Show Users and Groups.

3. Click Add to delegate permissions of the folder to users and/or groups. Or remove delegation permissions. When you are finished, click OK.

Finally, on the namespace properties page, you can view the namespace, the type, and the number of folders with targets. You can also choose the referral time and the ordering method of referrals for folders. You can also choose to optimize for consistency or scalability.

## Manage Replication

You can set up a new replication group by following these steps:

1. Select Actions, New Replication Group.

2. Choose the replication type: Multipurpose or Replication Group for Data Collection. Click Next.

3. Name the replication group, add an optional description, and choose the domain. Click Next.

4. Choose replication group members; add two or more servers to be a part of the replication group. Click Next.

5. Now choose options in the Topology Selection:

   ▶ **Hub and Spoke:** For this topology, three or more servers are needed. Spoke members are connected to one or two hubs, and hubs replicate data out to the spokes.

   ▶ **Full Mesh:** With this topology, each member replicates with all other members of the replication group. This topology should be used with 10 or fewer replication group members.

    ▶ **No Topology:** You use this option to create a custom replication topology. When you are done with the wizard, click Next.

6. Choose the replication schedule: either continuous replication or scheduled replication based on specific days and times. Then choose to throttle your bandwidth (16Kbps – 256Mbps) or use the full bandwidth for replication. Click Next.

7. Choose your primary member. This is the server that contains the content you want replicated to the other partners in the group. Select the server and click Next.

8. Select the folders on the primary member that you want replicated. Click Next.

9. Choose the local path where the data will be stored on the other group members. Click Next.

10. Review the settings and click Create to set up the replication groups.

When the replication group is created, you can view the memberships, connections, replicated folders, and delegations. You can also manage some items:

▶ **New Members:** You can add new member servers to the replication group.

▶ **New Replicated Folders:** You can add additional folders to the replication group.

▶ **New Connection:** You can create a connection between two members.

▶ **Create a Diagnostic Report:** You can create a health report or a propagation report, and you can perform a propagation test.

▶ **Verify Topology:** You can check that all partners in the replication group are connected and that data can replicate throughout the group.

# Understand the Improvement Windows Server 2008 R2 Brings to Server Roles

**Scenario/Problem:** Will the new Windows Server 2008 R2 features bring improvements to the management of the server roles you have installed in Windows Server 2008?

**Solution:** Windows Server 2008 R2 will introduce some new security and management features to the current release of Windows Server 2008.

For the DNS Server role, these are some of the improvements to look forward to:

▶ Added support for DNS Security Extensions (DNSSEC), so you can cryptographically sign a DNS zone, thereby providing better security for your networks.

▶ The addition of four new resource record types: RRSIG, NSEC, DS, and DNSKEY.

▶ The ability to sign a DNSSEC zone and host a signed DNSSEC zone.

For the DHCP Server role, these are some of the improvements to look forward to:

▶ Prevention of IPv4 address exhaustion at the scope level in redundant/highly available scenarios (Split-Scopes).

▶ Ability to migrate the DHCP Server role, using the Windows Server Migration tool.

▶ Operational enhancements such as auto-population of network fields (DNS Server, WINS, and so on) during scope creation and configuration; wizard-based split-scope configuration; and movement of the DHCP server service to the Network Service Account for enhanced security in the case of server compromises.

▶ Support for MAC-based network control access.

For the File Service role, these are some of the improvements to look forward to:

▶ **Improvements to NFS:** Netgroup support to simplify the control of users and group logins and support for RPCSEC_GSS, which enables NFS to use Kerberos authentication.

▶ **Improvements to the File Server Resource Manager (FSRM):** File classification to define classification properties and to allow you to create, update, and run classification rules to define properties in a specified folder; file management tasks to allow you to create and update file expiration tasks, create and update custom tasks (to run scripts or commands), and send e-mail; and event log notification or running of a command/script on a specified number of days before the task is to commence.

For more information on the improvements and changes available in Windows Server 2008 R2, see the following websites:

▶ **TechNet's File Services for Windows Server 2008 R2 (Beta):** http://technet.microsoft.com/en-us/library/dd463985.aspx

▶ **TechNet's What's New in DNS:** http://technet.microsoft.com/en-us/library/dd378952.aspx

▶ **Microsoft Windows DHCP Team blog:** http://blogs.technet.com/teamdhcp/archive/2009/02/26/new-features-in-dhcp-for-windows-server-2008-r2-windows-7.aspx

# CHAPTER 6

# Work with IIS 7.0

# Install the Web Server Role

> **Scenario/Problem:** You have been given the task of hosting an intranet site for your company. This will be the first website deployed for the company, and you will need to install the Web Server role on one of your Windows Server 2008 machines.

**Solution:** You can use Server Manager to install the Web Server role on a Windows Server 2008 machine. When you do so, IIS 7.0 is installed. IIS 7.0 has been restructured in order to improve the following:

- Security
- Support costs
- Web space management
- Time-saving workability

IIS 7.0 builds on the security enhancements made to IIS 6.0 to reduce surface area. IIS 6.0 improved security by locking down IIS; the default operating system installation did not include the installation of IIS services. When you installed IIS 6.0, not all the components were activated. IIS 7.0 takes security to a new level. Not only does IIS 7.0 not install by default, but when you do install the Web Server role, only the basic components are installed, to allow static websites supporting HTML and image files. All other components are not even installed. There are more than 40 installable components for the Web Server role. The ability to install only the components you need has many advantages, including the following:

- Having fewer installed components reduces the surface area for attacks.
- You have fewer components to manage, update, and maintain.
- Less components running in memory increases performance, reliability, and scalability.
- The footprint is smaller.

The steps to install the Web Server role are as follows:

1. Open Server Manager and click on Add Roles.
2. On the Select Server Roles page, select Web Server (IIS). If there are any dependent features needed, you are prompted to install them as well (see Figure 6.1). Click Add Required Features and then Next.

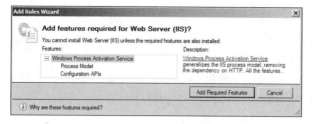

FIGURE 6.1
Installing dependent features.

3. You now see an introduction to the Web Server role, some things to take note of, and some links to get more information. Notice that the default installation allows you to host static content with only minor customizations, monitor and log server activity, and configure static content compression (see Figure 6.2). Click Next.

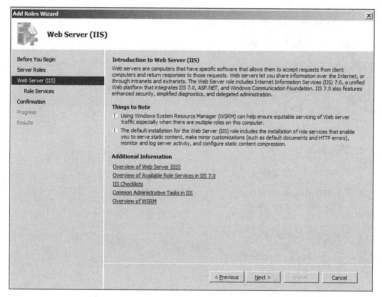

FIGURE 6.2
Introduction to the Web Server role.

4. The Select Role Services page allows you to add the services needed (see Figure 6.3). This is where you can see the componential design of IIS 7.0. Approach this page with care and add only the components or services that you definitely need. The idea here is to have the fewest possible components installed in order to reduce surface area. Make the following selections on this page:

▶ **Web Server**

    ▶ Common HTTP Features

        ▶ Static Content (selected by default)

        ▶ Default Document (selected by default)

        ▶ Directory Browsing (selected by default)

        ▶ HTTP Errors (selected by default)

        ▶ HTTP Redirection

    ▶ Application Development

        ▶ ASP.NET

        ▶ .NET Extensibility

        ▶ ASP

        ▶ CGI

        ▶ ISAPI Extensions

        ▶ ISAPI Filters

        ▶ Server Side Includes

    ▶ Health and Diagnostics

        ▶ HTTP Logging (selected by default)

        ▶ Logging Tools

        ▶ Request Monitor (selected by default)

        ▶ Tracing

        ▶ Custom Logging

        ▶ ODBC Logging

    ▶ Security

        ▶ Base Authentication

        ▶ Windows Authentication

        ▶ Digest Authentication

        ▶ Client Certificate Mapping Authentication

        ▶ IIS Client Certificate Mapping Authentication

        ▶ URL Authorization

        ▶ Request Filtering (selected by default)

        ▶ IP and Domain Restrictions

    ▶ Performance

        ▶ Static Content Compression (selected by default)

        ▶ Dynamic Content Compression

▶ **Management Tools**

    ▶ IIS Management Console (selected by default)

    ▶ IIS Management Scripts and Tools

    ▶ Management Service

    ▶ IIS 6 Management Compatibility

        ▶ IIS 6 Metabase Compatibility

        ▶ IIS 6 WMI Compatibility

        ▶ IIS 6 Scripting Tools

        ▶ IIS 6 Management Console

▶ **FTP Publishing Service**

    ▶ FTP Server

    ▶ FTP Management Console

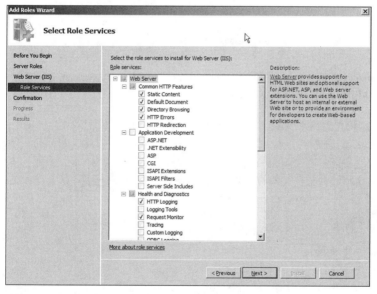

FIGURE 6.3
Adding only the services you need.

Leave the default services selected and click Next.

5. On the Confirm Installation Selections page, check your selections to make sure you have everything you need selected and make sure you have not selected any unnecessary services (see Figure 6.4). When you are sure that you have made the correct selections, click Install.

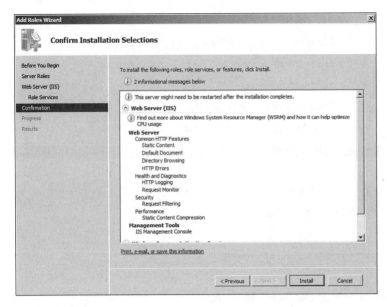

FIGURE 6.4
Confirming that you have added only the needed services.

6. As the installation is initialized, view the progress via the progress bar on the lower portion of the page (see Figure 6.5).

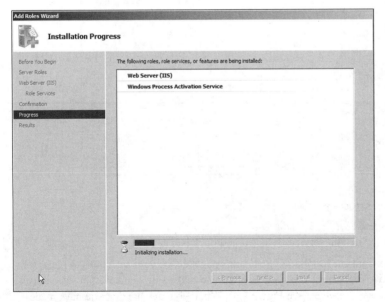

FIGURE 6.5
Viewing installation progress.

7. When the installation is complete, you are taken to the Installation Results page, which lets you know if there were any issues with the installation and whether the installation was successful, as shown in Figure 6.6. If you like, save, print, or e-mail the Installation Results page.

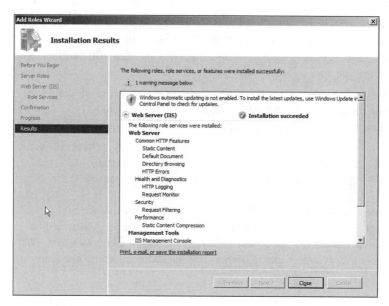

FIGURE 6.6
Installation Results page

8. Click Close. You have successfully added the Web Server role to Windows Server 2008.

9. To confirm that your installation is successful, open your browser and go to http://localhost. You should see an IIS 7.0 welcome screen.

The Web Server role can also be installed using the command-line tool pkgmgr.exe. pkgmgr.exe replaces sysocmgr.exe, which was used in earlier versions of Windows to install and uninstall optional features. One drawback to installing the Web Server role using the pkgmgr.exe tool is that you need to know the exact name of each package you want to install, as well as the names of any dependent packages. With the GUI interface in Server Manager, you just needed to check what you want from a list, and you are prompted if any dependent packages are needed.

To install the Web Server role via a command prompt, you will perform the following steps:

1. As an administrator, open a command prompt.

2. Type the following command:

```
start /w pkgmgr /iu:IIS-WebServerRole;WAS-WindowsActivationService;
➥WAS-ProcessModel;WAS-NetFxEnvironment;WAS-ConfigurationAPI
```

**NOTE** The /w in this command causes the command prompt to wait until the job
has completed before returning it to you.

When your command prompt is returned to you, the installation is complete.

3. To ensure that you have installed the Web Server role with only the default services, open Server Manager and navigate to the roles and then drill down on the
   Web Server role.

4. To add more components to your Web Server role, use pkgmgr.exe again. The
   following installs the FTP Publishing Service, FTP Server, and FTP
   Management components, along with their dependent components:

```
start /w pkgmgr /iu:IIS-IIS6ManagementCompatibility;IIS-Metabase;
➥IIS-WMICompatibility;IIS-LegacyScripts;IIS-LegacySnapIn;
➥IIS-FTPPublishingService;IIS-FTPServer;IIS-FTPManagement
```

As you can see, to install the FTP components, you must know what the
dependent components are. If you were to use Server Manager, you would be
prompted to add needed components or services. You can take a look at the Web
Server role in Server Manager to confirm that the additional components are
now installed.

**NOTE** You can use the pkgmgr.exe command-line tool in conjunction with an
unattend.xml file to perform unattended installations of this role.

Getting the Web Server role installed is just the beginning of publishing your intranet
site. You have, in effect, laid the foundation for your new intranet site. Now you need
to create a website.

## Create, Configure, and Manage New Websites

**Scenario/Problem:** You have successfully installed the Web Server role in
Windows Server 2008. Now you need to host an intranet site for your company.

**Solution:** You will use the IIS Manager to build your first website in Windows Server
2008. Follow these steps:

1. Open the IIS Manager by selecting Start, Administrative Tools, Internet
   Information Services (IIS) Manager. (You may see Internet Information Services
   [IIS] 6.0 Manager if you installed it in the previous section.)

2. When the IIS Manager appears, as shown in Figure 6.7, note that it displays these four sections:

   ▶ Recent Connections

   ▶ Connection Tasks

   ▶ Online Resources

   ▶ IIS News (disabled by default)

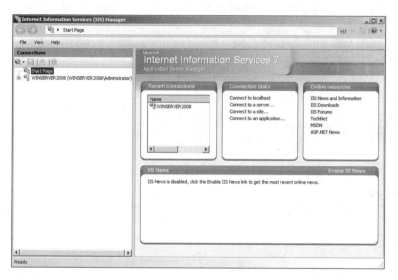

FIGURE 6.7
IIS Manager.

> **NOTE** You can enable IIS news by clicking the Enable IIS News link. The lower portion of the start page is then filled in with up-to-date information on IIS 7.0 and links to more information.

3. Expand the tree next to the server name and then select Sites.

4. On the right pane, click the Add Web Site link.

5. In the Add Web Site dialog box that appears (see Figure 6.8), supply the following details:

   ▶ **Site Name:** Call this site Company Intranet. Notice that as you define the site name, that name will also be entered in the Application Pool box. (You have the option to change the application pool by clicking Select to choose another available application pool.)

   ▶ **Physical Path:** Enter the path to the website content files. You can click the Connect As button to specify a user account to run the application pool's worker process. By default, a low-level privileged account is used. This is for security reasons; you would not want a high-level privileged account used to run your web services. You can also test the settings to make sure they will work.

▶ **Binding:** Select the type of website (HTTP or HTTPS), the IP address or All Unassigned, and the port that should be used. In this example, choose a different port number because the default website is using 80.

▶ **Host Name:** Insert the host name for your website. Leave this blank for now.

▶ **Start Web Site Immediately:** Ensure that this box is selected (which it is by default).

When you are done making these selections, click OK. You have now created a website.

FIGURE 6.8
The Add Web Site dialog box.

6. If you had valid web content files in step 5 and have set the default document, go to HTTP://<Servername>:<PortNumber> to see your site.

When you have created your website, you can add a web application—a collection of content at the root level of a website or a collection of content at a folder below the root level of a website. When configuring a web application in IIS 7.0, you define a directory as the application's root and then configure properties for the application (for example, the application pool in which the application will run).

**NOTE** Application pools in IIS 7.0 allow websites on the same web server to run as separate processes; this is also known as sandboxing. Application pools define the borders for the applications or websites they contain. Any application or website running outside the borders of an application pool will not affect applications or websites running within the application pool. The advantage to this is that if one website or application hangs, you can restart that website or application without having to restart the others.

You can use IIS Manager to manage your new website. With this tool, you can do just about all you need to do with your websites. Figure 6.9 shows the configuration tools available in IIS Manager.

FIGURE 6.9
Managing your websites with IIS Manager.

Here's how you set your default document for the company intranet site:

1. In IIS Manager, navigate to your website and highlight it to display your configuration tools.

2. Under the IIS section (if grouped by area), double-click the Default Document applet.

3. On the default document page, add the name of the default document (that is, the page you want to display first when visiting your website). You will find some files already in there, with the entry type Inherited. If these files are not

physically in the directory you configured the website to point to, they are not displayed. You can easily see what files are located in your home directory by clicking the View Content button at the bottom of the middle pane. Also, the order in which you place the files is the order in which IIS will search for the file to be displayed. If you do not see the web page file you want as the default document, you can add it now by clicking the Add link located at the top of the right pane. Enter the filename and click OK. The file is added to the top of your document list.

4. To get back to the website configuration page, double-click on the website in the left pane again.

As you can see, this is just one of many possible configuration changes. In fact, IIS 7.0 could be the subject of an entire book. However, this section shows the basics of where to go and how to use IIS Manager to create, configure, and manage your website. The next important area we need to cover is security.

# Secure Websites

> **Problem/Scenario:** You have successfully created a website for your company but would like to make sure you have not opened up your company to attacks. You need to make sure you have secured your website.

**Solution:** When considering the security of you web server and websites, you have at your disposal a variety of features and tools that are part of IIS 7.0:

- ▶ **Authentication:** By default, IIS7.0 uses anonymous authentication.
- ▶ **Authorization:** You can define which resources a user has access to.
- ▶ **Certificates:** You can verify the identity of a website.
- ▶ **ISAPI and CGI restrictions:** You can allow/deny dynamic content to run on your server.
- ▶ **SSL settings:** You can encrypt data between the server and the client.
- ▶ **HTTP filters:** You can restrict the type of HTTP requests allowed.
- ▶ **Roles:** You can control security for a group of users.
- ▶ **Trust levels:** You can grant permissions via ASP.NET code security policy.
- ▶ **Users:** You can configure user access to web applications.

There are, however, a few tools that you should look at and manually configure, depending on your environment, to make sure you have secured your website:

- ▶ Employ Minimal Install (This is covered earlier, in the section "Install the Web Server Role.")

- IP and Domain Restrictions
- Restrictive Authentication
- HTTP Request Filtering
- Restrict Directory Browsing

## IP and Domain Restrictions

With IP and Domain Restrictions, you can allow or deny access to a single IP address, a range of IP addresses, or a domain name. You need to take care when using domain names because they require reverse DNS lookups, which has an adverse affect on your server's performance. IP and domain restrictions can be applied to individual websites or an entire web server.

## Restrictive Authentication

You can employ many different methods of authentication:

- **Anonymous:** Any user can access content, with no prompt for username and password.
- **ASP.NET Impersonation:** You can run ASP.NET applications under a different security context than the default.
- **Basic:** This method requires a valid username and password.
- **Client Certificate Mapping:** This method allows automatic authentication for clients that log on with certificates.
- **Digest:** This method maps to a domain account for authentication, by using the domain controller. Also known as hashing.
- **Forms:** This method redirects unauthorized users to a form to provide credentials.
- **Windows:** You can use NTLM or Kerberos protocols to authenticate.

Only Anonymous authentication is enabled by default.

## HTTP Request Filtering

The HTTP request filtering tool was an add-on in earlier versions of IIS. This feature allows you to control the type of requests that will be run on your website. You can apply the following filters:

- **Double Encoded Requests:** This denies double-encoded requests.
- **High Bit Characters:** This denies non-ASCII characters.
- **Hidden Segments:** This identifies which segments are servable.
- **Base Extensions:** This identifies which extensions are allowed.
- **By Verbs:** This identifies verbs that IIS will accept.

- **Based on URL sequence:** This identifies a number of sequences to reject when requested.
- **Based on Request Limits:** This is a mix of `maxQueryString`, `MaxAllowedContentlength`, and `maxURL`.

## Restrict Directory Browsing

Directory browsing is disabled by default. If it is enabled, this feature allows the client to see the directories and drill down on the desired files. To use this feature, you must disable the default document feature. When Restrict Directory Browsing is enabled, you can restrict what the user will see while browsing. When you click the Directory Browsing applet in IIS Manager, you see these options:

- Time
- Size
- Extension
- Date (with a subfeature of long date)

> **NOTE**  Again, in this chapter, we are just scratching the surface of the security options provided in IIS 7.0. To get more information, see http://IIS.net.

For now, let's go through the steps to ensure that users must supply credentials to access content on your website:

1. Open IIS Manager.
2. Navigate to the website you would like to restrict.
3. Double-click the Authentication applet. The Authentication pane appears, as shown in Figure 6.10.
4. Notice that Anonymous Authentication is enabled by default. Click Anonymous Authentication and then click Disable in the Actions pane.
5. Click Basic Authentication and click Enable in the Actions pane.

You have successfully placed an authentication restriction on your website. Now when users try to view your web content, they get a logon prompt, as shown in Figure 6.11.

FIGURE 6.10
The Authentication pane in IIS Manager.

FIGURE 6.11
A prompt for credentials.

# Delegate Rights Assignments

**Scenario/Problem:** You have deployed your company's website and realize that you need to be able to delegate some management to the web content developers. The developers do not all work in the same location, so they will need to administer IIS remotely.

**Solution:** You can configure IIS 7.0 to be remotely administered, and you can minimize the amount of authority you give. Let's first look at how to configure IIS 7.0 to be remotely administered:

1. To add the IIS Management Service using Server Manager, begin by opening IIS Manager and selecting your web server in the left pane.

2. In the Management area (if grouped by area), double-click Management Service to open the Management Service pane (see Figure 6.12).

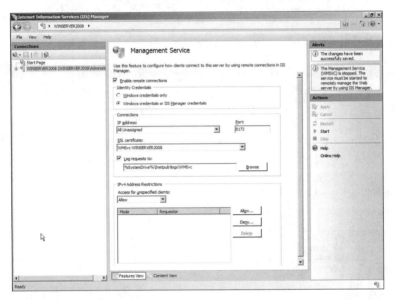

FIGURE 6.12
The Management Service pane in IIS Manager.

3. Make the following configuration changes:

   ▶ Check the box Enable Remote Connections.

   ▶ Select Windows Credentials or IIS Manager Credentials.

   ▶ Leave the default selections in the Connections section for IP address, port, SSL certificate, and logging.

   ▶ On the lower portion, if desired, restrict access by IP address.

   ▶ Notice at the top of the right pane that you are told that the Management Service (WMSVC) is stopped, and you need to start the service before remote connections can be made. Start WMSVC by clicking the Start button. By default, the service is set to Manual; you can set the service to Automatic if desired.

Now that you have successfully enabled remote connections to IIS 7.0, you need to define what the remote managers will be able to change within IIS. Follow these steps:

1. With your web server still selected in IIS Manager, double-click the Feature Delegation applet. The Feature Delegation pane appears, showing all the configurable features in IIS 7.0 and the level of delegation allowed for each.

2. Select Directory Browsing, and you see the different levels of delegation you can assign:

   ▸ **Read/Write:** This unlocks the configuration portion of the feature in the `Applicationhost.config` file.

   ▸ **Read Only:** This locks the configuration portion of the feature in the `Applicationhost.config` file.

   ▸ **Not Delegated:** This locks the configuration portion of the feature in the `Applicationhost.config` file.

   ▸ **Configuration Read/Write:** This unlocks the configuration portion of the feature in the `Applicationhost.config` file. You manage this setting outside IIS.

   ▸ **Configuration Read/Only:** This locks the configuration portion of the feature in the `Applicationhost.config` file, but it allows configuration changes outside IIS.

   ▸ **Not Delegated:** This locks the configuration portion of the feature in the `Applicationhost.config` file.

3. While we still have Directory Browsing selected, click Read Only.

4. Select your website in IIS Manager and double-click the Directory Browsing applet. A runtime error is generated, as shown in Figure 6.13, and you cannot configure directory browsing for the website.

FIGURE 6.13
The runtime error generated.

5. Click OK on the error message. In the top of the right pane, a message now states, "Could not retrieve the directory browsing settings."

You have seen how you can lock down specific configuration features in IIS 7.0. Keep in mind the following points when delegating rights with IIS:

▸ Back up the configuration files before performing modifications.

▸ Configure with the most restrictive settings possible.

▸ Do not change the system account.

When you're delegating rights, many features need to be considered. What if you have multiple IIS servers in your organization? How can you make sure your configuration is the same on all IIS servers? In this case, you can use the Shared Configuration applet under the Management section (when grouped by area) in order to use a shared configuration file or, if you have the master file, to export your file to a shared location for other servers to use.

> **NOTE** The Shared Configuration tool is not limited to the delegation and rights configuration of IIS 7.0. This tool shares all the configuration settings for IIS.

## Use the Command Line with IIS 7.0

**Scenario/Problem:** Now that you have installed and configured your web server, you realize that this is just another added responsibility in your already busy day. You would like to use some command-line tools to ease your administrative tasks.

**Solution:** The following are some of the command-line administrative tools you can use and their benefits:

- PowerShell:
    - Object-oriented data handling
    - Namespaces
    - Pipelining
    - Transparent access to command-prompt commands
    - Trusted scripts
- AppCmd:
    - Exposing key IIS Server management functionality
    - Easily controlling the server without using a GUI
    - Automating management tasks without writing code

In this chapter we focus on the Appcmd.exe utility, which is specifically designed to be used for IIS 7.0 management. Appcmd.exe can be found in the %systemroot%\ system32\inetsrv directory. The following is a list of supported object types that you can configure using this tool:

- **SITE:** Administration of virtual sites
- **APP:** Administration of applications
- **VDIR:** Administration of virtual directories

▶ **APPPOOL:** Administration of application pools

▶ **WP:** Administration of worker process

▶ **REQUEST:** Administration of HTTP requests

▶ **BACKUP:** Administration of server configuration backups

▶ **MODULE:** Administration of server modules

▶ **TRACE:** Working with failed request trace logs

---

**NOTE** You can add the %systemroot%\system32\inetsrv directory to your path environment variables to be able to run Appcmd.exe from any location.

---

The object that is being used defines the types of commands available for the object. To see what commands are available and a brief description of what the commands will do for a specific object, you can use appcmd <object> /?. For example, to see what commands are available for the APPPOOL object, follow these steps:

1. Open a command prompt.

2. Navigate to the inetsrv directory by typing CD \windows\system32\inetsrv.

3. Type appcmd apppool /?. The available commands are now listed for the APPPOOL object:

   ▶ **List:** List the application pools.

   ▶ **Set:** Configure the application pool.

   ▶ **Add:** Add a new application pool.

   ▶ **Delete:** Delete the application pool.

   ▶ **Start:** Start the application pool.

   ▶ **Stop:** Stop the application pool.

   ▶ **Recycle:** Recycle the application pool.

You can customize your command further by using an optional parameter such as the following:

▶ **/?:** Display help either from appcmd or appcmd <object>.

▶ **/text<:value>:** Generate output in text format.

▶ **/xml:** Generate output in XML format.

▶ **/in or-:** Read and operate on XML input from standard input.

▶ **/config<:*>:** Show configuration for displayed objects.

▶ **/metadata:** Show configuration metadata when displaying configuration.

▶ /**commit:** Set the path where configuration changes are saved.

▶ /**debug:** Show debugging information for command execution.

**NOTE** To see more details for these parameters, type `appcmd.exe /?`.

So now that you have a basic understanding of `appcmd.exe`, let's take a look at how we can use it. First let see how we can get a list of the websites on our server:

1. Type `appcmd list site`.

2. A new line appears for each website, as shown in Figure 6.14, with the following details:

   ▶ Name of the site

   ▶ ID

   ▶ Bindings

   ▶ State

FIGURE 6.14
Results displayed from `list sites`.

Now let's take a look at how to add, configure, and remove a site:

## Add a Website Using `appcmd.exe`

To add a website, you need to provide some configuration parameters for the site. Here's what you do:

1. Type the following:

   ```
   appcmd add site /name:NewSite /bindings:"http/*:802:"
   ➥/physicalpath:"c:\NewSite"
   ```

   The command returns three lines:

   ```
   object "NewSite" added
   APP object "NewSite/" added
   VDIR object "NewSite/" added
   ```

2. If desired, check in IIS Manager and confirm that the new website has been created.

## Configure a Website Using `appcmd.exe`

Here's how you reconfigure the port setting from 802 to 82 on the site you just created:

1. Type the following:

```
appcmd set site "NewSite" /bindings:"http/*:82:"
```

When the command prompt is returned to you, the task is complete.

2. If desired, you can check the bindings in IIS Manager to confirm the changes.

## Delete a Website Using `appcmd.exe`

The website you have created will have a short life. You are now going to delete it:

1. Type `appcmd delete site "NewSite"`. The command returns `SITE object "NewSite" deleted`.

2. Refresh the view in IIS Manager to confirm that the website `NewSite` has been deleted.

Now let's take a look at backing up and restoring the web server configuration.

## Back Up Your Configuration

To back up your configuration, type `appcmd add backup "Backup config"`. (If no name parameter is provided the backup will automatically generate a name, based on a timestamp.) The command returns `BACKUP object "backup_config" added`.

## View Available Configuration Backups

To view available configuration backups, type `appcmd list backup`. The command returns a list of all available backups of your configuration, including any backups that VSS automatically created.

## Restore Configuration Backups

To restore configuration backups, type `appcmd restore backup "backup config"`. This command returns `Restored configuration from backup "backup config"`.

Using `appcmd.exe` can ease the burden of managing your IIS environment. Being able to run many management tasks from a command line means that you will be able to script these tasks and schedule them as needed.

# Improve IIS 7.0 Performance

**Scenario/Problem:** If users experience slow performance from a website you have deployed, all your hard work will definitely not be appreciated. What are some things you can do to enable your websites to perform well (and receive the praise you have earned)?

**Solution:** When discussing performance, there are many factors to consider, such as hardware, other applications running, network bandwidth, and so on. We are going to focus on four options in IIS 7.0 that can be used to improve performance:

▶ Output caching

▶ Compression

▶ Logging frequency

▶ Windows Server Resource Manager (WSRM)

## Output Caching

If you enable output caching, IIS will keep a copy of previously requested pages in memory. Subsequent requests will be returned from memory and will not be reprocessed by IIS. You can really appreciate the advantages of this feature when you're using it with dynamic web content (for example, with an ASP.NET page that queries a SQL database for data to return to the client).

There are two output caching modes:

▶ User mode

▶ Kernel mode

Keep in mind the following when using kernel mode:

▶ Kernel mode will not cache modules that run in user mode, such as authentication or authorization. For example, if you are using basic authentication with the kernel mode option, the content will not be cached.

▶ Kernel mode supports the varyByHeaders attribute but not varyBYQuerystring.

Output caching can be configured on the web server or within individual websites on the server. You also have the option to choose when you would like to time out what is cached and force the server to reprocess the content. The timeout interval relies on how often the data changes in the web content. You can configure the File Caching Monitor to time out what is cached after either a specified amount of time or when a file changes. You can also define what file extensions the caching will apply to, as shown in Figure 6.15.

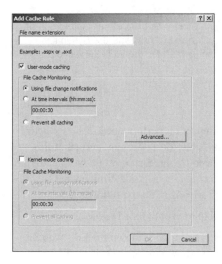

FIGURE 6.15
The Add Cache Rule dialog box.

## Compression

You can use HTTP compression to improve transmission of data by utilizing less bandwidth. Compression can be applied to static files and/or dynamic applications (see Figure 6.16). So in what type of scenarios would you use compression, and what are some things to keep in mind? Consider the following:

▶ **Static compression:** You use static compression when you need to improve transmission times and when working with graphic-intensive sites. Keep in mind that you use some CPU power for static compression, but compressed content can be cached.

▶ **Dynamic compression:** You use dynamic compression when you have a small number of requests and/or limited network bandwidth. Keep in mind that you use CPU power and RAM for dynamic compression, and compressed content cannot be cached.

Compression can be configured at the web server level or at each individual website.

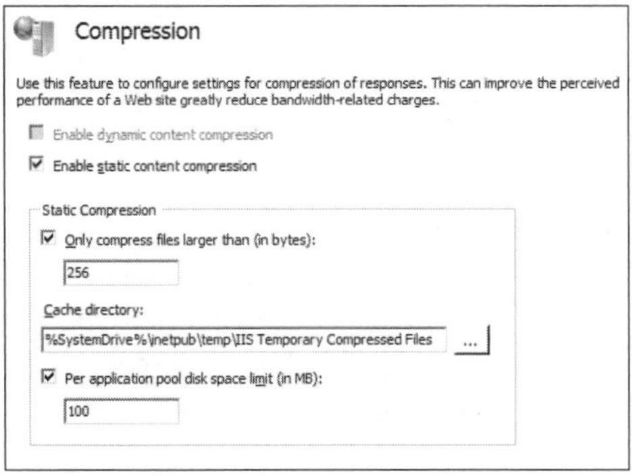

FIGURE 6.16
Configuring compression.

**NOTE** Dynamic Content Compression is not installed with the default installation of the Web Server role. To add this functionality, you need to first add the Dynamic Content Compression role service in Server Manager, under the Web Server role.

## Logging Frequency

Logging too much information has a negative impact on performance. A best practice with logging is to log as little information as possible for day-to-day normal utilization. If you are having issues with your site or web server, then it might be time to turn up the logging level to include failed request tracing and try to determine what is going on. To enable failed request tracing in IIS Manager, do the following:

1. Select the website on which you would like to enable failed request tracing.

2. In the Actions pane, click Failed Request Tracing to bring up the Edit Web Site Failed Request Tracing Settings dialog box, shown in Figure 6.17.

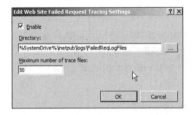

FIGURE 6.17
Configuring failed request tracing.

3. Click the Enable box and select the directory where you would like to create the log files and the maximum number of trace files desired. It is a good idea to move the log file creation to a separate volume because you usually do not want logging files to grow on your system drive.

To configure other day-to-day logging, use the Logging applet to set items such as the following:

▶ Format

▶ Directory

▶ Encoding

▶ Log file rollover

## Windows Server Resource Manager (WSRM)

WSRM enables you to control how server resources such as CPU and RAM are allocated to applications, services, and processes. You can use this tool to allocate CPU to application pools in IIS. You can see more information on WSRM and its use with IIS 7.0 at http://learn.iis.net/page.aspx/449/using-wsrm-to-manage-iis-70-apppool-cpu-utilization/.

# See What's New in Windows Server 2008 R2

**Scenario/Problem:** You have not deployed Windows Server 2008 in your environment yet, but you are considering doing so in the near future. You need to find out what improvements are included with R2 for your web server.

**Solution:** Some improvements are being made to IIS 7.0 with the release of Windows Server 2008 R2. In fact, with R2, you will receive a newer release of IIS (IIS 7.5). The following are some of the features and functionality that will be added:

▶ New management modules in IIS Manager

▶ Automation of administrative functions, utilizing PowerShell Provider for IIS

▶ Support for .NET on Server Core, enabling ASP.NET and remote management via IIS Manager

▶ Best Practices Analyzer (BPA) for IIS 7.5

For more details on IIS 7.5 and its improvements over IIS 7.0, see www.microsoft.com/windowsserver2008/en/us/R2-web-platform.aspx.

# CHAPTER 7

# Implement and Utilize Hyper-V

# Install the Hyper-V Role

**Scenario/Problem:** Your company has taken on a new initiative to "go green." Phase 1 of the green initiative requires all development servers from this point forward to be virtual servers. It is perceived that the benefits of virtualization will include the following:

- Server consolidation
- Improved server utilization
- Reduced power consumption
- Reduced data center footprint
- Improved flexibility

**Solution:** Windows Server 2008 has an installable role, Hyper-V, that enables you to configure an environment to support virtual servers. There are a variety of specific requirements that you need to keep in mind, including the following:

- The Windows Server Virtualization role can be installed only on a system that has a 64-bit processor.
- Hardware must support hardware-assisted virtualization (Intel VT or AMD-V) technology and hardware data execution prevention (DEP).
- Best practice is to have at least two physical network interface cards (NICs): one for management of the server and one or more for the virtual servers.

**NOTE** Why is there a Windows Server 2008 32-bit without Hyper-V edition available if you can only install the role on a 64-bit server? Although you can only install the Hyper-V role on a 64-bit server, you can install the management tools on both 64- and 32-bit machines. The Windows Server 2008 32-bit edition without Hyper-V does not give you the option to install the management tools.

Essentially, Hyper-V installs a hypervisor on top of your hardware but beneath your virtualized systems. This hypervisor makes it appear to all your virtualized systems as though they are running directly on the hardware, not sharing it with other virtualized systems. There is one parent system (running the full version of Windows Server 2008 or the Server Core version) that maintains the structure of Hyper-V.

**NOTE** What is a hypervisor? A *hypervisor*, also called a *virtual machine manager*, is a program that runs in a layer between your hardware (processor, memory, disk, network) and your OS. It allows you to install multiple operating systems as long as you have enough hardware power to support them. Different hypervisors work in different ways. For example, the VMware hypervisor includes drivers for your software in the hypervisor itself. The Hyper-V hypervisor does not include those drivers but relies on the OS to hold its own drivers, making the Hyper-V hypervisor "thinner," or smaller in size.

## Install Hyper-V on a Full Installation of Windows Server 2008

To install Hyper-V on a system that is already running the full installation of Windows Server 2008, perform the following steps:

1. Make sure your hardware is configured for Hyper-V in the BIOS:

    ► `Security: Execute Disable = On`

    ► `Performance: Virtualization = On`

    ► `Performance: VT for direct I/O access = On`

    ► `Performance: Trusted Execution = Off`

**NOTE** Name references in BIOS may differ, depending on the BIOS version. Also, you might need to actually power down your computer, rather than simply restart, for the settings to take hold.

2. Install the Hyper-V update KB950050 and then reboot.

3. In Server Manager click Add Roles and select the Hyper-V role.

4. Note the reminder to configure BIOS settings as well as the links to additional information. Click Next.

5. On the Create Virtual Networks page, select a network adapter to allow for a virtual network connection for the virtual machines, as shown in Figure 7.1. You can always add, remove, or modify your virtual networks later, through the Virtual Network Manager.

6. Review your role settings on the Confirm Installation Selections page and click Install.

7. When the installation is complete, restart your computer by clicking Yes.

8. After the computer restarts, you get a message about whether the installation was successful. If all went well, click Close. If you encounter errors, a good place to start your investigation is the event logs.

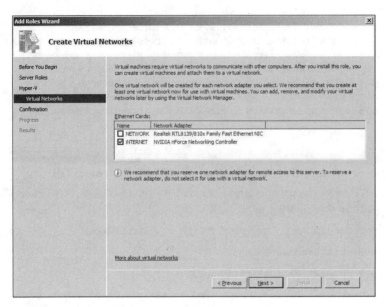

FIGURE 7.1
The Create Virtual Networks page to the Hyper-V installation process.

Now that you have it installed, you can use Server Manager or the Hyper-V Manager (shown in Figure 7.2) to see all the tools you have at your disposal to create and manage virtual machines.

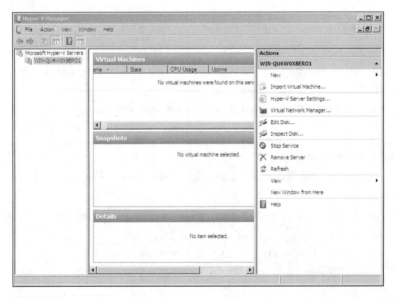

FIGURE 7.2
The Hyper-V Manager, postinstallation.

## Install Hyper-V on Server Core

To really improve server utilization and increase security, you might decide to install the Windows Server Virtualization role on the Server Core edition of Windows Server 2008.

To install on the Server Core edition, you follow these steps:

1. Set the BIOS settings as in the section "Install Hyper-V on a Full Installation of Windows Server 2008."

2. Check to see if the edition of Windows Server 2008 supports Hyper-V by entering wmic OS get OperatingSystemSKU. Windows Server 2008 returns a number, and only a few numbers refer to editions that support Hyper-V:

   ▶ **12:** Windows Server 2008 Datacenter Edition, Server Core

   ▶ **13:** Windows Server 2008 Standard Edition, Server Core

   ▶ **14:** Windows Server 2008 Enterprise Edition, Server Core

3. Ensure that you are running on 64-bit architecture by typing wmic OS get OSArchitecture.

4. Install the Hyper-V update KB950050 by typing wusa.exe <path to file>Windows6.0-KB950050-x64.msu /quiet. This update reboots the server

5. Actually install the Windows Server Virtualization Role by entering start /w ocsetup Microsoft-Hyper-V and restart the server when you're prompted to do so.

> **NOTE** Windows Server 2008 Standard edition includes a license for one free virtual instance, Enterprise edition includes a license for four free virtual instances, and Datacenter edition includes a license for an unlimited number of virtual instances.

At this point, you have installed the Windows Server Virtualization role. This is just a platform to build and manage virtual servers. Now let's look at how to manage this role to build and support virtual servers.

# Manage Hyper-V Remotely

> **Scenario/Problem:** Your infrastructure plan says that all Windows servers utilized for the virtualization project must be run on Server Core. How will you build and manage virtual servers on Server Core?

**Solution:** You need to install the Hyper-V Manager on client machines that are to be used to manage your Windows Server 2008 Hyper-V environment. Only two operating systems support the Hyper-V Manager:

▶ **Windows Server 2008:** You can add the Hyper-V Manager feature by using Server Manager. You can find the Hyper-V tools by selecting Remote Server Administration Tools, Role Administration Tools, Hyper-V Tools.

▶ **Windows Vista:** The Service Pack 1 KB925627 update package includes the Hyper-V Manager MMC snap-in and the Virtual Machine Console, a tool that enables you to establish an interactive session on a virtual server.

When you have the Hyper-V Manager installed, you can connect to remote Hyper-V servers that you need to administer by clicking the Connect to Server link in the Actions pane.

Hyper-V management leverages Windows Management Instrumentation (WMI) to manage Hyper-V. The Hyper-V WMI enables you to configure/manage all aspects of Hyper-V, such as the following:

▶ Configure server settings

▶ Build and configure virtual servers

▶ Create and manage virtual network switches

▶ Manage the state of virtual servers that are running

You can also remotely manage your Hyper-V server via Remote Desktop Protocol (RDP). The Terminal Services Remote application allows you to connect to Windows-based platforms from just about anywhere, which means you can connect to your Hyper-V server and, in effect, administer it locally. Virtual Machine Connection (vmconnect.exe) allows you to build and/or connect to the virtual servers that reside on your Hyper-V server. Virtual Machine Connection also uses RDP to establish connections.

**NOTE** The primary supported tools for remotely administering your Hyper-V infrastructure are the Hyper-V Manager and the System Center Virtual Machine Manager (VMM).

# Create Virtual Hard Drives and Machines

**Scenario/Problem:** Now that you have your Hyper-V server up and running, you are receiving multiple requests from the application team to build some virtual disks and virtual development servers, which the team needs in order to test and deploy a new application.

**Solution:** There are many reasons to create virtual drives. And you can do so before creating a virtual server or system when you have Hyper-V installed and can access the Hyper-V Manager.

## Virtual Hard Drives

You can create virtual drives when you create your virtual machines, or you can instead create them first. One reason for doing so may be to move data that is on a physical drive you are trying to consolidate into a virtual disk.

You have a few options when creating a virtual hard drive:

▶ **Dynamically expanding disks:** The virtual machine utilizes only the physical disk it is actually using. When more disk space is needed, the space used on the physical disk expands up to the defined amount of disk for the virtual machine. For example, if you configure the virtual machine with a 100GB drive, and only 25GB is being used, only 25GB of physical disk is used until the virtual machine needs more, up to 100GB. This type of disk is useful if performance is not a top priority, such as when building development or test servers.

▶ **Fixed-size disks:** The virtual machine utilizes the full amount of physical disk assigned to it, whether it is being used or not. With this type of disk, if the virtual machine is assigned 100GB and is using only 25GB, it would still utilize the full 100GB of physical disk. Fixed-size disks are typically used for production virtual machines where high performance is needed.

▶ **Pass-through disks:** A pass-through disk utilizes external storage without the use of a virtual hard disk. The virtual machine writes directly to the external storage. Some compatible data sources are physical disks, partitions, and LUNs.

> **NOTE** Configuring pass-through disks take extra work. This configuration is addressed by the Server Setup/Core Team at http://blogs.technet.com/askcore/archive/2008/10/24/configuring-pass-through-disks-in-hyper-v.aspx.

▶ **Differencing disks:** You can use a differencing disk if you are going to make a change to a virtual machine and want to have the option to roll back to the virtual machine before the changes are made, if needed. With a differencing disk, all changes are logged on this disk, and the original virtual hard drive is left intact. Therefore, if you need to roll back to a state before the changes, you can remove the differencing disk, and the original, untouched, disk will be used. Snapshots take advantage of this technology. A snapshot is a point-in-time copy of the virtual machine that creates a differencing disk with the file extension .avhd.

To configure these different types of disk, you use the Virtual Hard Disk Wizard. Let's configure a new dynamically expanding virtual disk:

1. Open Hyper-V Manager through Server Manager or from your server's Administrative Tools.

2. In the Actions pane, select New, Hard Disk.

3. On the Before You Begin screen, click Next.

4. The Choose Disk Type screen (shown in Figure 7.3) asks you what type of virtual hard disk you want to create (for example, dynamically expanding, fixed size, differencing). Choose one and click Next.

5. On the Specify Name and Location screen, provide a name and the location for the .vhd file. You can click Browse to select a new location if the default doesn't suit your needs.

6. On the Configure Disk screen, determine the size you require. You will be shown a default size under Create a New Blank Virtual Hard Disk and the maximum you can create. You can also choose Copy the Contents of the Specified Physical Disk if you want to use a physical disk and move the contents to the virtual drive. Make your choice and click Next or Finish.

7. On the Summary screen, confirm your choices and click Finish.

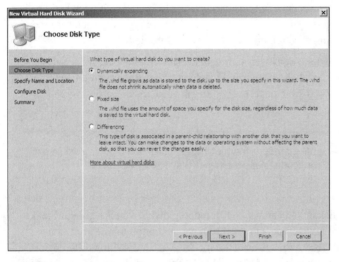

FIGURE 7.3
The Choose Disk Type screen.

When the disks are created, you can change or work with the disks by clicking the Edit Disk option from the Actions pane. (Note that below that option is the Inspect Disk option.) A wizard appears, and you can choose different options, depending on the type of disk you are editing. First, you need to locate the virtual hard drive, and then you can choose an action. You may be able to perform the following, depending on the disk type:

▶ **Compact:** This option allows you to shrink the disk size on a dynamically expanding disk, removing any empty spaces left behind when data was deleted.

▶ **Convert:** This option allows you to change a fixed disk to a dynamically expanding disk and vice versa.

▶ **Expand:** This option increases the size of either a fixed disk or a dynamically expanding disk.

▶ **Merge:** This option merges a differencing disk to the original parent disk.

▶ **Reconnect:** If you have chosen to use a differencing disk and the parent disk cannot be found, you are automatically asked to reconnect.

## Create Virtual Machines

Now that you have created the virtual disk, you are ready to build your first virtual machine. You can use the New Virtual Machine Wizard in Hyper-V Manager. To access this wizard, open the Hyper-V Manager and perform the following:

1. From the Actions pane select New, Virtual Machine.

2. On the Before You Begin screen, read the notes about the wizard and then click Next.

3. On the Specify Name and Location screen, provide a name for the virtual machine and then either leave the location set to the default or select the Store the Virtual Machine in a Different Location checkbox and choose a new location. Then click Next.

> **NOTE** The location for your virtual machines is set by default under the Hyper-V Server Settings, on the Actions pane.

4. On the Assign Memory screen, determine the appropriate amount of memory to use. Memory is a key factor for virtual systems, which is why you need as much as possible in a system where you plan on adding many virtual machines. When you're done, click Next.

5. On the Configure Networking screen, choose the network adapter that you want to use for that virtual machine. Then click Next.

6. On the Connect Virtual Hard Disk screen, create a virtual hard disk at this time (as shown in Figure 7.4) or choose to use an existing virtual hard disk that you may have already created (as you did earlier in this chapter). You can choose Attach a Virtual Hard Disk Later as well. Make your choices and click Next.

7. On the Installation Options screen (shown in Figure 7.5), choose one of the following:

   ▶ Install an OS later.

   ▶ Install an OS from a boot CD/DVD-ROM (which allows you to choose the media as a physical drive or an ISO file).

   ▶ Install an OS from a boot floppy disk (for a virtual floppy disk, or .vfd file).

   ▶ Install an OS from a network-based installation server.

When you're done, click Next or Finish.

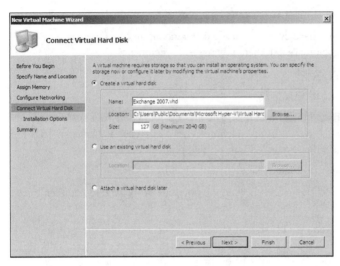

FIGURE 7.4
The Connect Virtual Hard Disk options.

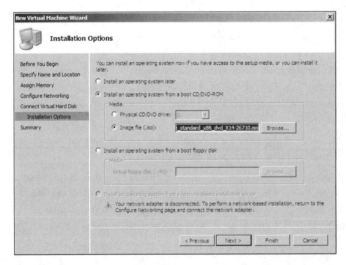

FIGURE 7.5
The Installation Options screen.

8. On the Summary screen, look over your chosen options and then click Finish or the checkbox Start the Virtual Machine After It Is Created and then click Finish.

**NOTE** Microsoft with Hyper-V supports a number of different guest operating systems. The list at the following site includes mostly Microsoft operating systems and various flavors of SUSE Linux: www.microsoft.com/windowsserver2008/en/us/ hyperv-supported-guest-os.aspx. This isn't to say other operating systems will not work; they just aren't supported—so they might or they might not work.

## Work with the Virtual Machine Connection Tool

You may have worked with a virtual machine tool in the past—maybe VMware or perhaps Virtual PC. If so, you'll find the Virtual Machine Connection tool a very simple tool to work with. If you haven't worked with such a tool, you need to learn a few concepts so that you can work with your virtual machines.

Note in Figure 7.6 that there are menus across the top of the Virtual Machine Connection tool, and there are little buttons as well. The buttons allow you to perform the same tasks that you see from the Action menu. You can use Ctrl+Alt+Delete, Turn Off, Shut Down, Save, Pause, Reset, Snapshot, Revert, and Insert Integration Services Setup Disk (which we discuss in the next section).

FIGURE 7.6
The Virtual Machine Connection tool.

**NOTE** If you click in the virtual machine, your mouse initially stays in the window until you press Ctrl+Alt+left arrow. So don't panic; just click those keys to release your mouse.

For the most part, if you click within the Virtual Machine Connection tool, you are working with your OS the same as you would if it were a real server. We therefore don't need to discuss those options further. However, note that you can make changes to the settings of your virtual machine in a much faster manner by selecting File, Settings.

One of the benefits of running a virtual machine is the ability to reconfigure the virtual hardware for the virtual machine. These are some of the items you can adjust:

- BIOS settings

- Processor settings

- Memory allocation

- IDE controller settings (add hard drive, CD/DVD drive)

- Addition and removal of network interface cards (NIC)

The settings for your virtual machine appear in an easy-to-select and easy-to-configure structure, as shown in Figure 7.7. You'll find that many of the settings you might want to configure, such as the amount of RAM assigned to the virtual machine, cannot be configured while the virtual machine is running. You need to power down the OS to make the adjustment. All in all, though, it is still a very fast adjustment to make compared to opening a system and literally having to place new RAM inside it. Now you simply allocate more RAM and turn the virtual machine back on.

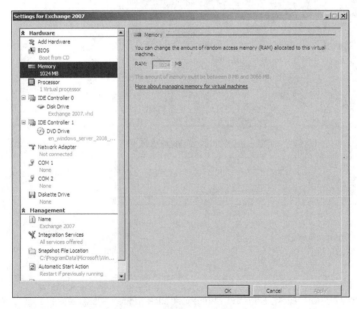

FIGURE 7.7
Virtual machine settings.

You should also note that there are some icons in the bottom-right corner of the Virtual Machine Connection tool that show you your input methods and security level.

> **NOTE** Hyper-V includes the ability to take snapshots of your virtual machines. By doing so, you create a point-in-time image of that system that you can restore at any time in the future to revert to that time. These snapshots can be taken at any time, while the system is running or stopped. This is an excellent way to recover your system in the event that you install something or make a change that is devastating. You simply create the snapshot, make your mistake (if it is a mistake), and restore the snapshot.

As you can see in Figure 7.8, you can use the Hyper-V Manager to monitor and manage your Hyper-V servers, the virtual machines they contain, and the snapshots of those virtual machines.

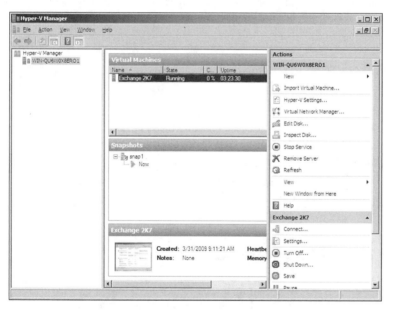

FIGURE 7.8
Hyper-V Manager.

## Install Integration Services

When your OS is installed in the virtual machine, you might want to install Integrated Services to provide a smoother experience in working with the virtualized OS. This is common in other virtualization solutions.

Integration Services installs drivers and services that allow your virtual machines to have a more consistent state and improve performance. Some of the benefits include the following:

- ▶ Improved desktop experience on the guest, via mouse pointer integration
- ▶ Time synch to keep guest OS time in synch with host OS time
- ▶ Access to the VMBus
- ▶ Use of synthetic devices
- ▶ Automation of start and stop processes
- ▶ VSS integration for live backup of running virtual machines

> **NOTE** The difference between a synthetic device and an emulated device has to do with how a virtual guest accesses the device. With synthetic devices, a request is packaged and forwarded to the host OS, over the VMBus, which in turn forwards the request to the needed physical device. Emulated devices emulate the physical hardware; for example, each virtual machine runs the emulation process `vmwp.exe`.

To install Integration Services, perform the following steps:

1. In the Virtual Machine Connection tool, select Action, Insert Integration Services Setup Disk.

2. The AutoPlay dialog appears because typically the system now views the Integration Services application as a DVD drive for you to install or run. Click the link to Install Hyper-V Integration Services.

3. When you are asked to restart your system, click Yes to restart immediately or No to wait until a later time.

# Monitor Hyper-V Performance

**Scenario/Problem:** In any IT infrastructure, performance of the servers is expected to meet specific thresholds. The same is true for virtual machines. How can you monitor the performance of your virtual infrastructure and use the information you obtain to help troubleshoot any issues you may be facing?

**Solution:** After you have installed the Hyper-V role, the Windows Performance and Reliability Monitor contains 24 specific counters for your Hyper-V environment. You can find detailed information on what counters to look at for specific resource issues at http://msdn.microsoft.com/en-us/library/cc768535.aspx. However, keep in mind that performance monitoring of a virtual machine is different from monitoring of a physical machine. Just one example is CPU monitoring. CPU utilization needs to be monitored in three different places:

▶ **Virtual Machine:** CPU utilization takes place within the virtual machine. Hyper-V Manager provides CPU utilization details here; in addition, you can look at the %Guest Runtime counter found in the Hyper-V Hypervisor Virtual Processor section.

▶ **Hypervisor:** CPU utilization also takes place in the Hypervisor. You can monitor this by using the %Hyper Runtime counter, also found in the Hyper-V Hypervisor Virtual Processor section.

▶ **Host Machine:** CPU utilization also takes place at the worker process level on the host machine. You monitor these CPU cycles on the host server.

**NOTE** For information on the Reliability and Performance Monitor see Chapter 12, "Monitor Performance and Troubleshoot."

## Utilize System Center VMM

**Scenario/Problem:** Your virtual infrastructure is growing at a very fast pace. You find that within a few months, you are going to have more than 200 virtual machines in your environment, and the count will continue to grow. You need a tool that will help you to stay in control of the virtual infrastructure.

**Solution:** The System Center VMM, a part of the System Center family of products used to manage IT infrastructure, enables you to take control and oversee the virtual infrastructure. It enables you to manage all your virtual machines and physical hosts. If you are familiar with VMware, this tool will compare with V-Center. An overview of some the benefits System Center Virtual Machine Manager are:

▶ Is specifically designed for Windows Server 2008

▶ Supports Virtual Server and VMware

▶ Optimizes performance and resources

▶ Maximizes data center resources

▶ Enables simple machine conversions

▶ Effectively provisions new virtual machines

▶ Enables organized placement of virtual machines

▶ Enables delegation of virtual machine management

▶ Centralizes management

▶ Integrates with PowerShell

**NOTE** The following are some of the other members of the System Center family:

- System Center Data Protection Manager
- System Center Operations Manager
- System Center Configuration Manager

These tools and System Center VMM all require the purchase of a license. You can find pricing and licensing information for the VMM at www.microsoft.com/ systemcenter/virtualmachinemanager/en/us/pricing-licensing.aspx.

Let's take a look at the different components of System Center VMM:

- **VMM server:** This is the core process that communicates with the host servers.
- **Virtual machine host:** Hosts can include the following:
  - Microsoft Virtual Server 2005 R2
  - Microsoft Windows Server 2008 Hyper-V
  - VMware ESX
- **Virtual machine library server:** The library is a catalog of resources that are available to build virtual machines within VMM.
- **Virtual Machine Manager administrator console:** This is a graphical user interface (GUI) you can use to manage your virtual infrastructure.
- **Windows PowerShell command-line interface:** You can use PowerShell to automate administrative tasks.
- **VMM Self-Service Portal:** This is a web-based interface that allows the delegation of building virtual guests in a controlled environment.
- **Microsoft SQL Server:** This is an information store of the virtual infrastructure that is contained in the Microsoft SQL Server 2005 database.

The following are some useful functions found in the VMM, besides the ability to create new and clone virtual machines:

- **Convert physical server:** You can convert a physical server to a virtual machine (P2V). This process captures an image of the source physical server's disk and then modifies the OS and drivers to be compatible with Hyper-V emulated devices. You can perform either an online P2V or an offline P2V. The online P2V does not require the source machine to be shut down as it uses VSS to capture the disk information.
- **Convert virtual to virtual:** This comes into play when (if) you decide to convert a VMware virtual machine to a Hyper-V virtual machine (V2V). There are two steps to performing this conversion:
  1. Copy the .vmx file and all the .vmdk files to the Virtual Machine Manager Library.

2.  Run the Convert Virtual Machine Wizard to identify the disk formats and
    virtual machine specifics and then convert the .vmdk files to .vhd files.

The VMM now prepares the virtual hard disks for the new virtual machine
creation.

As you can see, the Service Center VMM can ease your job of managing the virtual
infrastructure as it grows. You can even drill down your management to individual
virtual machines by performing the following tasks on them:

▶ Start a virtual machine            ▶ Save state/discard state

▶ Stop a virtual machine             ▶ Shut down a virtual machine

▶ Pause a virtual machine            ▶ Connect to a virtual machine

If you have System Center Operations Manager and reporting turned on, you can
generate reports via the Operations Manager to get a view of how your virtual infrastructure is doing and what you can do to improve the space. The following are some
of the reports that can be generated:

▶ **Virtualization Candidates:** This report takes a look at your environment and
  identifies physical servers that are good candidates for virtualization

▶ **Virtual Machine Allocation:** This report provides information on where virtual
  machines are allocated. This can be used to identify cost centers responsible for
  funding the virtual machine.

▶ **Virtual Machine Utilization:** This report discusses the resource utilization of
  virtual machines.

▶ **Host Utilization:** This report summarizes host utilization figures, such as the
  number of virtual machines running on the host as well as host CPU, memory,
  and hard disk utilization.

▶ **Host Utilization Growth:** This report discusses the growth on a specified host
  within a defined time period. Growth is presented in percentage and measures
  such things as number of virtual machines on the host and resource usage.

# Prepare for New Features to Hyper-V in Windows Server 2008 R2

**Scenario/Problem:** Microsoft has definitely made great improvements to its
virtual technology with Windows Server 2008 Hyper-V. However, it still has a way
to go when it comes to supporting virtual machines as well as VMware on ESX
hosts. You want to stick with Microsoft products in your environment and need
to know if its virtual technology is slated for improvements.

**Solution:** Windows Server 2008 R2 will provide many needed improvements to Hyper-V. The features we can look forward to include the following:

- ▶ **Live Migration:** This will enable guests' machines to move from one host to another without application interruption. It is similar to V-Motion for VMware.

- ▶ **Support for 32 logical processors on a host server:** This is twice the amount currently supported.

- ▶ **Hot add/remove of storage:** R2 will provide the ability to add and remove virtual hard disks without downtime. This ability will be supported only with SCSI disks.

- ▶ **Second-level translation:** You will be able to take advantage of new processor features and lighten the load on the Hypervisor.

- ▶ **Dynamic memory:** The memory pool will be dynamically distributed to virtual machines. Memory can be allocated and unallocated, depending on use, with no service interruption.

With the addition of these features in R2, Microsoft will definitely be putting itself on the same playing field as VMware running on ESX. There will still be some room for improvement, especially on the Linux support side.

In this chapter, we have just touched on all that is offered with Windows Server 2008 Hyper-V. To get more information, take a look at www.microsoft.com/windowsserver2008/en/us/hyperv-faq.aspx.

# CHAPTER 8

# Install and Configure Terminal Services

# Determine Which Terminal Services Roles to Install

**Scenario/Problem:** You have determined that there is a need for Terminal Services in your environment. Now you need to determine which features of the Terminal Services role you need to install.

**Solution:** Terminal Services is actually a group of five role services that you can install on Windows Server 2008 (see Figure 8.1). This group of role services allows you to host desktops and applications, manage client access licenses (CALs), load balance multiple terminal servers in a farm, grant access to terminal servers via the Internet, and use web browsers to access terminal servers.

A few factors determine whether you need to install all or some of these services. Let's begin with an overview of the services to begin to determine what your needs will be for implementation:

▶ **Terminal Server:** This role service allows the server to host applications or full desktop sessions. Clients connect to a terminal server and access programs or network resources directly from the server. This method of providing applications and resources has several advantages: It provides a single source for upgrading application and desktops, and it provides the ability to work securely on sensitive information without that information ever leaving the server. In addition, applications, resources, and data are available from virtually anywhere.

**NOTE** The ability to access resources from outside the internal network requires the installation of other Terminal Services roles. Later in this chapter, we discuss several different scenarios for gaining access to resources from outside the network.

▶ **TS Licensing:** This role service manages the CALs for Terminal Services. Each client (user or device) that requests to connect and use resources from a terminal server needs a CAL to do so. TS Licensing allows you to add, monitor, and issue terminal server CALs to those clients. Only one TS Licensing server is needed in a terminal server farm. Therefore, installation of this role service is necessary only in first installations of Terminal Services or in situations where redundancy or local geography necessitates the additional TS Licensing role service.

**NOTE** Remote Desktop supports two concurrent connections for the purpose of remote administration of a server. No CALs are required, and installing the TS Licensing server is not necessary for these remote sessions to work.

- **TS Session Broker:** This role service provides two functions. First, it allows you to split the load among several terminal servers in your farm. As a user signs in, the session broker looks for the server in the farm with fewest sessions and connects the user to that terminal server. Second, the session broker ensures that users who are disconnected from an active session can reconnect to that session without losing any work. This is accomplished by renegotiating the session on the original server or moving the session to an active terminal server if the original server in the load-balanced farm becomes unresponsive.

- **TS Gateway:** This role service allows users to connect to internal network resources from any device connected to the Internet. TS Gateway connects devices via RDP over HTTPS. The connectable resources can be terminal servers, computers running Remote Desktop, or terminal servers running RemoteApp programs.

- **TS Web Access:** This role service allows users to connect to a terminal server by using a web browser rather than the Remote Desktop client. TS Web Access also allows users to connect to a server or computers running Remote Desktop via a web browser, if they have appropriate permissions for that system.

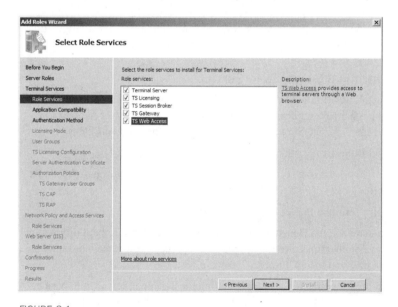

FIGURE 8.1
View of the available role services for Terminal Services.

Now that you have an understanding of what each of these applications can do, let's begin by installing each one of the Terminal Services roles. Then we will look at how to configure and manage each role.

# Install Terminal Services

> **Scenario/Problem:** Users in your environment need access to data and resources on a server. These resources require secure access and have certain restrictions due to compliance issues. The data and resources must be accessible both internally and from the Internet. They also need to be accessible via the Remote Desktop client and a web browser. Load balancing is essential to ensure that all users can access resources without too much load on any one server.

**Solution:** Install the Terminal Server role service to provide secure access to data, applications, and resources on your internal network. Add TS Licensing to install, manage, and monitor CALs. Create a terminal server farm and install TS Session Broker on all servers. Finally, install the TS Gateway and TS Web Access role services to allow access from the Internet via Remote Desktop or a web browser.

When you choose to install Terminal Services, you have the option of installing one, some, or all of the services on Windows Server 2008. We will look at installing each role service individually because in many cases each one requires some configuration during the installation phase.

## Install the Terminal Server Role Service

We begin by installing Terminal Server, which is the primary role service and must be installed. All the other role services depend on having Terminal Server in order to work. To install the Terminal Server role service, perform the following steps:

1. Click Add Roles from within Server Manager.

2. Read the Things to Note section and make sure all prerequisites have been met. Click Next.

3. Choose the Terminal Server role service and click Next.

4. The next screen is the Uninstall/Reinstall Applications for Compatibility screen. If you have applications already installed on this server, they may not function correctly after you install Terminal Server.

5. Uninstall those applications before installing the Terminal Server role service and then reinstall the applications after your installation of Terminal Server is complete. When you are done doing this, click Next.

6. Choose Require Network Level Authentication or Do Not Require Network Level Authentication and then click Next.

**NOTE** If you choose Require Network Level Authentication, only clients running a version of Remote Desktop Connection (RDC) version 6.0 and later will be allowed to use this terminal server. Remote Desktop Connection 6.0 is available for download for Windows XP and Windows Server 2003. Windows Vista and Windows Server 2008 come with RDC 6.0.

7. Specify the license mode. There are three choices here. The first one is a temporary solution: It allows you to configure the license mode later and gives you a 120-day grace period in which the terminal server will be fully functional. The other two options are per device and per user. The licensing mode chosen here must match the CALs available in your terminal server licensing server. Choose your licensing mode and click Next.

8. The next screen is the Select User Groups Allowed Access to This Terminal Server screen, and the default group is the Administrators group. Click Add to include other user groups that you want to have access to this terminal server, as shown in Figure 8.2. Click Next.

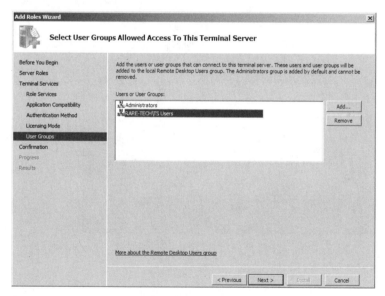

FIGURE 8.2
Adding user groups to grant access to a terminal server.

9. On the Confirm Installation Selections screen, review all your settings. You can also print, e-mail, or save this configuration information. When you are satisfied that all your selections are correct, click Install.

10. When the installation is complete, click Close. When you will receive a pop-up message to restart the server, click Yes. After the server has restarted, it finishes its setup of the terminal server. The installation results page lets you know whether terminal server has installed correctly. Click Close.

## Install the TS Licensing Role Service

To install the TS Licensing role service, perform the following steps:

1. In Server Manager go to the Terminal Server role, scroll down to the role services, and Click Add Role Service.

2. Choose the TS Licensing role service and then click Next.

3. In the Configure Discovery Scope for TS Licensing window (see Figure 8.3), choose one of the three possible choices:

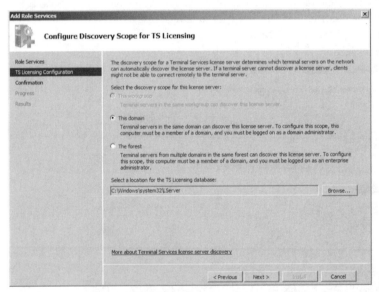

FIGURE 8.3
Discovery Scope selections for TS Licensing.

▸ **Workgroup:** Use this choice only where the TS Licensing server is installed on a server that is not part of a domain. A workgroup licensing server that joins a domain will automatically be changed from a workgroup scope to a domain scope.

▸ **Domain:** With this option selected, terminal servers in the same domain can discover this licensing server. To configure this scope, the server must be a part of this domain, and you must be logged on as a domain administrator.

**NOTE** If the TS Licensing role service is installed on a domain controller, terminal servers in the domain will be able to discover the licensing server automatically. TS Licensing can be installed on a member server but is not automatically discoverable.

▶ **Forest:** In this scope, terminal servers from multiple domains within the same forest can discover this licensing server. To configure this scope, the server must be a member of the domain, and you must be logged on as an enterprise administrator.

Finally, you can select the location for the TS Licensing database. By default, this database is placed in the following location: C:\Windows\system32\ LServer. After choosing your licensing scope, click Next.

4. On the Confirm Installation Selections screen, ensure that all your choices are correct and click Install.

5. When you receive a confirmation that the installation is complete, click Close.

## Install the TS Session Broker Role Service

To install the TS Session Broker role service, perform the following steps:

1. In Server Manager go to the Terminal Server role, scroll down to the role services, and click Add Role Service.

2. Choose the TS Session Broker role service and then click Next.

3. Pay attention to the informational alerts on the confirmation page that appears. They provide instruction and links to more information about the TS Session Broker. When you're done reading this page, click Install.

4. When you receive a confirmation that the installation is complete, click Close.

## Install the TS Gateway Role Service

The TS Gateway role service requires that IIS already be installed on the server where you will install TS Gateway. This role service also installs additional components in IIS. To install the TS Gateway role service, perform the following steps:

1. In Server Manager go to the Terminal Server role, scroll down to the role services, and click Add Role Services.

2. Choose the TS Gateway role service. The Add Role Services and Features pop-up box appears. This pop-up explains the additional role services and features that must be installed in order to install TS Gateway. Click Add Required Role Services and then click Next.

3.  The next screen is for the Server Authentication Certificate. TS Gateway uses the SSL protocol for encrypting network traffic. The recommended method is to choose an existing SSL certificate, which can be issued by an external Certificate Authority (CA) or issued by your internal CA. You can create a self-signed certificate from this terminal server. This certificate must be added manually to each client that will connect to the terminal server. The last option is to choose to assign an SSL certificate later. Choose this option if you plan to request a certificate from a CA and will import it later. TS Gateway requires that a valid SSL certificate be configured on the server before it will function. Click Next.

4.  Create Terminal Services connection authorization policies (TS CAPs) and Terminal Services resource authorization policies (TS RAPs).

> **NOTE** TS CAPs let you specify the users who can connect to this TS Gateway server. TS RAPs let you specify User Groups and the computers they can connect to through TS Gateway.

You can choose to create the authorization policies now or later. Users cannot access resources through TS Gateway until TS CAPs and TS RAPs have been created. Choose to set up authorization policies now and click Next.

5.  Select and Add the User Groups that can connect through TS Gateway. The Administrators group is the default. Add other user groups to allow users to access resources through TS Gateway. Click Next.

6.  Create a TS CAP in this screen, enter a name for this TS CAP, and choose to authenticate via password, smart card, or both. Click Next.

7.  Create a TS RAP in this screen, enter a name for this TS RAP, and then specify which computers are accessible. You can choose to allow access to computers in a particular group, or you can choose to allow access to any computer through Remote Desktop. Click Next.

8.  Next is the Network Policy and Access Services informational screen, which provides an Introduction to Network Policy and Access Services, Things to Note, and links to additional information. Click Next.

9.  Choose the role services for Network Policy and Access Services. These are the choices:

    ▶ **Network Policy Server (NPS):** You can create and enforce network access policies for clients, and you can set organizationwide policies for client health and for connection-request authentication and authorization. You can also deploy Network Access Protection (NAP) in your organization.

▸ **Routing and Remote Access Services (RRAS):** This role service provides users access to resources over a VPN connection. It is made up of two parts: the Remote Access Service, which provides access to an internal network through a VPN, and the Routing portion, which provides support for NAT, RIP, and multicast routers.

▸ **Health Registration Adding Authority (HRA):** This role service validates requests from clients and issues health certificates for connectivity to resources for clients who meet the health criteria. Adding HRA requires the additional step of selecting a valid CA before HRA is functional.

▸ **Host Credential Authorization Protocol (HCAP):** This role service allows you to integrate Microsoft's NAP solution with Cisco's NAP solution. Deploying HCAP, NPS, and NAP allows NPS to perform authorization of Cisco Network Access Control clients. To add HCAP, you must assign a CA-issued SSL certificate before HCAP is functional.

Choose the Network Policy and Access Services you want to add to your terminal servers and click Next.

10. The next screen is another information screen about IIS. It includes an introduction to IIS, Things to Note, and links to Additional Resources. When you are ready to proceed, click Next.

11. TS Gateway adds the additional IIS role services (see Figure 8.4) necessary to make TS Gateway function. Some selections are added based on how you have configured TS Gateway. Check these services and Click Next.

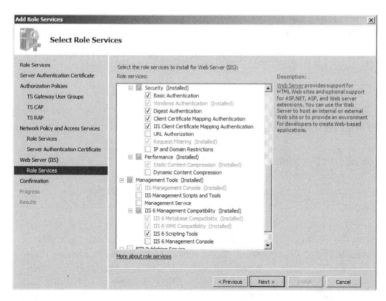

FIGURE 8.4
Additional role services added to IIS for TS Gateway.

> **NOTE** It is important to confirm all your installation selections in this screen. Ensure that all the parts that are necessary have been added and are configured correctly.

12. This screen can be printed, e-mailed, or saved to refer to later, if necessary. When you are sure the selections are correct, click Install.

13. Check that all the components installed correctly and pay special attention to any informational alerts that exist. Click Close.

## Install the TS Web Access Role Service

To install the TS Web Access role service, perform the following steps:

1. In Server Manager, go to the Terminal Server role, scroll down to the role services, and click Add Role Services.

2. Choose the TS Web Access role service and then click Next.

> **NOTE** If all the necessary services are not installed, you will receive the Additional Role Services pop-up. When you accept this, the Web Server IIS page appears. After reading the Things to Note and Additional Information page, click Next.

3. In the Confirm Selections screen, take note of the default web access site, which is generally http://<servername>/ts. Click Install.

4. When the results screen show that the installation has succeeded, click Close and restart the server.

# Configure Terminal Services

> **Scenario/Problem:** All the Terminal Services components have been installed on your network. You now need to add applications, add additional policies, and configure the Terminal Services clients' settings for your organization.

**Solution:** By using the Terminal Services snap-in within Server Manager, you can create applications that can be accessed using RemoteApp Manager. You can add additional policies, configuration, and settings with TS Gateway Manager. Terminal Services configuration allows greater configuration of client settings.

## Configure the TS RemoteApp Manager

The purpose of Terminal Services is to allow users to access applications and resources on a remote machine and operate on these applications and resources as if they existed locally. To make these applications accessible, you need to consider a few options. Let's take a look at the different methods of delivering applications and some additional configurations available using the RemoteApp Manager.

Begin by going to Server Manager and Terminal Services. When you expand Terminal Services, you see the RemoteApp Manager. Click the RemoteApp Manager, and you are immediately presented with a lot of information (see Figure 8.5).

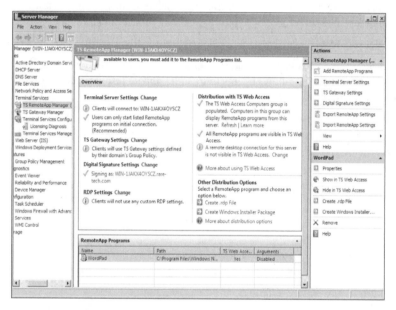

FIGURE 8.5
A look at the TS RemoteApp Manager.

The Overview section provides summary information and the ability to configure or adjust settings for the RemoteApp deployment settings:

▶ **Terminal Server Settings:** These are the settings used by clients connecting to this terminal server. You can configure the following:

  ▶ **Connection settings:** Enter or change the server name. If the terminal server were part of a farm, you would enter the DNS name of the farm in this box. You can also set the RDP listening port (3389 by default) and choose to require server authentication (in which case you need to provide the FQDN of the server).

  ▶ **Remote desktop access:** Check this box to show a Remote Desktop connection to this terminal server within TS Web Access.

▶ **Access to unlisted programs:** Choose Do Not Allow Users to Start Unlisted Programs on Initial Connection (recommended) or Allow Users to Start Listed and Unlisted Programs on Initial Connection.

▶ **TS Gateway Settings:** Use this tab to configure clients to connect through a specific TS Gateway server when they use RemoteApp programs on this server. You can choose to do the following:

  ▶ Automatically detect TS Gateway server settings.

  ▶ You can choose the TS Gateway server name, logon method (ask a user to select at connection, ask for password [NTLM], or smart card). You can also choose whether a user will use the same credentials for TS Gateway and terminal server and/or bypass TS Gateway for local addresses.

  ▶ Not use TS Gateway server.

▶ **Digital Signature Settings:** You can sign .rdp files used for RemoteApps with a digital certificate. This allows clients to trust the remote resources coming from your internal network.

▶ **RDP Settings:** These are common settings clients use when connecting to this terminal server. This section is broken down into two subsections—Devices and Resources and User Experience.

Devices and Resources lets you select the devices and resources on the remote computer that the user can access in a remote session. They include the following:

▶ Printers

▶ Clipboard

▶ Support for plug-and-play devices

▶ Disk drives

▶ Smart cards

User Experience allows you to configure the display settings for the remote session. You can choose from 256 colors up to 32-bit color. In addition, you can allow font smoothing for a better display of text in remote sessions.

### Methods of Distributing RemoteApp Programs

Within the Overview section of TS RemoteApp Manager, in the right pane are options for distributing RemoteApp programs to clients:

▶ **Distribution with TS Web Access:** When this is selected, users click on a link using TS Web Access to access the program. TS Remote App Manager automatically detects whether the TS Web Access group is populated within Active Directory. TS Remote App Manager also detects whether a Remote Desktop connection is visible in TS Web Access for this server.

▶ **Other Distribution Options:** In this section, you select the RemoteApp and click one of the following delivery options:

  ▶ **Create .rdp File:** Using this option, you can create an .rdp file to distribute to users. This file can then be distributed using software distribution software such as System Center Configuration Manager or through a file share. Users double-click the .rdp file to launch the RemoteApp program.

  ▶ **Create a Windows Installer Package:** Using this option, you can create an .msi package. This can be delivered using software distribution software such as System Center Configuration Manager, via a file share, or through Group Policy. Users double-click a program icon on their desktop or in their Start menu to launch the RemoteApp program.

> **NOTE** These methods of distributing RemoteApp programs are available only to clients that are running the Remote Desktop Connection client version 6.0 or later.

Installed RemoteApp programs are listed below the Overview section. This list shows the name and path of the remote application, the status of TS Web Access, and the status of command-line arguments.

The last section in the RemoteApp snap-in is the Actions pane. We have already looked at configuring Terminal Server Settings, TS Gateway Settings, and Digital Signatures Settings. Using the Actions pane is another way to access these settings. We will look at how to add RemoteApp programs and how to import and export their settings when we consider managing Terminal Services, later in this chapter.

## Configure the TS Gateway Manager

In Terminal Services, if you expand the TS Gateway Manager and then highlight the TS Gateway Server for your organization, you see the connection and configuration status of your TS Gateway Server (see Figure 8.6).

Although you configured many of these settings during the installation, there are a few things you can go back and change or set (if you did not do so during the initial installation). For instance, if you were waiting for an SSL certificate issued by a CA, you could add that SSL certificate now.

Under Properties in the Actions pane are six tabs you can configure. Let's review them:

▶ **General:** Set the maximum connections to this TS Gateway. You can limit the maximum number of simultaneous connections, allow the maximum supported simultaneous connections, or choose to disable new connections (in which case active connections will not be automatically disconnected).

▶ **SSL Certificate:** In this tab, you can create a self-signed SSL certificate or select an existing SSL certificate for the TS Gateway. This tab also shows the current SSL certificate and its expiration date.

▶ **TS CAP Store:** In this tab, you can indicate whether to use a connection access policy from a local or central NPS server. If you choose a central NPS server, you need to add the name or IP address of the NPS server to be used. You can also choose to request that a client send a statement of health (SoH) to enable the policy.

▶ **Server Farm:** Here you can add the various TS Gateway servers to participate in a server farm. To create a TS Server farm, you must include all the TS Gateway servers (including the one you are now working on) in the server farm.

▶ **Auditing:** In this tab, you select the events you want to enable for logging. Table 8.1 provides the events and description of the events, as expressed in "Understanding TS Gateway Event Types" on Microsoft's TechNet website.

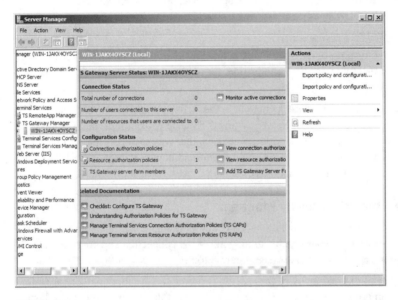

FIGURE 8.6
The server status screen in the TS Gateway Manager.

TABLE 8.1    **Auditing Events**

| Event Name | Description |
|---|---|
| Successful User Disconnection from the Resource | By monitoring the timestamp for this event and the related Successful User Connection to the Resource event, you can verify the user session time and the amount of data (in kilobytes) sent and received by the client through the TS Gateway server. |

TABLE 8.1    **Auditing Events** (continued)

| Event Name | Description |
| --- | --- |
| Failed User Connection to the Resource | The remote client met the conditions specified in the TS CAP and the TS RAP but could not connect to the internal network resource (computer) through the TS Gateway server because the computer was unavailable. By auditing this event, you can determine which connectivity issues are caused by problems with Terminal Services and Remote Desktop rather than the TS Gateway server. |
| Failed Connection Authorization | The remote client could not connect to a TS Gateway server because the client did not meet the conditions specified in the TS CAPs. |
| Failed Resource Authorization | The remote client could not connect through a TS Gateway server to the specified computer because no TS RAPs are configured to allow the user access to the specified computer. |
| Successful User Connection to the Resource | The remote client successfully connected to a computer through the TS Gateway server. |
| Successful Connection Authorization | The remote client successfully connected to the TS Gateway server because the client met the conditions specified in at least one TS CAP. |
| Successful Resource Authorization | The remote client successfully connected through the TS Gateway server to the specified internal network resource because the client met the conditions specified in at least one TS RAP. |

- ▶ **SSL Bridging:** To enhance security, you can configure TS Gateway to use ISA or a third-party product to perform SSL bridging. You can also choose to use HTTPS–HTTP bridging (this will terminate the SSL requests and initiate new HTTP requests).

Expand the TS Gateway server and highlight its policies folder in the console tree. In the Actions pane you can now create and configure additional TS CAP and TS RAP authorization policies. The Properties tabs for each of these authorization policies expose some additional configuration settings. Expand the Policies folder and high-light Connection Authorization Policies. Choose the TS CAP you want to configure in the Actions pane. Click Properties. The properties page has three tabs:

- ▶ **General:** This tab shows the policy type, the policy name, and the order in which the policy is applied. You can choose to enable or disable a policy from this tab.

- ▶ **Requirements:** In this tab, you set the requirements users must meet to connect to the TS Gateway server. You can adjust the authentication methods (password and smart card) here, and you can add other user groups. Optionally, you can choose to add computer groups that will have access to this TS Gateway server. (The option of adding computer groups was not available at installation.)

▶ **Device Redirection:** This tab contains other configurable items that were not present during the installation. Here you can enable or disable device redirection for clients connecting to the TS Gateway server. You have the option of also disabling only certain device types.

---

**NOTE**  In all scenarios, a smart card cannot be disabled as a device because it is used as an authentication method for connecting to the TS Gateway server through the TS CAP.

---

Expand the Policies folder and highlight Resource Authorization Policies. Choose the TS CAP you want to configure and in the Actions pane click Properties. The properties page has four tabs:

▶ **General:** In this tab, you can view or adjust the policy name. You can also add a description and enable or disable this policy.

▶ **User Groups:** This tab allows you to add additional user groups to this policy.

▶ **Computer Group:** This tab allows you to specify computer groups that can be accessed by clients. You can select an existing Active Directory security group or an existing TS Gateway managed group or allow users to access any network resource.

▶ **Allowed Ports:** In this tab, you can choose to allow connections through port 3389, allow connections through a list of specified ports (added manually), or allow connections through any port.

## Configure a Load-Balanced Farm with TS Session Broker

You installed the TS Session Broker role service earlier. This server will be the one that is used to track user sessions within the load-balanced farm. However, there are still a few steps needed to create a load-balanced environment. To begin with, session load balancing is supported only on terminal servers that are running Windows Server 2008, so all members of this group must be running Windows Server 2008. Follow these steps to complete the configuration:

1. Add each terminal server for the load-balanced farm to the Session Directory Computers local group.

2. Configure DNS round-robin entries for all the terminal servers participating in the farm. Here's an example:

   ▶ TS_FARM_1    host (a)    192.168.0.50

   ▶ TS_FARM_1    host (a)    192.168.0.51

   ▶ TS_FARM_1    host (a)    192.168.0.52

3. Configure terminal servers in the farm to join a farm in the TS Session Broker. This step is covered in detail later in this chapter.

## Configure Terminal Services

With all the installation and configuration you have done so far, you feel pretty well set for Terminal Services. However, this section could actually be accurately called "Terminal Services Client Configuration." It differs from the initial setup you have done so far in that this management snap-in concentrates on the configuration of user settings. To configure Terminal Services, follow these steps:

1. In the Terminal Services management snap-in, expand the Terminal Services Configuration.

2. An RDP-Tcp connection was created upon installation (see Figure 8.7). From the Actions pane, create a new connection: Highlight the current RDP-Tcp connection and click twice to bring up the properties page, which has eight tabs for configuration.

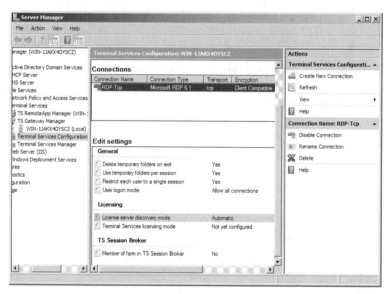

FIGURE 8.7
The RDP-Tcp connection properties page.

▶ **General:** This tab shows the connection type (RDP-TCP) and transport method (tcp).You can include a comment for the connection. In the Security section, you can choose the security layer and encryption level, you can choose to allow only connections from computers running Remote Desktop with Network Level Authentication, and you can select an SSL certificate.

▶ **Log On Settings:** In this tab, you choose how clients log on. You can specify that they can use client-provided information or a fixed set of credentials (not recommended). You can also choose to always prompt for a password.

▶ **Sessions:** You use this tab to set Terminal Services timeout and reconnection settings for the client. If you choose nothing, the server defaults to the user's Active Directory session settings. You can override the user settings for disconnected and active sessions. You can also override user settings for how Terminal Services reacts when a session limit is reached or a connection is broken.

▶ **Environment:** You can allow or disallow an initial program to be launched when a user logs on. You can also choose to start a particular program when the user logs on.

▶ **Remote Control:** This tab features settings for remotely viewing or controlling user sessions. You can use remote control with default user settings (taken from Active Directory), disallow remote control, or use custom settings such as requiring user permission and the level of remote control allowed (view or interact).

▶ **Client Settings:** These settings can limit the maximum color depth. These setting override the Remote Desktop client settings for color depth. You can also choose to disable redirection of individual devices for this connection.

▶ **Network Adapter:** You can choose the network adapters to use for connection to this terminal server. You can choose all adapters configured with this protocol or select particular adapters to use. You can also choose to allow unlimited connection or to set connection limits.

▶ **Security:** This tab is the security principals that have permissions to this terminal server. You can view, add, and remove users or groups who have access and modify permissions.

Below the connections section are the terminal server settings, which directly affect the performance of the terminal server. They are broken down into three sections. You can highlight any item under Edit Settings and double-click any setting to bring up the properties page. There are three tabs here:

▶ **General:** For best results, you should leave all three boxes checked:

  ▶ Delete Temporary Folders upon Exit

  ▶ Use Temporary Folders per Session

  ▶ Restrict Each User to a Single Session

These are the user logon mode settings:

  ▶ Allow All Connections

  ▶ Allow Reconnections but Prevent New Logons

  ▶ Allow Reconnections but Prevent New Logons Until the Server Is Restarted

▶ **Licensing:** Specify the licensing mode:

  ▶ Not Yet Configured

  ▶ Per Device

  ▶ Per User

And the licensing discovery mode:

- Automatically discover a licensing server
- Use the specified licensing servers

You can add multiple licensing servers, separated by commas, and even check license server names. If licensing servers are specified, the terminal server attempts to locate them first. If they are unreachable, it uses automatic discovery.

- **TS Session Broker:** In this tab, you add connections to a TS Session Broker farm by configuring the following:

  - Join a Farm in TS Session Broker. (This must be checked to activate the other fields.)
  - Insert the TS Session Broker name or IP address in this dialog box.
  - Insert the farm name for the TS Session Broker.
  - Click this box to participate in Session Broker load balancing.
  - Choose the relative weight of this server.
  - Click this next box to use IP address redirection (recommended).

Finally, you can select the IP addresses to be used for reconnection. Clients running Remote Desktop 5.2 or earlier will only use the first IP address in this list for reconnection.

# Manage Terminal Services

**Scenario/Problem:** Now that you have your Terminal Services role services installed and configured, how do you install applications and make them available to users connecting to your terminal server? You also need to consider how to manage settings for these programs. Finally, you need to consider how to monitor users, sessions, and processes in your terminal server.

**Solution:** Install software packages on the terminal server and then use the tools in the Terminal Services management snap-in to make applications available to users and manage settings for these installed applications. With these available tools, you can also monitor and manage users, sessions, and processes.

Begin by opening Server Manager and expanding Terminal Services. Under Terminal Services you see RemoteApp Manager, TS Gateway Manager, and Terminal Server Manager. Let's look at how to manage the terminal server environment using these tools.

One of the most important administrative tasks you will undertake in Terminal Services is installing applications that will be available to remote users. However, before you can make these applications available to users, you must first install them on your terminal server. There are two ways to accomplish this task:

▶ If you are installing applications from a Windows Installer package, the package will automatically install the application in terminal server mode.

▶ If the application uses another installer technology, you will have to put the terminal server in installation mode. To put the terminal server in installation mode, open a command prompt and type change user /install after the application has installed successfully from a command prompt. Type change user /execute to exit from installation mode.

Now you are ready to make these programs available to users in your organization.

## Add RemoteApp Programs

In Server Manager, go to the Terminal Services management snap-in. Expand Terminal Services and click RemoteApp Manager. To add applications, perform the following steps:

1. From the Actions pane, click Add RemoteApp Programs. The RemoteApp Wizard starts.

2. Read the section titled Before You Run This Wizard Ensure That. If you have met all the requirements, click Next.

3. On the next screen, Choose Programs to Add to the RemoteApp Programs List, the list is prepopulated with applications to add. You can select all, select none, or choose applications individually.

> **NOTE**  If the application is not shown, you can browse to the .exe file to add the program. In this screen, you can also see the properties page for this program. In the properties page, you can set the RemoteApp program name, location, and alias. You can make RemoteApp available through TS Web Access by adding command-line arguments, and you can change the default icon (see Figure 8.8).

After you have chosen your programs and selected the properties, click Next.

4. On the next screen, review the settings. This page shows the program name and path, and it shows whether RemoteApp will be available through TS Web Access and whether command-line arguments have been added. When you are done reviewing the settings, click Finish.

When you have added programs to RemoteApp, you have the option of making these programs available through TS Web Access (see Figure 8.9), an .rdp file, or a Windows Installer package.

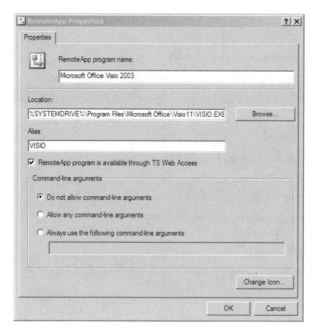

FIGURE 8.8
A look at the RemoteApp programs list and properties of an application.

FIGURE 8.9
RemoteApp programs available in TS Web Access.

Let's now look at how to create an `.rdp` file and a Windows Installer package for RemoteApp programs.

In the RemoteApp Manager, perform the following steps:

1. Highlight the application you want to distribute and click Create .rdp File.

2. When the RemoteApp Wizard starts, providing information for creating an `.rdp` file, click Next.

3. Specify the package settings:

   ► Enter the location to save the packages. (This can be a file share.)

   ► Enter the terminal server settings: Choose the server, required authentication, and port for this `.rdp` file.

   ► Enter the TS Gateway settings: Choose to automatically detect TS Gateway, use a specific TS Gateway server, or not use any TS Gateway server for this `.rdp` file.

   ► Enter certificate settings: Choose a certificate to use in signing files or do not use a certificate to sign files for this `.rdp` file.

   Finish specifying package settings and click Next.

4. Review the settings and click Finish. The location where the `.rdp` file was created will be opened automatically after the wizard closes.

Next, create a Windows Installer package by doing the following:

1. Highlight the application you want to distribute and click Create Windows Installer Package.

2. When the RemoteApp Wizard starts, providing information for creating a Windows Installer Package, click Next.

3. Specify the package settings (which are the same as the `.rdp` file package settings) and click Next.

4. Select where the shortcut icons will appear on client computers:

   ► Desktop

   ► Start menu folder (specify a folder name; "Remote Programs" is the default)

   Check the box to take over client extensions. This way, users can open local files with programs that are installed on the terminal server. Click Next.

5. Review the settings and click Finish. The location where the Windows Installer package was created is opened automatically after the wizard closes.

## Monitor Terminal Services

There are two places to monitor Terminal Services: the TS Gateway Manager and the Terminal Services Manager. We will begin by looking at monitoring in the TS Gateway Manager.

In Terminal Services, expand the TS Gateway Manager and server. You can then monitor active connections to the TS Gateway server. The monitoring events include the following:

- Connection ID
- User ID
- User Name
- Connected On
- Connected Duration
- Idle Time
- Target Computer
- Client IP Address
- Note
- Target Port

To receive details about a TS Gateway connection, click the connection, and the details appear below the summary pane. If necessary, from here, you can disconnect one or all TS Gateway connections for a user.

Monitoring connections in the Terminal Services Manager includes the ability to monitor users, sessions, and processes. Expand Terminal Services and find the Terminal Services Manager.

Expand this console tree and highlight the server you want to manage. From the action menu you can connect or disconnect to a terminal server. In the console view (Figure 8.10), there are three tabs to monitor/manage:

- **Users:** In this tab, you can view information about all users connected to this terminal server, including Server, User, Session, ID, State, Idle Time, and Log on Time. From the Actions pane you can disconnect, reset, send message, check the user's status (see Figure 8.10), or log off the user.

- **Sessions:** In this tab, you can view information about all sessions connected to this terminal server, including Server, Session, User, ID, State, Type (identifies the Remote Desktop client version), Client Name, Idle Time, Log on Time, and Comments. From the Actions pane you can disconnect, reset, send message, or check the user's status (see Figure 8.11).s

- **Processes:** In this tab, you can view processes that are running on this terminal server, and you can end processes running on this terminal server.

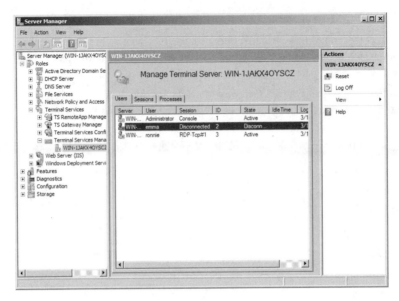

FIGURE 8.10
Monitoring users in a terminal server.

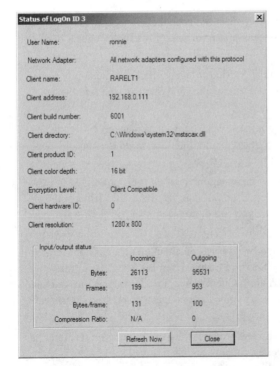

FIGURE 8.11
User Status information in the
Terminal Services Manager.

In a large environment with RemoteApp programs being deployed both internally and externally, it is important to monitor your terminal servers. Disconnected sessions staying active on a terminal server can affect performance for all users. The tools discussed in this section can help keep your terminal server running efficiently.

# Get More from Terminal Services in Windows Server 2008 R2

**Scenario/Problem:** With Windows Server 2008 R2, what changes should you expect to see in Terminal Services?

**Solution:** Terminal Services is one area where Microsoft has been working hard to improve usability and manageability. In fact, Terminal Services has undergone major changes in R2. Actually, in R2, it is not even called Terminal Services anymore. It has been renamed Remote Desktop Services. If you have heard news of this already, you might be in a panic, but don't be overly concerned; the overall look and feel will remain the same. We will look at the name changes and talk about some of the new features provided. Tables 8.2 and 8.3, provided by Microsoft, show the name changes that will take place in Windows Server 2008 R2.

TABLE 8.2     **Name Changes of Roles and Services**

| Former Name of Roles and Role Services | Name in Windows Server 2008 R2 |
|---|---|
| Terminal Services | Remote Desktop Services |
| Terminal Server | Remote Desktop Server |
| Terminal Services Licensing (TS Licensing) | Remote Desktop Licensing (RD Licensing) |
| Terminal Services Gateway (TS Gateway) | Remote Desktop Gateway (RD Gateway) |
| Terminal Services Session Broker (TS Session Broker) | Remote Desktop Connection Broker (RD Connection Broker) |
| Terminal Services Web Access (TS Web Access) | Remote Desktop Web Access (RD Web Access) |

TABLE 8.3     **Name Changes of Management Tools**

| Former Name of Management Tools | Name in Windows Server 2008 R2 |
|---|---|
| Terminal Services Manager | Remote Desktop Server Manager |
| Terminal Services Configuration | Remote Desktop Server Configuration |
| TS Gateway Manager | Remote Desktop Gateway Manager |
| TS Licensing Manager | Remote Desktop Licensing Manager |
| TS RemoteApp Manager | RemoteApp Manager |

The change from Terminal Services in Windows Server 2008 R2 has created some major changes to the role services and management tools in Remote Desktop Services. Next we look at the new services; the following list details which functions they will provide going forward.

- Remote Desktop Server
  - Client experience configuration page
  - Remote Desktop IP virtualization
  - Windows Installer RDS compatibility
  - Fair Share CPU Scheduling
  - Roaming user profile cache management
- Remote Desktop Licensing
  - Automatic licensing server discovery no longer supported for Remote Desktop servers
  - Changes to Licensing tab in Remote Desktop Server Configuration
  - The Manage RDS CALs Wizard
  - Service connection point registration
- Remote Desktop Gateway
  - Configurable idle and session timeouts
  - Background session authentication and authorization
  - Service and consent messages
  - Secure device redirection enforcement
- Remote Desktop Services Provider for Windows PowerShell
  - View/edit configuration settings for a Remote Desktop server.
  - Create and configure a Remote Desktop server connection.
  - Publish or remove a RemoteApp program.
  - Create and configure a Remote Desktop server farm.
  - Configure RemoteApp and Desktop Connection for virtual desktops and RemoteApp.
  - Manage a Remote Desktop licensing server.
  - Manage a Remote Desktop Gateway server.
- Remote Desktop Client Experience
  - Audio and video playback redirection
  - Multiple monitor support
  - Audio recording redirection

- ▶ Desktop composition
- ▶ DirectX redirection
- ▶ Language bar redirection

For details on the changes, check the following sites:

- ▶ **What's New in Remote Desktop Services, from the Microsoft Download Center:** www.microsoft.com/downloads/details.aspx?displaylang= en&FamilyID=821fa300-edb0-4396-a443-64890cc0fcbd
- ▶ **Terminal Services in Windows Server 2008 R2 becomes Remote Desktop Services, What's New? From Bink:** http://bink.nu/news/terminal-services-in-2008-r2-becomes-remote-desktop-services.aspx

# CHAPTER 9

# Understand and Manage Active Directory

# Understand the Functionality of Active Directory

**Scenario/Problem:** Perhaps Windows Server 2008 is your first server OS or, in your current environment you haven't had Windows 2000/2003 servers in place, so you haven't had the opportunity to work with Active Directory. In either of these situations, you probably need to know more about Active Directory before you begin implementation.

**Solution:** Active Directory, first introduced with Windows 2000 Server, is a directory service. In the most basic of comparisons, you might liken it to a telephone directory, which is an organization of people based on various fields (name, address, number, and so forth). However, Active Directory has identity management, which allows for more advanced control than simply looking up a person to locate his or her number.

Active Directory allows you to create objects (user accounts, groups, computers, and so forth) for which you can then define attributes (such as name, address, and department) and that you can utilize in a network to determine login settings, permissions for access to resources, computer behavioral auditing, policy settings, and much, much more. It goes beyond a simple, static directory and is much more dynamic, or active, in its functionality.

**NOTE** It's important to note that this chapter provides a basic understanding of Active Directory and a foundation on which to build. However, if you need to go further, we recommend that you purchase a book that focuses completely on Active Directory (such as *Active Directory Domain Services 2008 How-To* by John Policelli, ISBN 978-0-672-33045-2) and research Active Directory further on Microsoft's TechNet site (http://technet.microsoft.com).

## Visualize the Physical and Logical Sides of Active Directory

Active Directory was designed to take into consideration the physical and logical sides of a network environment. Consider two persons who work in the same building on the same floor for, what appears to be, the same company. These two persons might sit only feet apart from each other, but they might have completely different physical and logical Active Directory features.

From a physical perspective, Active Directory allows you to group computers (both workstations and servers) into sites. A site would typically include a single subnet or subnets, all located within the same physical area. So, you might have two offices, one in New York and one in Los Angeles. You should, rightist seems, have two different sites. But going beyond that, you might have multiple subnets in New York due to the size of that location. You can break that physical location up into multiple sites as well (or keep them under one site). Active Directory is designed to allow for that level of flexibility so that the final design decisions aren't forced on the administrative team.

Sites are helpful because they curtail the amount of replication that occurs between the sites, and that gives you the ability to control the amount of bandwidth utilized for replication traffic that may be caused by Active Directory itself.

Beyond the physical side, however, there is also the logical side, which allows for even more flexibility in your design of Active Directory objects. Forests, domains, organizational units...this is the lingo of logical Active Directory.

A *forest* contains trees, of course. You can see in Figure 9.1 that a tree, in this case, is called a *domain*. There is a parent domain, and there can be subdomains called child domains. So, you might have a forest with a single domain tree (although this would be a very small forest), or you might have multiple domains with multiple child domains, all interconnected by transitive two-way trusts.

**Forest**

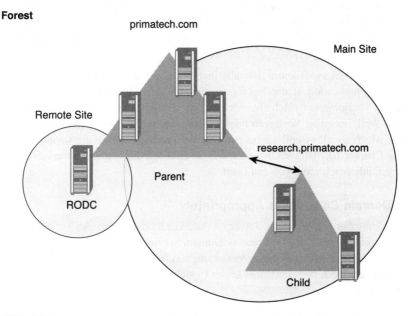

FIGURE 9.1
Physical and logical Active Directory.

What is a transitive two-way trust? Well, with domains of the same forest, there might be resources (printers, file servers, and so forth). If a user wants to access a resource in another domain within the same forest, he or she would need the permission to do so. But the trust is automatic between domains. One might liken it to two countries that allow persons to pass back and forth without a specific visa to do so. For example, if a U.S. citizen attempts to enter Canada, while she might need her passport and go through customs, she isn't required to obtain a visa the way she would for another country; the trust is already in place to that extent.

You might wonder why you would create multiple domains. Is it based on locations or departments? Actually, it could be for many different reasons. A parent domain such as primatech.com (note the DNS naming structure) might have a research division that is top secret. That research division might want to have special security in place and thus require its own domain. So, you might create the research.primatech.com domain.

---

**NOTE**  Active Directory is based on a standardized directory service called LDAP. LDAP evolved from the X.500 set of standards and a protocol called Directory Access Protocol. The revised, lighter version is called LDAP, for Lightweight DAP, which serves as both the service and protocol. Active Directory relies on the same naming structure as DNS. (Hence primatech.com should be registered for the Internet community at large, but the internal DNS doesn't need to be.)

---

Beyond domains being used to create reasonable security or departmental divisions there are organizational units (OUs) that are simply containers that hold objects (such as users, groups, printers, and computers) for the establishment of policies or administrative control.

So, the Active Directory structure basically involves sites based on IP subnets, which help to control replication. It also has forests, domains, and OUs, which help to logically control your objects (which are users, groups, computers, printers, and so forth). Is that all? Well, not quite. We haven't delved deep into the world of LDAP, Kerberos, and DNS, which are all essential aspects to Active Directory, and we are saving Group Policy for Chapter 10, "Utilize Group Policy," so although this is a solid overview, there is certainly much more you can learn.

## Utilize Domain Controllers Appropriately

A domain controller is a Windows Server (2000/2003/2008) running Active Directory services. These services (Active Directory Domain Services [AD DS]) can be shut down for maintenance (such as defragmentation) and restoration purposes, which essentially makes the server a member server (which is any server that is not running Active Directory).

What exactly does a domain controller (DC) do? A full domain controller retains a copy of every object within the forest, although only a DC that is designated a global catalog (GC) server has a copy of every attribute for those objects. Typically a DC retains both objects and attributes for members within that domain (unless it is a GC server).

When users log in to the domain, a DC validates the login and issues a token that can be used to grant or deny permissions to access resources within the domain (or perhaps across domains). Responding to security authentication requests is one of the key responsibilities of a DC.

DCs are the only types of servers that can serve as one of the five primary FSMO (Flexible Single Master Operation) roles. While, typically, every DC is equal, these five roles make for uniqueness within the domain.

These are the FSMO roles:

> **Schema Master:** There is one of these per forest. It is responsible for schema modifications.

> **Domain Naming Master:** There is one of these per forest. It is responsible for the addition or removal of domains in the forest.

> **Relative ID Master (RID Master):** There is one of these per domain. It allocates security RIDs to the DCs so that Active Directory can assign unique numbers to security principles (such as users, groups, and/or computers).

> **Infrastructure Master:** There is one of these per domain. It keeps track of security identifiers and globally unique identifiers (GUIDs). It is useful only if you have a multidomain arrangement because it specifically keeps track of users being placed in cross-domain groups and so forth.

> **PDC Emulator:** There is one of these per domain. It handles password changes and authentication failures.

These five roles are important to the continued life of a domain (and, in some cases, the entire forest), so in the event that a server holding one of these roles crashes, you need to seize the role (using the ntdsutil command). Otherwise, if you have a modicum of advance warning, you would want to transfer the role before the system crashes (or comes offline for maintenance).

---

**NOTE** Some best practice advice is that you should separate these roles if possible, although initially they will all reside on the first DC in the forest (and the three domain FSMO roles will reside automatically on the first DC of the domain). The Infrastructure Master role shouldn't reside on a global catalog server (which is also the first server of a forest or domain), so you should move this role. The PDC Emulator and RID Master roles should be on the same DC, if possible, and the Schema Master and Domain Name Master roles should reside together.

---

For the sake of fault tolerance, you should have two DCs in each domain. That way, if one fails, the other can seize FSMO roles and will also have a copy of all the objects in that domain (all objects and attributes).

## Read-Only Domain Controllers (RODCs)

One of the features in the days of Windows NT 4 domain architecture was that we had a primary domain controller (PDC), and all other controllers were backup domain controllers (BDCs). Those BDCs held only a readable copy of the database. Active Directory functions quite a bit differently in that every DC has a complete copy of the database that can be written to. However, with Windows Server 2008 we see the return of the RODC, but with a specific purpose.

RODCs are designed with branch offices in mind. Having an RODC in a remote location (perhaps even a less secure location) than a standard DC will mean persons can log in without sending credentials over a WAN connection (which may be a slow connection), but a person cannot break into the RODC and make any domain configuration changes because it is read-only.

In addition, rather than having a full copy of the domain database sent over to the branch office location across a WAN link (which, again, may be very slow), you can configure the RODC to hold only a copy of the site it is located within. You can also assign permission for a local administrator to maintain and handle that server, without giving that person any level of control over the domain objects.

> **NOTE** There are times when other application servers require a writable DC, as in the case of Exchange 2007, Service Pack 1. So you need to be careful when deciding to implement an RODC.

# Promote Servers as Domain Controllers

> **Scenario/Problem:** The decision has been made to create a new Active Directory domain, and so DCs will be installed in several locations throughout the building, as well as in branch locations. How should you, as an administrator, proceed?

**Solution:** An Active Directory domain begins with the installation of a single DC. To ensure that the first controller will work, however, you might need to make decisions about your DNS infrastructure. If you have one already, you need to ensure that it is ready for Active Directory. If you do not have one, you may choose to install DNS when you install your first DC.

However, you also need to consider the installation of additional DCs and possibly RODCs. You will need to design your forest (starting with its name) and possible child domains. (As you read the previous section, you learned about sites and physical boundaries that may come into play.) You may also want to install DCs through an unattended installation with answer files. Yes, it can all become quite complicated.

But let's go back a step and install the first DC, with DNS included in the installation.

## Install the First DC of the Forest

Although there are a variety of different ways to set up DCs, in setting up this first one, you are going to start with the basics:

1. To begin the process, from a Windows Server 2008 system that is acting as a member server (that is, not running AD DS), click Start and enter dcpromo in the Instant Search pane (or in the Run dialog). The system checks whether AD DS binaries are installed, and then it installs them. These might already be installed if you ran dcpromo command at an earlier time and cancelled the operation.

2. On the Active Directory Domain Services Installation Wizard startup screen (shown in Figure 9.2), click Next or select the checkbox Use Advanced Mode Installation and then click Next. (You might want to check the box because you might want to see some of the valuable configuration screens that are added to the installation.)

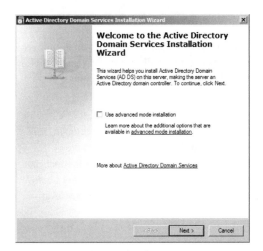

FIGURE 9.2
The Active Directory Domain Services
Installation Wizard.

3. If you have selected advanced mode, you see some information regarding OS compatibility (because of the improved security settings in Windows Server 2008). Read the information and click Next.

4. Under Choose a Deployment Configuration, because this is the first DC in the forest, choose Create a New Domain in a Forest and click Next.

5. Provide the fully qualified domain name (FQDN) of the new forest root domain (for example, corp.contoso.com). Normally, you'd think about your company name and the name you have registered and then, if you choose to use the same name, enter that here. In this scenario, however, enter primatech.com and click Next.

6. The wizard checks to see if this name is already in use, and if it is not, it takes you to the Domain NetBIOS Name screen, which it fills in for you. Change it if you like and click Next.

7. When you are asked to set the forest functional level, choose Windows 2000, Windows Server 2003, or Windows Server 2008. Because this is a brand new forest, you would most likely want to choose Windows Server 2008 and click Next.

**NOTE** As you select the functional level you want, you are shown details that indicate what features are being added with each choice. There are new features between the Windows 2000 and Windows Server 2003 options; however, there are no new features in choosing Windows Server 2008 over Windows Server 2003. The only valid distinction to keep in mind with choosing Windows Server 2008 is that you will be able to add to this forest only DCs that are running Windows Server 2008 or later.

8. If you select Windows Server 2008 as the forest functional level, you do not see Set Domain Functional Level because it is automatically set to Server 2008. If, however, you did not choose Windows Server 2008, you need to choose a domain functional level and click Next.

9. In the Additional Domain Controller Options page, choose to install DNS as an additional option. Because this is the first DC of the forest and/or domain, it is automatically a global catalog server, and that option is selected. There is another option to install as an RODC, but it will be disabled due to the fact that this is your first DC in a new forest and/or domain and therefore cannot be an RODC. In this case, you leave the default settings that install DNS with Active Directory and click Next.

**NOTE** You may see a warning sign because the wizard is not able to create a delegation for the DNS server. In this case, because you are not integrating with an existing DNS server and are making this server a DNS server, you do not have to worry about this warning. Click Yes to continue.

10. Provide the location for the database, log, and SYSVOL folders:

   ▶ **Database:** Stores information about the objects (such as users and computers) on the network

   ▶ **Logs:** Record activities related to Active Directory (such as object updates)

   ▶ **SYSVOL:** Contains Group Policy objects and scripts

   Each of these is important. Select locations (or leave the default) and click Next.

11. On the Directory Services Restore Mode Administrator Password page, provide a password for the Administrator account that will be used when the DC is started in Active Directory Directory Services Restore Mode (AD DSRM).

Make sure the password you use meets the complexity requirements, or you receive an error.

12. On the Summary page, examine the settings you have chosen or click Export Settings to create an answer file for use with unattended Active Directory configurations. Click Next.

13. A variety of different options are established (DNS, Group Policy Management Console installation, and so forth). When this process is complete, click Finish on the final screen.

14. Restart the server, and the AD DS goes into action.

After you reboot the system, note the new tools available Administrative Tools. They include the following:

- Active Directory Domains and Trusts
- Active Directory Sites and Services
- Active Directory Users and Computers
- ADSI Edit
- DNS
- Group Policy Management

## Setting Up Additional DCs

To add more DCs to an existing forest (after the first DC has been created), you run the Active Directory Domain Services Installation Wizard again through dcpromo.

The difference with setting up an additional DC is that when the wizard brings you to the Choose a Deployment Configuration page, you now select Existing Forest, as shown in Figure 9.3.

You can now choose to do one of the following:

- Add a domain controller to an existing domain.
- Create a new domain in an existing forest. (This server will become the first DC in the new domain.)
- Create a new domain tree root instead of a new child domain.

On the Network Credentials page, type in the name of the domain you are looking to add this server to and indicate whether there are alternate credentials you want to use.

---

**NOTE** To add a DC to a domain, you need to be a member of the Enterprise Admins group and the Domain Admins group for that domain.

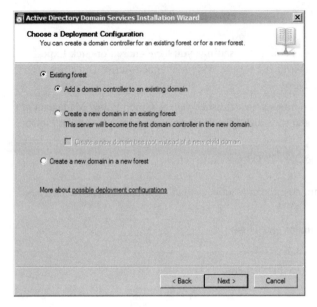

FIGURE 9.3
Choosing a deployment configuration.

You then select a domain and a site or choose the option Use the Site That Corresponds to the IP Address of This Computer.

When you come to the Additional Domain Controller Options screen, you need to decide whether you want to make this server a DNS server, a global catalog server, or an RODC.

On the Install from Media page, you would most likely choose Replicate Data over the Network from an Existing Domain Controller, unless you have a reason to choose otherwise.

On the Source Domain Controller page, you can choose Let the Wizard Choose an Appropriate Domain Controller or Use This Specific Domain Controller and choose the one you think is best.

**NOTE** A replication partner imposes certain logical restrictions. For example, an RODC cannot be an installation partner. If you are installing an RODC, you need a DC that runs Windows Server 2008 for an installation partner. Only DCs within a domain can be installation partners for one another.

For the most part, the rest of the options and dialog screens in the wizard are the same as in the preceding section.

## Install an RODC

Recall that an RODC is a DC that you might utilize when you are working with a branch office situation that doesn't require write capability to the domain (and might be a security risk if you did use a traditional DC).

During the installation procedure, when you reach the Additional Domain Controller Options page, you can choose the Read-Only Domain Controller (RODC) option, as shown in Figure 9.4.

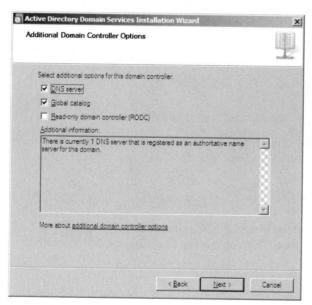

FIGURE 9.4
Choosing an RODC.

When you select this option, you need to select other options as well. You need to establish a password replication policy in the Specify the Password Replication Policy window, as shown in Figure 9.5. This policy determines which users and their user object information will be replicated to the RODC and stored locally. You can select Deny or Allow as setting choices.

**NOTE** Typically you want to allow password replication for the accounts that belong in the site where the RODC is located. Then those accounts can authenticate locally against that RODC. However, accounts that are perhaps used only at main sites should not be replicated down to this RODC. It is recommended that you use global groups to control the replication and replicate only those accounts you need to replicate.

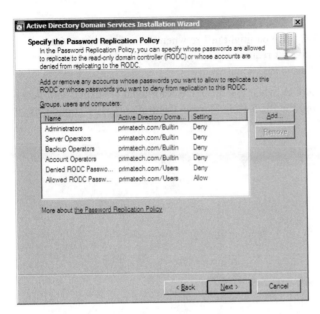

FIGURE 9.5
The password replication policy.

An interesting feature is the Delegation of RODC Installation and Administration page, where you can specify a user or group that can administer the RODC locally.

## Install from Media

At times you might want to install from media for your DCs because the amount of data transfer over your network lines may be excessive. This is especially the case when you have remote locations with slow WAN links. Installation from Media (IFM) begins with the process of capturing the Active Directory database from an existing DC and then pulls it into your remote DC.

To capture the existing DC, you would use NTDSUTIL. There is some flexibility as to what you can capture. You can choose one of the following four options:

▶ Create IMF media for a full AD DC or an AD LDS instance.

▶ Create IMF media without SYSVOL for a full AD DC or AD LDS instance.

▶ Create IMF media for an RODC.

▶ Create IMF media without SYSVOL for an RODC.

Depending on which version you choose, you use the NTDSUTIL command on a DC to create the IMF.

When you are doing the installation, you come to the Install from Media screen (shown in Figure 9.6,) where you can select Replicate Data from Media at the Following Location and select the location.

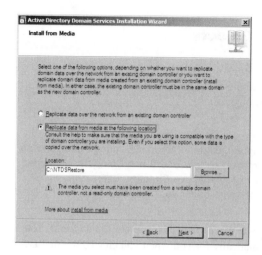

FIGURE 9.6
The Install from Media page.

## Prepare an Existing Domain Schema

In the event that you are attempting to install a Windows Server 2008 machine running AD DS into an existing Windows 2000 Server/Windows Server 2003 domain, you need to modify the schema to reflect this. To accomplish this, you use the adprep command.

To access this command, you use your Windows Server 2008 media and locate the \sources\adprep folder for the command under the command prompt. The adprep command comes with familiar switches (familiar because they were also available in Windows Server 2003) and one new one, /rodcPrep. These are the switches:

- ▶ **/forestPrep:** Updates forest information. Must be run on the Schema Master role.

- ▶ **/domainPrep:** Updates domain information. Must be run on the Infrastructure Master role. Must be run after /forestPrep is finished.

- ▶ **/domainprep /gpprep:** Updates permissions on Group Policy objects in AD DS and SYSVOL. Must be run on the Infrastructure Master role. Must be run after /forestPrep is finished. (You use this switch only if your DCs are running Windows 2000 Server. Otherwise, /domainPrep is fine.)

- ▶ **/rodcPrep:** Updates permissions on Nondomain Naming Context (NDNC) partitions to enable replication for RODCs. Runs remotely and contacts an NDNC replica to update permissions. Must be run after /forestPrep is finished. Can be rerun at any time. You should run this in particular when you have DNS application partitions in your forest.

# Create Active Directory Objects

**Scenario/Problem:** When Active Directory is up and running, how do you create users, groups, and computers? The whole purpose is to create a directory of objects, but how do we create those objects?

**Solution:** The creation of objects (computer, contact, group, OU, printer user, and so on) can all be handled with the tool Active Directory Users and Computers. To open this tool, you select Start, Administrative Tools, Active Directory Users and Computers. You then see a hierarchy of items under your domain.

Note that there are automatic containers in place (such as Computers and Users). You also see objects that were created automatically for you when you created the first DC. The computer that is the first DC becomes an object (for example, in the DCs built-in OU). As you add new DCs, they are automatically added. Computers you join to the domain go in the Computers container automatically. Users and groups—such as the Administrator account and various groups, such as the Enterprise Admins and Domain Admins security groups—already exist in the Users container.

Before you begin inadvertently creating new objects, it's a good idea to consider an OU structure to put in place.

## Design and Create an OU Structure

Creating an OU design is important when you first establish your Active Directory domain. Over time, your OUs may grow beyond your initial plan, but you should start things off right. Now, the matter of "right" is a matter of opinion. For example, you might create an OU structure based on location. Or perhaps on department. Or perhaps a combination of both. Each environment is a little different, so this requires some thought.

Let's consider an example. Primatech is a company that has a main headquarters with four branch offices. Let's say the offices are all under a single domain structure. In this case, you might create an OU based on each branch office location. However, if each branch has its own child domain, you might create departmental OUs within each domain.

In keeping with the first scenario, you could create OUs that relate to locations and then sub-OUs for individual departments. If it seems like a lot of planning and work, well...planning takes the majority of the time. Actually creating an OU once you have the design in place takes seconds.

To create an OU in Active Directory, perform the following steps:

1. Select Start, Administrative Tools, Active Directory Users and Computers.

2. Your first OU is at the domain level, so begin by right-clicking the domain name and then choosing New, Organizational Unit (as shown in Figure 9.7).

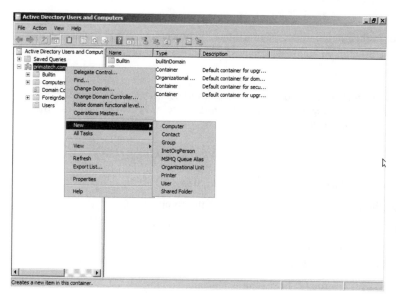

FIGURE 9.7
Creating an OU.

3. When you are asked for a name, provide the name and click OK.

You should see your OU in the hierarchy now, and it will stand out as being different from containers because the folder will have a little graphic inside.

> **NOTE** When creating an OU, you see the Protect Container from Accidental Deletion checkbox, which is enabled by default. Enabling this checkbox denies all administrators or users of the domain and DC the ability to delete this object.

> **NOTE** To create OUs within OUs, you simply right-click the OU you want to nest within and then select New, Organizational Unit. The console knows you are attempting to create the OU within that particular OU.

## Create Computer Objects

Typically, a computer object is created automatically if you add that computer to the domain manually at the workstation level. At that time, you are asked for the credentials necessary to accomplish the addition, and the computer is added to the Computers container. You can choose to move it from there to an OU at a later time.

However, you can also add computers to Active Directory ahead of time, but you need to be a member of the Account Operators group, the Domain Admins group, or the

Enterprise Admins group (or been assigned the correct permissions). Adding computer objects prior to their deployment may facilitate the process when you are deploying many systems through an automated deployment across your organization.

> **NOTE** The concept of linking physical computers to computer account objects is called *prestaging*. (Prestaged clients are also referred to as known computers.) The benefits of prestaging include added security and greater flexibility.

To add a computer object, perform the following steps:

1. Select the domain or OU you want to add the computer to.

2. Right-click the domain/OU and then select New, Computer.

3. Provide a computer name (for peer connections) and a computer name (for legacy pre-Windows 2000).

4. Select a user or group. The default is Domain Admins.

5. Select the Pre-Windows 2000 Computer checkbox if applicable.

6. Click OK.

After the computer account is created, you can right-click the account and select Properties. You then see seven tabs you can work with to include further details regarding that account:

▶ **General:** This tab provides mostly preset information regarding the name, DNS name, DC type, site, and a configurable description. (On DCs there is a button for NTDS options.)

▶ **Operating System:** This is another tab that shows the OS name, version, and service pack.

▶ **Member Of:** This tab indicates the groups or built-in security principles the computer belongs to.

▶ **Delegation:** Delegation is a security-sensitive operation that allows services to act on behalf of another user. Options include trusting or not trusting the computer for delegation and combinations of trust for Kerberos only or specified services.

▶ **Location:** On this tab, you can indicate the location of the system.

▶ **Managed By:** Here you can configure the user or built-in security principle that manages this computer. If attributes are configured for the user (for example, office, street, city), those options are automatically displayed on this tab.

▶ **Dial-in:** This tab offers a variety of important settings, as you can see in Figure 9.8. You can allow or deny or control network access permission. You can verify caller ID, set callback options, and assign static IP addresses and static routes.

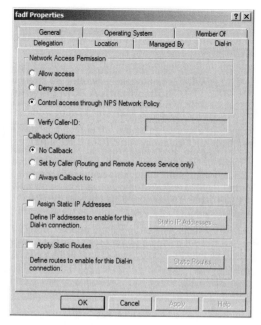

FIGURE 9.8
Configuring computer dial-in properties.

## Create User Objects

Ultimately, it all comes down to the user, doesn't it? What is the point of setting up a directory service if a user cannot sit down at his system, type in a user name and password, and access the network? From the administrator's perspective, it's the fact that you can track, control, and enforce policy over users that gives Active Directory its true value. In either case, however, the user object must be created first.

To create a new user, you perform the following steps:

1. Select the domain, built-in users container, or specific OU and then right-click that element. Choose New, User.

2. In the New Object – User dialog shown in Figure 9.9, provide basic information such as first name, initials, last name, and full name. Also provide the user logon name and the domain it belongs to. The pre-Windows 2000 portion fills itself in when you put in the logon name. Make alterations to these items, if needed, and then click Next.

3. Create a password and confirm that password. Also choose any of the following four checkboxes, as necessary:

   ▶ User Must Change Password at Next Logon

   ▶ User Cannot Change Password

   ▶ Password Never Expires

   ▶ Account Is Disabled

After you've selected your options, click Next.

4. Review your options and create the user by clicking Finish.

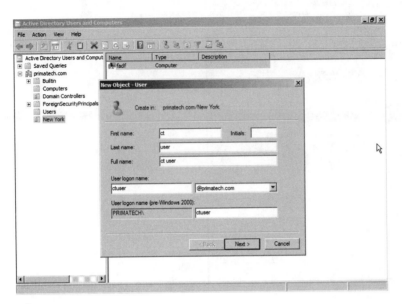

FIGURE 9.9
Creating a new user.

After the new user is created, you can right-click the user and click Properties to see the many tabs with available properties to configure regarding a user. These are the tabs:

▶ **General:** This tab allows you to include quite a bit of personal information regarding the person: name, description, office, telephone, e-mail address, and more.

▶ **Address:** This tab allows you to provide the full address of the person, including city, state, zip, and country.

▶ **Account:** This tab is an important one for administrators because you can configure items such as logon hours (to determine a set time when a person can log in), logon options (to establish which machines the individual can log on to), account options, and expiration date settings.

▶ **Profile:** This tab allows you to configure the location of a computer profile (which includes items such as your wallpaper and personal settings that make up your unique profile) and logon script. It also allows you to determine the location of a home folder.

▶ **Telephones:** This tab allows you to configure all the possible phone numbers a person might use (home, pager, mobile, fax, and IP phone) and also has a Notes section.

▶ **Organization:** This tab contains the person's job title, department, company, manager name, and a Direct Reports section.

▶ **Remote Control:** This tab allows you to manually configure Terminal Services remote control settings. You can enable/disable, require the user's permission, and specify a level of control.

▶ **Terminal Services Profile:** You use this tab to configure the Terminal Services user profile, such as the profile path and home folder.

▶ **COM+:** This tab allows you to configure a COM+ partition set for the user.

> **NOTE** COM+ partitions are a very specific set of COM components that are developed to work together for services such as queuing, role-based security, and so forth. Unless you have a need to configure multiple COM+ partitions, such as when you need to make two or more versions of an application available to users within your domain, you don't typically need to worry about this feature.

▶ **Member Of:** This tab indicates the groups a person belongs to or is a member of.

▶ **Dial-in:** Much like this identical tab for computer properties, this tab allows you to configure a variety of settings, such as allow/deny or control network access permission. You can verify caller ID, set callback options, and assign static IP addresses and static routes.

▶ **Environment:** You use this tab to configure the Terminal Services startup environment. You can configure a starting program and whether you want certain devices to be connected (drives, client/main printers).

▶ **Sessions:** You use this tab to set Terminal Services timeout and reconnection settings.

> **NOTE** In the event that a user leaves the company and you aren't certain about deleting the account right away, you can right-click the account and choose Disable Account (and, conversely, if the person returns, you choose Enable Account). You can also right-click an account and choose Reset Password if a user has lost her password. And if a user account has property settings you need to duplicate for other users you need to create, you can right-click the account and choose Copy. Finally, if you need to move a user or computer account from one container or OU to another, you can right-click the object(s) and choose Move.

# Work with Site and Domain Consoles

**Scenario/Problem:** Perhaps you have a solid grasp of the basics of Active Directory, including installation and object creation, but as your domain grows and perhaps has more advanced scenarios to contend with, how do you handle your domains and sites? More specifically, how do you work with the other Active Directory consoles, Active Directory Sites and Services, and Active Directory Domains and Trusts?

**Solution:** Every console contains a bevy of tools. It's good to know which ones might overlap with other consoles—remember that there is always more than one way to accomplish a task—and which ones are unique to the console you are working in. In addition, it is important to know why you would reach out to these consoles because in smaller environments, you might never need them.

## Active Directory Sites and Services

While there are many different configuration options with the Sites and Services tool, the following are a few of the most common items you might want to consider.

### Change the Default-First-Site-Name Name

An administrator with a single site will typically leave the setting Default-First-Site-Name, even though it is quite easy to change. To change the name, perform the following steps:

1. Select Start, Administrative Tools, Active Directory Sites and Services.

2. Expand the Sites folder and look for the Default-First-Site-Name option.

3. Right-click Default-First-Site-Name and choose Rename.

4. Type in the new name and press Enter.

### Enable Global Catalog

It is easy to see whether your DCs are also global catalog servers (meaning that they hold a copy of all the objects and attributes for your entire domain). It's also a simple matter of selecting a checkbox to allow an existing DC to also be a GC.

**NOTE** You should have at least one GC per site.

To enable a GC, perform the following steps:

1. Select Start, Administrative Tools, Active Directory Sites and Services.

2. Expand the Sites folder and then expand the site that has the server you are looking for.

3. Expand the Servers folder and select the server on which you are going to enable GC.

4. Expand the server, right-click NTDS Settings, and choose Properties.

5. On the General tab, shown in Figure 9.10, select the Global Catalog checkbox and click OK.

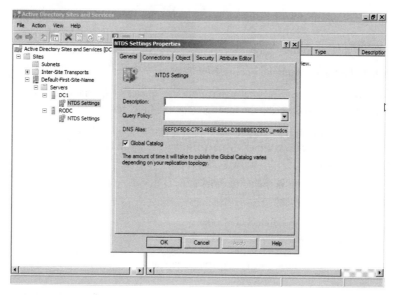

FIGURE 9.10
Enabling the Global Catalog setting.

**NOTE** You can establish this same setting from within the Active Directory Users and Computers tool. To do so, go to the Domain Controllers container, and when you access the properties of any of the systems, you can see on the General tab a button that says NTDS Settings. When you select this, you then see the checkbox on the General tab that allows you to enable/disable the GC.

While working with the NTDS settings, you might want to take note of some of the other tabs and settings.

## Create a New Site

Sites and subnets are logical representations of physical realities. Your network has routers and IP addressing already in place that you want to utilize in order to ensure that replication breaks exist between your Active Directory sites. The goal is to mirror your physical topology.

Multiple physical subnets may exist within a single site. You can maintain those subnets under one site for Active Directory if the replication factor is not a bandwidth issue, or you can break them up based on those subnets. You may also have multiple sites (physical locations) that have unique subnetting. That would lend itself more easily to a site design because you can quickly see the value and necessity of creating new logical sites based on the physical sites within your organization.

To begin, you need to create a new logical site. To do this, perform the following steps:

1. Select Start, Administrative Tools, Active Directory Sites and Services.

2. Right-click the Sites folder and choose New Site.

3. Enter a name for the site. Note that you cannot use spaces or special characters. A typical name would describe the location (for example, NewYork).

4. Select a site link object. By default, there is only one, DEFAULTIPSITELINK. Then click OK. You receive a message explaining what you need to do, with a list of configuration necessities to make this site function:

   ▶ Ensure that the site is linked to other sites with site links, where appropriate.

   ▶ Add subnets to the Subnets container.

   ▶ Install or move DCs to the site.

5. Click OK, and you are now able to see your new site.

After the site is created, you can assign IP subnets to it, and you can then move servers over to it (or add them directly to the site when you set them up as DCs).

## Create a New Subnet

To create a new subnet, perform the following steps:

1. Select Start, Administrative Tools, Active Directory Sites and Services.

2. Expand the Sites branch, right-click Subnets, and choose New Subnet.

3. At this point, you are asked to enter the address prefix, using the network prefix notation *address/prefix length*. So, for an IPv4 prefix, you might use 157.54.208.0/20, and for an IPv6 prefix you might use 3FFE:FFFF:0:C000::/64

4. Select a site object for the prefix.

5. Click OK.

Keep in mind that you can add more subnets to the mix and assign them under the same site. A site can hold multiple subnets.

### Move a DC to a New Site

To move a DC to a new site, follow these steps:

1. Select Start, Administrative Tools, Active Directory Sites and Services.

2. Expand the Sites branch and expand the site that has the server you want to move (for example, Default-First-Site-Name). Expand the Servers branch.

3. Right-click the server you want to move and choose Move.

4. Select the site that should contain the server and click OK.

### Working with Site Links and Replication

Typically, sites contain servers that replicate to one another through intrasite replication and replicate between sites through intersite replication.

The Active Directory Knowledge Consistency Checker (KCC) automatically builds the connections to allow for replication. Understanding that WAN links between sites may have limited bandwidth, the KCC is able to configure a topology that uses a least-cost spanning tree design. In other words, in a large environment where items need to replicate from one site to the next, the KCC considers the big picture of bandwidth and makes an estimated best-guess topology based on how items should replicate.

While you do not have to create the connection objects for your sites, you may want to intervene in the timing of intersite replication. To adjust your site link settings, perform the following steps:

1. Select Start, Administrative Tools, Active Directory Sites and Services.

2. Expand the Sites branch and expand the Inter-Site Transports folder.

3. Select IP. DEFAULTIPSITELINK is probably all you see if you are just getting started with your site topology.

4. Right-click the site link and choose Properties.

5. On the General tab, look at which sites are in the site link and look at the cost, the replication frequency (the default is 180 minutes), and the Change Schedule button. Use these settings to manually adjust the site link replication properties.

### Check Replication Topology

Although the KCC manages replication quite amazingly, there are times when you might remove a DC from your environment, and the replication topology doesn't catch up quickly. To correct this, you can initiate Check Replication Topology. To do this, perform the following steps:

1. Select Start, Administrative Tools, Active Directory Sites and Services.

2. Expand the Sites branch and expand the site. Expand the Servers folder and expand a server.

3. Right-click NTDS Settings and choose All Tasks and Check Replication Topology.

## Manage and Modify Replication

There are tools for working with replication a bit more. For example, you can use the Replication Diagnostics utility (`Repadmin.exe`) to verify and troubleshoot replication.

> **NOTE** To locate `Repadmin.exe` and a host of other advanced tools, you can open Server Manager on the DC. Expand the Roles branch and select Active Directory Domain Services. Scroll down to Advanced Tools, and you see the many different AD DS tools that can help you.

# Active Directory Domains and Trusts

We mentioned earlier that domains within a forest form automatic two-way transitive trusts with other (child- and parent-level) domains within the forest. You can therefore grant permissions for resources.

There are times when you might want to form an external trust relationship with another forest/domain. The tool for this is Active Directory Domains and Trusts. However, this tool also includes other somewhat hidden features.

## Raising Domain and Forest Functional Levels

Determining the level of forest and domain function involves the ability for Active Directory to either assume all the functionality that comes with a Windows Server 2008 level or maintain a functionality with legacy servers and systems (Windows 2000/Windows Server 2003), depending on the functional level you choose.

However, if you want to raise the domain or forest functional level, you can do so from the Active Directory Domains and Trusts tool.

> **NOTE** You can also raise the functional level of a domain by using the Active Directory Users and Computers tool.

To raise the forest functional level, perform the following steps:

1. Select Start, Administrative Tools, Active Directory Domains and Trusts.

2. Right-click the top of the hierarchy, where it says Active Directory Domains and Trusts, and select Raise Forest Functional Level.

3. Select the level you want (unless you are already at the highest level).

**NOTE** This is a one-way process, not something you can undo after you agree to raise it.

To raise the domain functional level, perform the following steps:

1. Select Start, Administrative Tools, Active Directory Domains and Trusts.

2. Right-click the domain and select Raise Domain Functional Level.

3. Select the level you want (unless you are already at the highest level).

**NOTE** Again, this is a one-way process, not something you can undo after you agree to raise it.

### Changing Operations Master Roles

You can change the Domain Naming Master role from within the Active Directory Domains and Trusts tool. To do this, perform the following steps:

1. Click Start, Administrative Tools, Active Directory Domains and Trusts.

2. Right-click the top of the hierarchy, where it says Active Directory Domains and Trusts, and select Operations Master.

3. Click Change to transfer the role to another DC.

At times a server may crash before you are able to transfer the role to another server. If the server is not repairable in a reasonable amount of time and you need to perform a task that requires one of the Domain Naming Master roles, then you will need to seize that role. To do this, you use the `ntdsutil` command. You can learn more about this command from the Microsoft Help and Support site, at http://support.microsoft.com/kb/255504.

**NOTE** To change the RID Master, PDC Emulator, and Infrastructure Master roles, you use the Active Directory Users and Computers tool. You right-click the top of the hierarchy and select Operations Masters to see the tabs where you indicate changes. To change the Schema Master role, you would use the Active Directory Schema snap-in. You can also perform these transfers by using PowerShell with `Move-ADDirectoryServerOperationMasterRole`.

### Create an External Trust

To establish manual trusts with external domains, perform the following steps:

1. Select Start, Administrative Tools, Active Directory Domains and Trusts.

2. Right-click the domain and select Properties.

3. Select the Trust tab and click the button on the bottom that says New Trust. The New Trust Wizard launches. You can use this wizard to create a trust to connect to one of the following:

   ▶ A Windows domain in this forest or in another forest

   ▶ A Windows NT 4.0 domain

   ▶ A Kerberos V5 realm trust

   ▶ Another forest

4. Click Next and follow the prompts to complete the trust relationship. Depending on your choices, you will be presented with a variety of different options.

> **NOTE** To see detailed instructions for every type of trust you might create and the step-by-step method for doing so, visit the Windows Server TechCenter from TechNet, at http://technet.microsoft.com/en-us/library/cc816837.aspx.

## Utilize Other Active Directory Services

> **Scenario/Problem:** AD DS is clear in your mind at this point, but you notice that there are several other types of services that begin with the words *Active Directory*. What are they, and how/when do you implement them?

**Solution:** Additional Active Directory services, including the following, can be installed for specific purpose:

▶ **Active Directory Certificate Services (AD CS):** This tool is used to create CAs and related role services that allow you to issue and manage certificates used in a variety of applications.

▶ **Active Directory Federation Services (AD FS):** This tool provides simplified, secured identity federation and Web single sign-on capabilities.

▶ **Active Directory Lightweight Directory Services (AD LDS):** This tool provides a store for application-specific data for directory-enabled applications that do not require the infrastructure of AD DS.

▶ **Active Directory Rights Management Services (AD RMS):** This tool helps you protect information from unauthorized use. It establishes the identity of users and provides authorized users with licenses for protected information.

It may be difficult for you to see the practical value of these tools up front.

AD LDS, for example, is the update to what was called Active Directory Application Mode in Windows Server 2003. It's really just an LDAP database where you can store information such as application credentials (although not security principles). One example of its use is in Exchange 2007 Edge Transport role servers. An Edge Transport server resides in the DMZ and is not a part of Active Directory. However, you need to install AD LDS in order for it to work and function.

From a practical standpoint, AD FS provides a single sign-on for enterprise scenarios. Consider, for example, two companies, Company A and Company B. Let's say that Company A has Active Directory, and users log in without a problem. Company B has a website that requires login using internal credentials. Through AD FS, you can establish a connection between the two so that users who log in in Company A can access the website (or SharePoint, perhaps) resources without logging in with an account in Company B.

AD RMS allows you, as one person put it, to "bake" permissions into a document. These RMS permissions go beyond standard NTFS permissions and relate to documentation issues such as printing, copying to the clipboard, and so forth. So you might be able to view a document but not copy it or e-mail it to another person.

AD CS goes beyond certificate services in times past, where you might have set up a certificate server, but it provides a full-production Public Key Infrastructure (PKI) for an enterprise.

# Improve Active Directory with Windows Server 2008 R2

**Scenario/Problem:** Changes to Active Directory are typically subtle, performance-oriented changes. The overall structure has remained the same since Windows 2000 Server. Will Windows Server 2008 R2 be much different?

**Solution:** Yes and no. There have been impressive improvements (seen and unseen) in Active Directory with each release of Windows Server. Windows Server 2008 R2 carries on that tradition but brings with it enhancements that make it unique. Those enhancements include the following:

▶ **A new Active Directory module for Windows PowerShell:** This new module (named ActiveDirectory) replaces the large variety of command-line tools that used to work with Active Directory in times past. Now you have a centralized method of administering Active Directory from the command line. There are about 85 Active Directory–oriented PowerShell cmdlets, enabling you to script Active Directory tasks through PowerShell much more easily.

▶ **Active Directory Administrative Center:** A new GUI interface allows you to access the same features in the Active Directory Users and Computers tool but with a few new features, such as a list view and breadcrumb bar navigation; it is really a task-oriented interface based on the new PowerShell cmdlets that will provide another method of administration.

▶ **A Recycle Bin:** Have you ever accidentally deleted an item (for example, a document, an e-mail message)? Now you can retrieve those items from an Active Directory Recycle Bin. It requires the R2 forest functional level (so that may be a bit of a task for companies that are not ready to go full R2), but it is nice to know it exists.

▶ **Active Directory Best Practices Analyzer:** This tool goes through your AD DS and determines whether you are meeting best practice standards and reports back the good, the bad, and the ugly. It also provides instruction on what you need to do to meet best practices for Active Directory.

These features are joined by a few others, including offline domain joining, managed service accounts, the Active Directory Management Pack (for working with System Center Operations Manager, the upgrade to MOM), authentication management assurance, and Active Directory Web Services.

# CHAPTER 10

# Utilize Group Policy

# Grasp the Structure of Group Policy

**Scenario/Problem:** With Active Directory up and running, you want to see the benefits of applying policies that apply to your users. However, this may be a complicated task if you have never used Group Policy before. There are thousands of policy settings, and it feels a bit overwhelming. Where do you begin?

**Solution:** Trying to focus on the thousands of settings will certainly hurt your mind a bit. Over time, you will remember settings or keep a log of which ones you feel are required, but to begin with, you should start with small, easy-to-grasp settings so you can see immediately if and how your policies are being applied. Before you begin, however, it is a good idea to gain a full understanding of what Group Policy settings do and how they work.

## Group Policy Objects

You can apply a Group Policy object (GPO), which is created within Active Directory, to particular systems or users. A GPO is made up of two parts: a Group Policy container (GPC), which lives within Active Directory, under the System\Policies container and is replicated with Active Directory items, and a Group Policy template (GPT), which is stored in the SYSVOL folder.

**NOTE** SYSVOL is a collection of folders that contain a domain's public files, including logon scripts, GPTs, and system policies. In Windows Server 2003, SYSVOL was replicated using the File Replication Service (FRS), but with Windows Server 2008, if the domain is upgraded to the Windows Server 2008 domain functional level, the SYSVOL folder is replicated through Distributed File System (DFS) replication.

## The Group Policy Central Store

In addition to the typical settings within Group Policy, Microsoft provides template files (previously called ADM files) that you download in order to manage items through Group Policy. A good example of this is Microsoft Office templates for Group Policy.

With legacy versions of Group Policy (Windows 2000 Server/Server 2003/Server 2003 R2), there is too much replication occurring with the SYSVOL folder because the GPT included all the default Group Policy templates and any ADM templates for the GPO, and they replicated (with a minimum of 4MB each) around the entire domain. That made for excessive replication.

Instead of having all the templates replicate, the solution is to point everyone to a single central store.

**NOTE** The template files that were previously called ADM files have been split into two parts, ADMX and ADML. ADMX holds the settings, while ADML holds the language. So, in Windows Server 2008, a single ADMX can have multiple ADML files that support multiple languages. This allows administrators in various countries to read Group Policy definitions that have been established in their own language.

To create the central store, you have to perform the following steps:

1. Log in to any domain controller as an Administrator for the domain.

2. Create a new folder in the SYSVOL folder called PolicyDefinitions. That folder is typically c:\Windows\SYSVOL\domain\Policies\ PolicyDefinitions.

3. Create a subfolder in the PolicyDefinitions folder for each of the languages you need to support (for English, it is \en-US).

4. When the central store is created (it is empty at the moment), add templates that you want to use. To find templates, go to the c:\Windows\PolicyDefinitions folder on a Windows Vista or Server 2008 system and copy the ones you like. Keep in mind two points: You need the ADMX and the ADML files (and the ADML will go in the language folder you created). Also, you should not copy all these—only the ones you need.

## The Application Order of Group Policy

You can create and apply Group Policy in a variety of ways. Within Active Directory, you can apply GPOs at the site, domain, and organizational unit (OU) levels. In fact, with OUs nested within other OUs, you can apply policies at every level.

However, a local system may also have policies applied. Pre-Vista systems had only one local Group Policy, whereas Vista and Windows 7 systems allow for Multiple Local Group Policy Objects (MLGPOs).

Group Policy is relatively easy to understand when you have one policy applied to one OU, and a user logs in and receives those policy settings. That seems to make perfect sense. But what happens when there are policies at the site level, the domain level, the OU level, and the local level?

When local policy settings conflict with Active Directory policies, the local settings always lose. Beyond the local level, the order of precedence is site, domain, OU (with OU taking the highest precedence).

For example, if you have wallpaper settings in several policies which state wallpaper should be blue applied to the site level, green applied to the domain level, and yellow applied at the OU of a user named John, and John logs in, the wallpaper will be yellow. If, however, there is no conflict, and each of those policies has different settings that can be applied, they will accumulate, and all settings that do not conflict will be applied to the user or computer.

**NOTE** A Block Inheritance attribute can be selected to stop the application of policies from higher levels of precedence. However, if an administrator wants to force a policy setting to be applied down to the lower levels, he can set the Enforced setting.

# Use Starter GPOs

**Scenario/Problem:** Group Policy already seems a bit overwhelming. Is there a way to get started without all the complexity?

**Solution:** Windows Server 2008 has a new feature called Starter GPOs. These provide a starting point for administrators to create policies on aspects of the system configuration that are typically necessary.

To use Starter GPOs, perform the following steps:

1. Select Start button, Administrative Tools, Group Policy Management.

2. Expand Forest, expand Domains, and expand the domain in which you want to form GPOs.

3. Select the Starter GPOs container.

4. Click the button Create Starter GPOs Folder if this is the first time you are using a Starter GPO.

5. At this point, you can choose the Load Cabinet option to select CAB files that will include recommended settings to apply as policies. However, if you want to create your own Starter GPO, right-click in the Content dialog and choose New.

6. Provide a name, add comments if you like, and click OK.

7. To edit the Starter GPO, right-click it and choose Edit.

Notice that the only settings are user and computer configuration settings, and only for administrative templates.

One of the nice things about Starter GPOs is that you can export your settings as CAB files that can be distributed and imported so that policy settings that work for your organization (best practices, for example, or important management settings) can be shared and imported by others.

When you have Starter GPOs enabled, you can use them as a source for creating new GPOs.

# Create and Apply Group Policies

**Scenario/Problem:** You have everything in place to begin the creation and application of Group Policy within Active Directory. You just need to take the next step and actually do it. Where do you begin this process?

**Solution:** First of all, you need to be more than a creator of Group Policy. You also need to be a designer, or an architect. To accomplish this, you have to spend some time clicking through the different policy settings so you know what exists.

We are going to walk through some of the basics of policy possibilities, and ultimately we provide the steps for you to create two policies: one for securing password settings through greater complexity and another for hiding the Screen Saver tab in your Display Properties. These examples will help you get your feet wet with Group Policy settings and application.

## Access Group Policy Settings

There are multiple ways to access Group Policy settings, some of which are more complicated than others. Let's start simply. If you select Start, Administrative Tools, Group Policy Management, you are taken to a one-stop-shop location for Group Policy settings, the Group Policy Management console, shown in Figure 10.1. In this console, you can see a hierarchy of forest, including your domain(s), OUs, and sites.

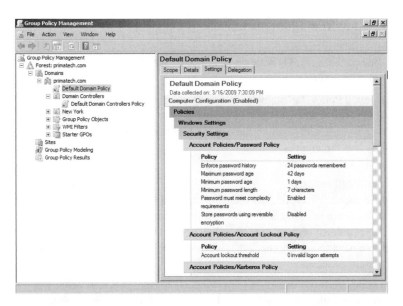

FIGURE 10.1
The Group Policy Management console.

Consider a few elements of your policy:

▶ What exactly are you looking to configure?

▶ Will you combine multiple items into a single GPO, or will you use multiple GPOs due to the nature of the settings and persons you are applying them to?

▶ Where is the best place to apply a GPO once it is created?

To begin with, you might want to see where security settings for your domain are configured. That happens on policies created that are applied at the domain level. To see an existing policy, you can perform the following steps:

1. Expand your forest branch by clicking the plus sign.

2. Expand the domain by using the plus sign.

3. Select Default Domain Policy. Note the four tabs displayed in the console:

   ▶ Scope

   ▶ Details

   ▶ Settings (shown in Figure 10.1)

   ▶ Delegation

4. Right-click the policy and click Edit. The Group Policy Management Editor appears.

5. Make adjustments to the Default Domain Policy, including the security settings in the Settings tab.

## The Group Policy Management Editor

The Group Policy Management Editor provides a very simple way of seeing what is happening in one particular GPO. Within a single GPO, however, you have the ability to make many configuration changes.

The Default Domain Policy, for example, is already configured with certain options, mainly related to security. You can see that there is a basic hierarchy of Computer Configuration and User Configuration. Beneath each of these, for both configuration sets, are Policies and Preferences sections.

### Policies Versus Preferences

What is the difference between Group Policy Policies and Group Policy Preferences? Well, it may come down to enforcement. Users cannot change Group Policy settings. Preferences do not enforce settings over users and computers, but they apply settings, although in the same tattooing approach that we saw back in the days of Windows NT 4.0 with system policies.

Group Policy Preferences (GPP) arrived with Windows Server 2008 after Microsoft purchased a company called Desktop Standard and its PolicyMaker line of products.

For clients other than Vista to process GPP settings, they have to install the GPP Client Side Extension (CSE), available from Microsoft. So, how do GPP and CSE differ?

Group Policy settings do not tattoo the registry, they supersede an application's configuration settings, and/or they are recognized by an application. Preferences settings, however, do tattoo and can overwrite an application's configuration setting, but they are not recognized by an application. With GPP settings, there are more than simply Apply or Don't Apply type options. Now you can choose to remove items that no longer apply and can also choose Apply Once and Do Not Reapply, which gives you greater flexibility.

> **NOTE** One aspect of Preferences settings that make them as flexible as they are powerful is the ability to perform item-level targeting. Using the Targeting Editor tool, you can define where you want a policy applied (laptops, only certain OS versions, disk space, or RAM settings...it is truly item-level targeting).

While policies are the key element to Group Policy, let's consider one type of Preferences setting that may help you see the value in using a GP Preferences policy: the ability to create shortcuts in Internet Explorer that you can then use to implement intranet sites directly within your users' Favorites.

To create a policy of this sort, you perform the following steps:

> **NOTE** We assume that you are using the existing policy for the domain in this case. We will show how to create new policies in the next section.

1. In the Group Policy Manager, right-click the appropriate policy and choose Edit to open the policy with the Group Policy Management Editor.

2. Under User Configuration, expand Preferences. Then expand Windows Settings.

3. Right-click Shortcuts and select New Shortcut.

4. Notice in Figure 10.2 that you can specify the action, name, target type, and location. Provide a reasonable name to your shortcut, such as Company Intranet Site. (You can put your shortcut in a special folder if you like—one that exists or one that will be created—by making the name Folder\Name.)

5. Select Target Type and change it to URL.

6. Select Location and choose Explorer Favorites.

7. Indicate the target URL.

8. Click OK.

Because that policy is set for the domain (as mentioned earlier), users will have that shortcut in their Internet Explorer Favorites the next time they log in.

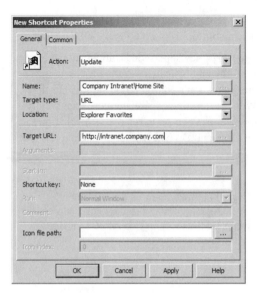

FIGURE 10.2
Creating a shortcut Preferences setting.

**NOTE** While a user policy applies when the user logs out and back in again, you can force it to happen by opening a command prompt and typing `gpupdate`.

### Policy Settings

Within either Computer Configuration or the User Configuration, you see three sets of folders: Software Settings, Windows Settings, and Administrative Templates (see Figure 10.3).

The settings in Computer Configuration and in User Configuration are not the same. If you open each of the folders, you see that some settings are connected to only one or the other. For example, establishing account policies is something you can only do from the Computer Configuration side of a policy.

As you click among the many different settings, you may begin to wonder what each one does and how it functions. With many of the policies, you can see in an extended view, showing the requirements for and description of the policy, as shown in Figure 10.4.

In addition, you can double-click to open any policy setting and click see the Setting tab (where you can configure settings), the Explain tab (where you can see a very detailed explanation of the setting), and the Comment tab (where you can make comments and observations regarding that setting).

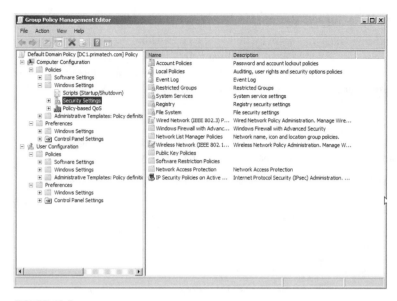

FIGURE 10.3
The Group Policy Management Editor.

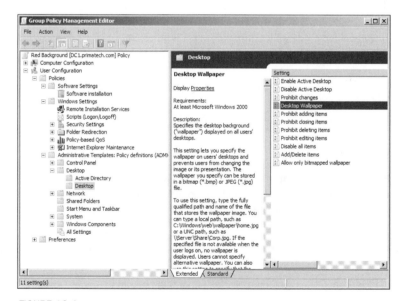

FIGURE 10.4
The extended view of a policy, showing a description.

## Change an Existing GPO

To alter an existing GPO, you begin by finding the GPO within the Group Policy Management console. If you look under the hierarchy for a folder called Group Policy Objects, you see that, by default, there are only two policies: Default Domain Controllers Policy and Default Domain Policy. You can add others, as discussed in the next section.

We mentioned a little earlier that we will walk through two different policy settings. The first is a security setting, which means it has to be set at the domain level. In this case, you are simply going to alter the Default Domain Policy.

To alter the Default Domain Policy to require, in this case, complexity of passwords, you perform the following steps:

1. In the Group Policy Management console, expand the hierarchy, and under Domains select the Group Policy Objects folder. (As noted earlier, you could also expand the domain name to find the Default Domain Policy.)

2. Right-click the policy and choose Edit.

3. From the Group Policy Management Editor tool, expand Computer Configuration, expand Policies, expand Windows Settings, expand Security Settings, and expand Account Policies.

4. Select Password Policy.

5. Note the option Password Must Meet Complexity Requirements; this option is most likely enabled by default, but make sure it is selected.

6. Double-click the policy setting. Note the Security Policy Setting and Explain tabs.

7. After you alter a policy setting, click OK, and the change becomes part of the GPO.

## Create a New GPO

There are many ways to create a new GPO. One simple way is to create a policy without initially being concerned with its application. The policy can reside under the Group Policy Objects branch of the Domain section of the Group Policy Management console.

To create a new policy in the Group Policy Objects branch, perform the following steps:

1. In the Group Policy Management console, expand the hierarchy under Domains and select the Group Policy Objects folder.

2. Right-click the Group Policy Objects folder and choose New.

3. Give your new policy a name. In this case, call it No Screensaver Tab.

4. Select a Starter GPO if you have an existing GPO that you want to use as your base set of configuration settings, like a template. In this case, choose None and click OK. The No Screensaver Tab policy should show up under your Group Policy Objects folder.

5. Right-click the No Screensaver Tab policy and choose Edit.

6. Expand User Configuration, expand Policies, expand Administrative Templates, and expand Control Panel.

7. Select the Display folder and double-click the Hide Screen Saver setting to open it.

8. Select the Enabled radio button. Note the Explain and Comment tabs. Click OK.

9. Close the Group Policy Management Editor tool.

Now, when you have this new policy in the Group Policy Objects section of the Group Policy Management console, you can select it and see information about it. Figure 10.5 shows an at–a-glance view of the settings.

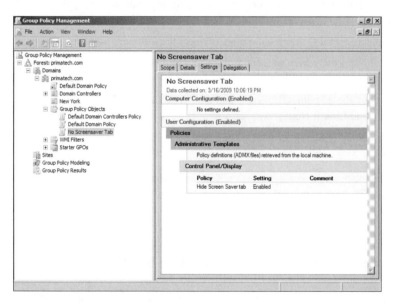

FIGURE 10.5
Policies in the Group Policy Objects folder exist but may not be applied.

Even though you have the policy, unlike the default domain and domain controller policies, this one hasn't been applied to anything yet. You can apply it to the domain, the OU, or the site level. The choice is really up to you.

## Apply a GPO

To apply policies, you need to know what a policy does and who it is supposed to affect. Because policies can be applied at the site, domain, and OU levels, you have to prepare policies with the appropriate application in mind.

To link an existing GPO to the domain, site, or OU level, perform the following steps:

1. In the Group Policy Management tool, right-click the domain, OU, or site to which you want to apply the policy and then click Link an Existing GPO.

2. From the Select GPO dialog, look in your domain (or other domains) for the GPO. When you locate the GPO name, click it. Click OK.

Now you can see that the GPO is linked because you can see it in the Linked Group Policy Objects tab when you select the domain, OU, or site.

## Create and Apply a GPO

If you want to avoid taking multiple steps to create and apply a GPO (although that is the more organized method of GPO deployment), you can create and apply the GPO at the same time.

To create and apply a GPO at the same time, perform the following steps:

1. In the Group Policy Management tool, select the domain, OU, or site to which you want to apply the policy.

2. Right-click the domain, OU, or site and then click Create a GPO in This Domain and Link It Here.

3. In the New GPO dialog, provide a name and a Starter GPO.

> **NOTE** Remember that creating the GPO and having it applied is only half the process. You still have to edit the GPO and create the settings you want applied.

# Configure Group Policy Application Settings

**Scenario/Problem:** Now that you understand the basics of creating and applying a GPO, what type of flexibility is afforded in regard to the application of those policies? How do you alter the default application of policies?

**Solution:** It's true that creating and applying a policy can be relatively easy to do. However, over time there have developed ways of manipulating policies to alter the way they apply, to change the order in which they apply, and even to remove all or part of their application.

In this section we will discuss the following alterations:

► Raising or lowering the link order

► Disabling a policy

► Disabling half a policy

► Deleting a link or a policy

► Block inheritance

► Enforce a policy

► Filter GPO application

## Raise or Lower the Link Order

Within each level of Group Policy application (site, domain, OU) is a ranking precedence order in which policies are applied.

For example, in Figure 10.6, you can see two policies applied to the New York OU. One says No Screensaver Tab, and the other says Include the Screensaver Tab. Which will be applied?

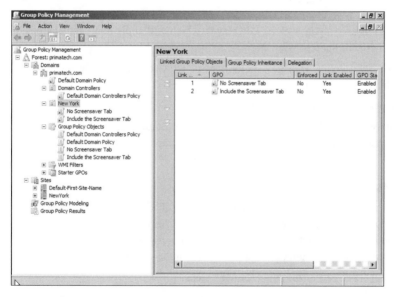

FIGURE 10.6
Linked GPO settings.

The way these will be processed is from lowest link to highest link. So, number 2 will be processed first and then number 1. In this case, the No Screensaver Tab policy will win in the conflict.

If two policies within the same level contain values for the same setting, the link order takes precedence. Therefore, if you look at the options to the left of the table, you see that you can alter the link order to ensure that the policy you want to be applied last is number 1 or higher up in the process order than the policy that you want to win.

## Disable a Policy

There are many reasons you might want to disable a GPO. Perhaps you are trouble-shooting or reorganizing your policy settings. Whatever the case, there are multiple ways to disable (without deleting) a GPO.

One way is to disable it on the level where you are having difficulty. For example, if you have a policy that is applied to multiple OUs, but only one OU is having trouble, you can disable it from that OU by performing the following steps:

1. In the Group Policy Management tool, locate the OU where you want to disable the policy. Right-click the policy.

2. Note the checkmark next to Link Enabled. Click Link Enabled to remove that checkmark.

3. That policy, although still applied to the OU, is now disabled for that OU. The icon now appears slightly dulled.

If you want to disable a policy at the GPO level (which will apply to all applications of that policy), perform the following steps:

1. In the Group Policy Management tool, locate the Group Policy Objects container under the domain.

2. Locate and right-click the policy.

3. Hover over GPO Status and select the option All Settings Disabled. The icon now appears dulled.

## Disable Half a Policy

Every policy adds a slight bit of performance overhead to your system during bootup and login. Therefore, if you have a policy that contains only user configuration settings, you might want to disable the computer configuration portion of the policy. That might save you a tiny amount of performance on the policy.

To disable half a policy, perform the following steps:

1. In the Group Policy Management tool, locate the Group Policy Objects container under the domain.

2. Locate and right-click the policy.

3. Hover over GPO Status and under the option All Settings Disabled, elect one of the following options, depending on your needs:

   ▶ User Configuration Settings Disabled

   ▶ Computer Configuration Settings Disabled

**NOTE** Be warned here. You gain only a minor performance increase by disabling half a policy. If, after you disable half a policy, you forget that you've done so and have to figure out why a policy you reconfigure isn't applying, you will have a frustrating search on your hands. Use this feature sparingly and don't forget to document your settings.

## Delete a Link or a Policy

To delete a policy, you can right-click it and click Delete, but depending on where you do this, you will have different results. For example, if you right-click an applied policy within an OU (you can tell it is applied because it has a little shortcut arrow in the bottom corner that you do not see in the Group Policy Objects container) and then click Delete, you will receive the message "Do you want to delete this link? This will not delete the GPO itself." On the other hand, if you select a policy directly from the Group Policy Objects container, right-click it, and choose Delete, the message you receive is "Do you want to delete this GPO and all links to it in this domain? This will not delete links in other domains."

**NOTE** Because you are deleting a GPO that may be linked to other parts of your domain, you should take a look at the Scope tab for the policy first and note the other sites, domains, and OUs that have it linked so you can inform any other administrators that you are deleting this policy before you do it.

## Block Inheritance

While the typical method of policy application occurs from sites to domains to OUs, and so forth, there may be times when you want to block a policy from being applied. You can use the setting Block Inheritance to block GPOs and their policies from applying down to areas you feel are not applicable.

To accomplish this, you locate the OU (or domain, if you are seeking to block from the site level), right-click, and select Block Inheritance. The OU now has a blue circle with a white exclamation point. This setting will block all policies from above from applying to the OU. Now only the policies applied to that OU will apply. However, there is a way for administrators with greater power to enforce their policies and trump your block inheritance. Read on.

## Enforce a Policy

Any time an administrator wants to ensure that a policy is absolutely applied down the food chain, regardless of Block Inheritance settings, you can enforce your policy by using the Enforced option.

**NOTE** In first-release versions of Group Policy with Windows 2000, Enforced was called No Override.

Enforcing policy settings is quite simple: You right-click the GPO link (so you won't find this in the Group Policy Objects container, but on the links within an OU, at the domain or site level where the policies are actually linked) and then choose Enforced. Note that the link icon changes slightly, to reveal a little lock.

## Filter GPO Application

There are several ways to alter the application of a GPO. While turning off the user or computer configuration options may alter the way the policy is applied to a site, domain, or OU (as do the Block Inheritance and Enforced policy options), it does not change the persons or computers within a site, domain, or OU that have the policy applied toward them.

For example, if a group of settings among multiple policies are added up and applied to an OU that has 100 people in it, all 100 will typically have those policies applied.

Now one way to filter this is by using the Security Filtering settings. When you select a policy in the Group Policy Management tool, you see in the Security Filtering portion of the Scope tab (shown in Figure 10.7) that the default setting is to apply the policy to authenticated users.

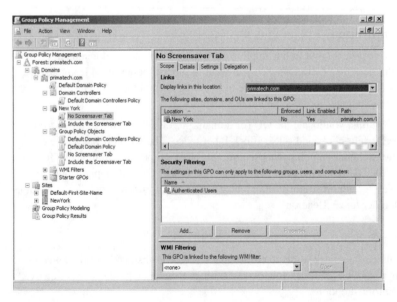

FIGURE 10.7
Filtering GPO application with security filters.

If you wanted certain persons or computers but not others to have the policy applied, you can create different groups and then add those persons/computers to the groups. You can then remove Authenticated Users by clicking Remove and add in the security groups you have created that you want those policies applied to.

**NOTE** Technically, you cannot attach a GPO to a group. However, you can attach it to an OU and then use security filtering to attach it to a group that is in the OU.

Now this method certainly provides a way to apply policies to only those you want, but you might want to drill down a little deeper and not have a policy apply to someone in the group to which you just applied the policy. You could remove this person from the group, but that might cause other problems. So, how would you alter individuals or groups of individuals who seem locked in to receive this policy?

The key is knowing what is going on under the hood with the GPO. Users who have the policy applied to them have two permissions settings that are explicitly set: Allow Read and Apply Group Policy. These two settings are absolutely necessary if you want the policy applied to the group. You can explicitly deny those abilities to an individual in a group that has the permissions, and this Deny setting will override anything else. You can do this for multiple persons or create a group and deny the group those permissions.

To access the options you want to be in the policy, you select the Delegation tab from within the Group Policy Management tool. Imagine, in this scenario, that you have created special groups to which to apply the policy, and you have removed the Authenticated Users group from the security filtering options. At this point, you need to select the Delegation tab and add the user or group to which you want to explicitly deny access to the policy settings.

In the Delegation tab, click Add, enter the object name to include, and click OK. When it is included, select the object and click Advanced. You now see the security settings over that object. You can purposely select Deny for both the 'Read' and 'Apply Group Policy' settings.

With the Deny setting chosen, those persons or groups with the Deny setting will be passed over during the security check for policy application because Deny takes precedence over everything else.

**NOTE** You have just learned two different approaches to filtering GPOs from application. One is to apply a GPO through security filtering so that only those you approve apply the policy. The other is to deny the application to those you don't want the policy applied to. The real difference between the two methods appears when you are tracking a problem. The security filter easily shows you who has it applied, and that should be enough—unless you use the Deny feature. In that case, you have to go to the Delegation tab and click Advanced on every object in the tab to find out if any have the Deny setting on. So it just depends on how methodical you want to be when creating and applying policies in the first place. The preferred, recommended, and cleaner method is the first one: applying a GPO through security filtering.

# Work with Group Policy Modeling and Results

**Scenario/Problem:** Over time, the number of policies grows. Ultimately, it becomes more and more confusing to know what is in a policy, what will be applied to a user, and so forth. Are there methods for determining the what-if scenario of a user logging in with regard to policy settings being applied?

**Solution:** When Group Policy was first introduced to the IT world, it was such a relief to have powerful but flexible tools in comparison with NT 4.0's system policies structure that tattooed the registry (with evil intent, I might add). However, very quickly we became aware that something was missing: a what-if calculator that would add up policies and settings and spit out a simple "if user A logs in on computer B, these policies and settings will be applied."

With Group Policy, we saw some wonderful advancements in Windows Server 2003, and now we have them in Windows Server 2008. For example, the Group Policy Modeling Wizard helps you determine what would happen if, say, User A were to change sites or OUs. How would policies apply differently as a result of this change?

## The Group Policy Modeling Wizard

To use the Group Policy Modeling Wizard, follow these steps:

1. Open your Group Policy Management tool, select the Group Policy Modeling folder, right-click in the Contents pane, and select Group Policy Modeling Wizard.

2. On the Group Policy Modeling Wizard welcome screen, click Next.

3. Select the DC on which you want the simulation performed (or leave it as Any Available Domain Controller Running Windows Server 2003 or Later) and click Next.

4. In the User and Computer Selection pane (shown in Figure 10.8), select the user and/or computer information and click Next.

5. Under Advanced Simulation Options, choose the following, as appropriate:

   ▶ Slow network connection (for example, a dial-up connection)

   ▶ Loopback processing (with replace or merge)

   ▶ Site

6. From Alternate Active Directory Paths, click the Browse option and determine a new location with which to simulate the settings and click Next.

7. Under User Security Groups, look at which security groups the user belongs to. Add others or remove some to see what happens if their group membership changes. Click Next.

8. Under Computer Security Groups, look at which security groups the computer belongs to. Add or remove groups to see what happens and then click Next.

9. Under WMI Filters for Users, include WMI filters in the simulation and click Next.

10. Under WMI Filters for Computers, include WMI filters in the simulation and click Next.

11. Review the options on the Summary of Selections page and then click Next.

12. After the processing takes place, click Finish on the completion screen.

13. When you see the report of the what-if model in your Group Policy Modeling container, select it and view the settings that would apply if that simulated scenario were, in fact, reality.

---

**NOTE** Throughout the Group Policy Modeling Wizard, which appears to be very long, there is a checkbox at the bottom that says Skip to the Final Page of This Wizard Without Collecting Additional Data. You can use it to shorten the wizard once you have provided the necessary information to perform the simulation.

---

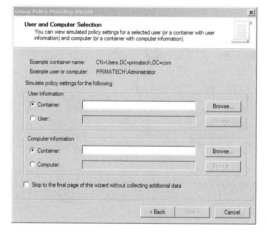

FIGURE 10.8
The Group Policy Modeling Wizard.

## The Group Policy Results Wizard

The Group Policy Results Wizard actually tells you the policy settings for a specific user or computer. Rather than a simulation, it is actually a real environment result for that user or computer. To run the wizard, you perform the following steps:

1. Open your Group Policy Management tool and select the Group Policy Results folder. Right-click in the Contents pane and select Group Policy Results Wizard.

2. On the Welcome screen, click Next.

3. On the Computer Selection screen, select the computer from which you want to display policy settings:

   ▶ You can choose This Computer or Another Computer.

   ▶ You can select the checkbox Do Not Display Policy Settings for the Selected Computer in the Results (Display User Policy Settings Only).

   When you're done, click Next.

4. On the User Selection screen, choose any of the following, as appropriate:

   ▶ Display Policy Settings for Current User

   ▶ Display Policy Settings for Specific User

   ▶ Do Not Display User Policy Settings in the Result (Display Computer Policy Settings Only)

5. Review the Summary of Selections screen and click Next.

6. After the wizard processes the results and shows the completion screen, click Finish.

7. When you see the report on the results options you've requested under the Group Policy Results folder, select the results report and review a summary of items that will apply based on your selected options.

# Prepare for Windows Server 2008 R2 Enhancements to Group Policy

**Scenario/Problem:** What new features should you expect from Group Policy in Windows Server 2008 R2? Is it possible that Group Policy will be enhanced any further?

**Solution:** There are always changes that can and should be made to Group Policy to make it work better and make it more manageable for administrators. In addition, new tools are being developed all the time to assist in handling Group Policy on many levels.

Windows Server 2008 R2 will bring four main improvements to Group Policy:

▶ **Windows PowerShell cmdlets for Group Policy:** The cmdlets will allow you to manage Group Policy from the command line and run PowerShell scripts during logon and startup.

▶ **Group Policy preferences:** There will be additional preference items, making this a stronger feature in the future. Some items include Power Plan (for Vista and later), Scheduled Task, Immediate Task, and Internet Explorer 8 preferences.

▶ **Starter Group Policy objects:** The Starter GPOs will be improved. For example, some GPOs will be included automatically rather than need to be downloaded and added. These include the following:

   ▶ Windows Vista Enterprise Client (EC)

   ▶ Windows Vista Specialized Security Limited Functionality (SSLF) Client

   ▶ Windows XP Service Pack 2 (SP2) EC

   ▶ Windows XP SP2 SSLF Client

▶ **Administrative template settings:** There will be an improved user interface and additional policy settings. In addition, there will be support for multistring registry and QWORD value types.

> **NOTE** A good example of changes occurring in the Group Policy world is the PolicyPak tools that are provided by Jeremy Moskowitz for the development of your own personal policies, based on other applications. See www.policypak.com.

# CHAPTER 11

## Configure Security

# Understand Security Improvements in Windows Server 2008

**Scenario/Problem:** You have installed Windows Server 2008 because you want to take advantage of the many improvements, including those in the area of security. How do you understand what improvements have been made to Windows Server 2008 security, and what do these improvements mean for your network?

**Solution:** Windows Server 2008 has made a number of changes to security features. Some changes can be readily seen, such as Windows Firewall and Network Access Protection (NAP). But these configurable components are only part of the big picture. Some security components in Windows Server 2008 are installed by default and need no configuration or management. Others call for very little setup and configuration.

We begin this section by looking at the "less configurable" security pieces, and then we move on to the components that could be considered highly configurable. Regardless of how configurable they are, all these components are parts of a whole, and it's important to understand them in order to build a secure environment.

## Built-in Security Features

To begin, let's look at the security features that are added when Windows Server 2008 is installed. These features require little to no configuration, and some of them can be managed:

▸ **Authorization Manager:** This is a role-based management tool for controlling access to resources by assigning users to roles in Windows Server 2008. You can also track what permissions are granted to each role in your network.

▸ **Security Auditing:** This tool allows you to track security events on your server. Auditing allows you to monitor the creation, access, and modification of objects. It tracks user activities and provides warnings about potential security problems.

▸ **Security Configuration Wizard:** This tool determines the minimum required functionality of the server to perform tasks, based on its installed roles. All other ports, services, and functionality are disabled. To run the Security Configuration Wizard, perform the following steps:

1. In Server Manager, highlight Server Manager in the console tree. In the Details pane you can see that the Server Summary Security Information is directly below the Computer Information.

2. Click Run Security Configuration Wizard.

3. On the first screen of the Security Configuration Wizard, click Next.

4. On the Configuration Action screen, choose to create a new security policy. The following other choices are available on this screen:

   ▶ Edit an existing security policy

   ▶ Apply an existing security policy

   ▶ Rollback the last applied security policy

   Click Next.

5. In the next screen, select a server to use as a baseline for this security policy. You need to have Administrator permissions to this server. Choose the DNS name or IP Address and Click Next.

6. On the Security Configuration screen, review the database configuration (you will receive a pop up warning asking to allow Active X controls, click Yes) and then click Next.

7. On the Role-Based Service Configuration screen, click Next.

8. Select the server roles that this server performs and click Next.

9. Select the client features this server performs and click Next.

10. Select the options used in administration of this server and click Next.

11. Select any additional services that this server is running and click Next.

12. Choose how to handle unspecified services. You can choose not to change the startup mode of the service or to disable the service. Click Next.

13. Confirm the selections in this screen and click Next.

14. Get ready to configure Network Security. (This section of the wizard configures the Windows Firewall settings for this server.) Click Next.

15. Select or unselect the network security rules or add additional rules and click Next.

16. Get ready to configure the registry settings. (This section of the wizard configures the protocols used for communication with other computers.) Click Next.

17. Choose whether Server Message Block (SMB) security signatures are required. Select the attributes and click Next.

18. Choose settings for whether you Require LDAP Signing; click the radio box to choose the minimum default security level for LDAP; then click Next.

19. Choose the outbound authentication methods and click Next.

20. Choose Outbound Authentication using Domain Accounts and click Next.

21. View the Registry Settings Summary section and click Next.

22. Set the audit policy for this server; these are the settings that will be used for success/failure audits for the server. Click Next.

23. Choose one of the following choices from the Auditing Objectives list:

   ▶ Do Not Audit

   ▶ Audit Successful Activities

   ▶ Audit Successful and Unsuccessful Activities

   Click Next.

24. Confirm your selections and click Next.

25. On the Save Security Policy screen, click Next.

26. Name the security policy file (the .xml extension will automatically be added later), change the location, add a description, view the security policy, or include security templates to this policy, and click Next.

27. Choose to apply this policy later or to apply it now. Click Next.

28. On the final screen of the wizard, note the location of this security policy file and the name and then click Finish.

▶ **Software Restriction Policies:** This tool is used to identify and control the ability of software to run on a local computer, organizational unit (OU), domain, or site. Managing these polices at the OU, domain, or site level requires the use of the Group Policy Management console. To manage software restriction policies on the local computer, do the following:

   1. Select Start, Administrative Tools, Local Security Policy.

   2. In the console tree, click Software Restriction Policies.

   3. Either right-click and select New Software Restrictions Policy or select Action, New Software Restrictions Policy.

   4. In the object view, choose security levels, enforcement, designated file types, trusted publishers, and additional rules.

> **NOTE** Under additional rules, you have the option of creating a new rule for certificates, hashes, network zones, and paths. The rules are used to override the default security level in place on the local machine.

> **NOTE** These software restriction policies will apply only to the local computer. If restriction policies need to be implemented on a large scale, you should instead use the Group Policy Management console.

▶ **Security Configuration and Analysis:** This tool analyzes and configures the local security policy for the server. It provides recommendations alongside the current security settings and flags areas where the current security settings do not match recommendations. It also enables you to resolve those security issues by directly configuring the local security policy and importing security templates.

▶ **Encrypting File System (EFS):** This tool provides a transparent file-encrypting technology for storing encrypted files on an NTFS volume. EFS is managed through Group Policy or the Encrypting File System Wizard. To encrypt a file or folder using the Encrypting File System Wizard, perform the following steps:

1. Open the Control Panel and double-click User Accounts.

2. Under Tasks, click Manage Your File Encryption Certificates.

3. On the first page of the Encrypting File System Wizard, click Next.

4. Select a certificate to use or create a new certificate and click Next.

5. Choose to back up the certificate and key now or later and then click Next.

6. Select the folder or volume(s) with encrypted files. You can choose to update encrypted files later by checking the box below the folder and volume selections. Click Next.

7. Review the certificate details and click Close.

▶ **Internet Explorer Enhanced Security Configuration (IE ESC):** This security component reduces your server's exposure to web-based attacks. The only configuration is to turn IE ESC on or off for the Administrators and Users group. (By default, IE ESC is turned on for both groups.)

## User Account Control (UAC)

You are familiar with User Account Control (UAC) from Windows Vista. Windows Server 2008 has added UAC into its security repertoire. Like some of the other security components in Windows Server 2008, UAC is installed when you install Windows Server 2008. It is usually managed using Group Policies, although you can set up UAC under the local security policy. So what does the inclusion of UAC mean for Windows Server 2008, and how does it improve overall security?

UAC provides the ability to enter credentials during a user session to perform administrative tasks without switching users or using the Run As command.

To view and set UAC settings in the Local Security Policy tool, perform the following steps:

1. Select Start, Administrative Tools, Local Security Policy.

2. In the console tree, expand Local Policies and click Security Options. Scroll down to the bottom of the screen to see the available UAC options (see Figure 11.1).

3. Double-click each UAC setting you want to configure, select the UAC option, and click OK.

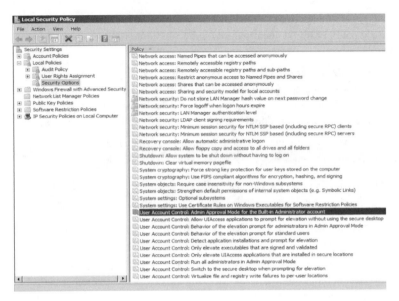

FIGURE 11.1
Available UAC settings in the Local Security Policy tool.

## Additional Security Components

Windows Server 2008 comes with additional security components that need to be set up after Windows Server 2008 is installed:

- **Smart cards:** Windows Server 2008 has built-in capabilities to work with smart cards. Smart card readers should be installed and configured according to manufacturers' specifications.

- **Trusted Platform Module (TPM) management:** TPM is a hardware-based security architecture for providing access to systems. An installed TPM chip (v.1.2) and TCG-compliant BIOS are needed. Windows Server 2008 has an MMC snap-in for managing TPM devices on the local server. No further configuration is needed to take advantage of TPM.

- **BitLocker drive encryption:** BitLocker provides full drive encryption and an integrity check of boot components. You install BitLocker by using the Add Features Wizard, as follows:

  1. In Server Manager choose Add Feature, BitLocker Drive Encryption and click Next.

  2. On the next page, which asks you to confirm that you want to install the feature, click Install.

  3. On the results page, which inform you that you must restart your server to finish the installation of BitLocker, click Close. When you are prompted to restart the server and finish the installation, click Yes.

  4. When the BitLocker installation is complete, click Close.

An important and often-overlooked part of the security picture is Windows Update. In fact, when you look at the security information in Server Manager, you see that Configure Updates is directly below Windows Firewall. It is important to ensure that Windows Server 2008 is kept up to date by using either Windows Update or another update management package, such as WSUS or System Center Configuration Manager. All the security you put in place is useless if you forget to patch a hole that has been discovered.

## Configure Windows Firewall with Advanced Security

**Scenario/Problem:** Windows Firewall is installed and activated by default. How do you configure Windows Firewall to enhance security, and how do you customize Windows Firewall to work for your organization?

**Solution:** Windows Firewall with Advanced Security is a fully integrated and very configurable security solution. In fact, it is two security solutions combined: a host-based firewall and IPsec. Working in conjunction with a perimeter firewall, it provides a layer of security at the OS level. A second advantage of Windows Firewall is protection from attacks from within the network. Because all inbound requests to the server require both a firewall and connection rule, your server is protected from inadvertent attacks from within your organization.

Windows Firewall is a stateful firewall, which means each packet is inspected and allowed or disallowed based on the state of the packet. This is determined by the firewall rules and the connection security rules implemented by Windows Firewall.

Windows Firewall with Advanced Security comes preconfigured, but what if you need to add additional rules for the firewall and for connections to this server? To configure Windows Firewall with Advanced Security, perform the following steps:

1. From Server Manager, under Security Information, click Go to Windows Firewall.

**NOTE** Alternatively, you can expand the configuration tree in Server Manager and select Windows Firewall. Or you can select Start, Administrative Tools, Windows Firewall.

2. On the overview screen that shows the settings for the Domain, Private, and Public profiles (see Figure 11.2), click Windows Firewall Properties.

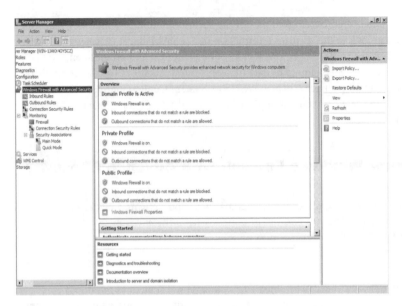

FIGURE 11.2
Overview of Windows Firewall with Advanced Security.

3. Note that the properties page has four tabs (see Figure 11.3), where you can set
   the behavior of Windows Firewall for the three profiles as well as the IPsec
   settings:

   ▶ **Domain Profile:** On this tab, you specify the firewall behavior for when a
   computer is connected to a domain. You can change the firewall state (On
   or Off) and set how the firewall will handle inbound and outbound
   connections (Block, Allow, or Block All Connections). You can customize
   settings for the firewall profile, including displaying notifications, allowing unicast responses, and merging rules. You can also customize logging
   for the profile, set the name and location of the log, choose the log size,
   and choose to log dropped and/or successful packets.

   ▶ **Private Profile:** On this tab, you specify the firewall behavior for when a
   computer is connected to a private network. You can change the firewall
   state (On or Off) and set how the firewall will handle inbound and
   outbound connections (Block, Allow, or Block All Connections). You can
   customize settings for the firewall profile, including displaying notifications, allowing unicast responses, and merging rules. You can also
   customize logging for the profile, set the name and location of the log,
   choose the log size, and choose to log dropped and/or successful packets.

   ▶ **Public Profile:** On this tab, you specify the firewall behavior for when a
   computer is connected to a public network. You can change the firewall
   state (On or Off) and set how the firewall will handle inbound and
   outbound connections (Block, Allow, or Block All Connections). You can

customize settings for the firewall profile, including displaying notifications, allowing unicast responses, and merging rules. You can also customize logging for the profile, set the name and location of the log, choose the log size, and choose to log dropped and/or successful packets.

▷ **IPsec Settings:** In this tab, you can customize the IPsec defaults. You can change and customize the key exchange, data protection, and authentication method. You can also set IPsec exemptions.

Customize settings here, as needed. (We recommend that you leave the firewall profiles active and use the firewall and connection rules.)

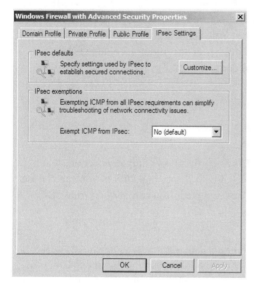

FIGURE 11.3
Connection profiles properties page.

## Create Inbound and Outbound Rules

If you expand the Windows Firewall and Advanced Security console tree and highlight Inbound or Outbound Rules, you will notice that Windows Server 2008 has already predefined rules for Windows Firewall. The number of rules defined depends on which roles and features have been installed. From the Action menu, you can filter the results by profile, state, and group. Here's how you create inbound and outbound rules:

1. To create a new firewall rule, click New Rule.

2. When the New Inbound/Outbound Rule Wizard begins, choose which type of rule to create:

   ▷ **Program:** Rules that control connections for a program

   ▷ **Port:** Rules that control connections for a TCP or UDP port

   ▷ **Predefined:** Rules that control connections for a Windows experience

   ▷ **Custom:** A customized rule based on all or part of the previous three types

Choose the custom rule type (this will allow you to see the set up options for all the rule types) and click Next.

3.  On the next screen, apply the rule to all programs, apply the rule to a specific program path (for example, <c:\path\executable>), or apply the rule to a service. You can customize service rules as well, applying them to all programs and services, to services only, or to a specific service. After you choose how you want to apply this rule, click Next.

4.  In the Protocol and Ports screen, choose the protocol type, local port, and remote port. (If you choose ICMP, you can customize ICMP types.) Click Next.

5.  Choose the scope for this rule. You can choose to apply the rule to any IP address, a single IP address, a subnet, or a range of IP addresses. The scope is set for local and remote connections. You can also customize the interface types, choosing to apply the rule to all interfaces or specifying local area network, remote access, or wireless. Choose the scope settings for your rule and click Next.

6.  In the next screen, note that you have the following options:

    ▶ **Allow the Connection:** Allows connections, regardless of whether they have been protected by IPsec.

    ▶ **Allow the Connection if It Is Secure:** Allows only connections that have been authenticated and protected with IPsec. In addition, you can choose to require the connection to be encrypted. You can also override block rules (only for inbound rules).

---

**NOTE**   If you choose the option Allow the Connection if It Is Secure, you also need to specify authorized computers or computer groups for inbound rules. In addition, you need to choose authorized computers if this is selected for an outbound rule.

---

    ▶ **Block the Connection:** Does not accept any connection to this port, service, or program.

    In this case, choose Allow the Connection if It Is Secure and click Next.

7.  Choose the computers and users that will be allowed to connect to this computer using this inbound rule and click Next.

8.  Choose when this rule applies by choosing a profile. Again, the profile types are Domain, Private, and Public. Click Next.

9.  Name this inbound rule and provide an optional description that will help you identify this inbound rule on your network. Click Finish.

After the rule is created, you can change any of the settings you configured by clicking the properties page in the Actions pane. You can also set an option that is not available while you are creating the rule: You can allow edge traversal (see Figure 11.4). You can also disable this inbound rule from the Action menu.

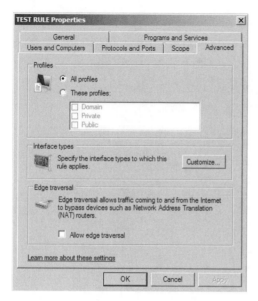

FIGURE 11.4

A rule properties page with advanced settings shown.


## Create Connection Security Rules

Along with the Windows Firewall rules, you can set connection security rules. Expand the Windows Firewall and Advanced Security console tree and highlight Connection Security Rules. In the Action menu, you can filter these rules by profile and by state. To create a new connection security rule, follow these steps:

1. Select Action, New Rule. There are five different connection security rule types to choose from:

   ▶ **Isolation:** Restrict connections based on authentication prerequisites (for example, health status, domain membership).

   ▶ **Authentication Exemption:** Do not authenticate connections from specified computers.

   ▶ **Server-to-Server:** Authenticate connections between specified servers.

   ▶ **Tunnel:** Authenticate a connection between gateway computers.

   ▶ **Custom:** Create custom authentication and endpoint criteria for connection security (see Figure 11.5).

   Choose Custom to create a custom rule and click Next.

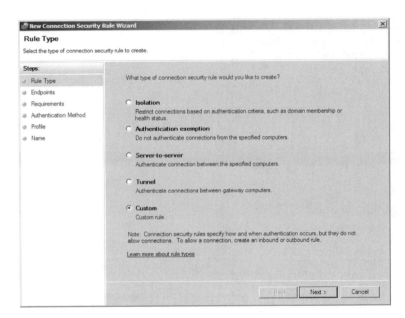

FIGURE 11.5
The New Connection Security Rule Wizard.

2. Select the endpoints for a secured connection. These are set as endpoint 1 and endpoint 2. (For tunnel endpoints, you need to provide the IP address for the tunnel computers closest to endpoint 1 and endpoint 2.) You can also customize the interface types, choosing to apply the rule to all interfaces or specifying local area network, remote access, or wireless. Choose the endpoint settings for your rule and click Next.

3. In the requirements page, select one of the four choices:

   ▶ **Request Authentication for Inbound and Outbound Connections:** Authenticates whenever possible, but authentication is not required.

   ▶ **Require Authentication for Inbound Connections and Request for Outbound Connections:** Inbound connections must be authenticated. Outbound connections are authenticated whenever possible, but authentication is not required.

   ▶ **Require Authentication for Inbound and Outbound Connections:** Both inbound and outbound connections must be authenticated.

   ▶ **Do Not Authenticate:** No authentication is necessary for connections.

   Click Next.

4. On the authentication methods page, choose one of the five choices:

   ▶ **Default:** Uses the method specified in the profile properties page.

   ▶ **Computer and User (Kerberos V5):** Restricts communications to connections from domain-joined users and computers.

▶ **Computer (Kerberos V5):** Restricts communications to connections from domain-joined computers.

▶ **Computer Certificate:** Restricts communications to connections from computers that have a certificate from a specified CA.

▶ **Advanced:** Allows you to choose two authentication methods. You also have the option of making either the first or second authentication method optional.

Click Next.

5. Specify when this connection security rule applies by choosing a profile. Again, the profile types are Domain, Private, and Public. Click Next.

6. In the final step, name this connection security rule and provide an optional description that will help identify this inbound rule on your network. Click Finish.

When the connection security rule is created, you can change any of the settings you configured by clicking the properties page in the Actions pane. You can also disable this connection security rule from the Action menu.

## Monitor Windows Firewall and Advanced Security

After you add inbound and outbound rules and set up connection security rules for Windows Firewall, you can then monitor these, along with the predefined rules established by Windows Server 2008. Expand the console tree under Windows Firewall with Advanced Security and click Monitoring.

You will notice at first that this screen looks like the overview screen shown in Figure 11.1, except that here you can see more details about each profile, including the general settings and the logging settings. By default, the monitoring page is opened to the profile that is currently active.

When you expand the console tree, you see three more monitoring options:

▶ **Firewall:** Monitors all active firewall rules for the active profiles. Also monitors firewall rules distributed by GPOs.

▶ **Connection Security Rules:** Monitors all enabled connection rules. Also provides detailed information about those connections.

▶ **Security Associations (SA):** Monitors communications from senders and receivers, based on the security connections rules defined to create the SA. Monitoring SAs consist of two types: Main Mode and Quick Mode. Both provide a view of the IP address of each endpoint.

Policies that are created using the IPsec Security Policy snap-in cannot be monitored using this tool.

# Configure NAP

**Scenario/Problem:** You need to allow access to resources on your network. However, you need to ensure that all clients that connect (including vendors or consultants) to your network meet the minimum standards for a healthy client computer. Computers that do not meet the requirements need to have limited connectivity in order to install necessary updates to meet the health requirements.

**Solution:** You need to deploy the Network Policy and Access Services role and add the Network Policy Server (NPS) role service to validate health policies in your network. Then you can configure Network Policy Server (NPS) to create and enforce those health policies on clients.

Clients that connect to a NAP server and do not meet the health requirements are placed in a restricted network until updates are performed and the machine meets the health requirements.

## Install the Network Policy Server

To install the NPS role service and configure NAP, perform the following steps:

1. In Server Manager, select Add Roles.

2. Choose the Network Policy and Access Services role and then click Next.

3. On the next screen, which has the sections Introduction to Network Policy and Access Services, Things to Note, and Links to Additional Information, click Next.

4. Choose the role services for Network Policy and Access Services:

   ▶ **Network Policy Server (NPS):** Creates and enforces network access policies for clients and sets organizationwide policies for client health and for connection request authentication and authorization. Also enables you to deploy NAP in your organization.

   ▶ **Routing and Remote Access Services:** Provides users access to resources over a VPN connection. It is made up of two parts: Remote Access Service provides access to the internal network through a VPN, and the Routing portion provides support for NAT, RIP, and multicast routers.

   ▶ **Health Registration Adding Authority (HRA):** Validates requests from clients and issues health certificates for connectivity to resources for clients that meet the health criteria. Adding HRA requires the additional step of selecting a valid CA before HRA is functional.

▷ **Host Credential Authorization Protocol (HCAP):** Allows you to integrate Microsoft's NAP solution with Cisco's NAP solution. Deploying HCAP, NPS, and NAP allows NPS to perform authorization of Cisco Network Access Control clients. Adding HCAP requires that you assign a CA-issued SSL certificate before HCAP is functional.

> **NOTE** Routing and Remote Access Services is part of access services but does not fall under the category of an NPS or NAP server role. Rather, NPS and NAP are used to validate the health of clients before they connect to a VPN through Routing and Remote Access clients.

5. When prompted to choose the network policy and access services you want to add, select NPS, HRA, and HCAP. Click Next.

6. On the next screen, where you can choose to install a local CA, choose a remote CA, or select a CA later, select your choice for a CA and click Next.

7. Choose the authentication requirements. You can choose to require that requestors be authenticated as domain members (recommended) or allow anonymous requests for health certificates. Click Next.

8. Select an SSL server certificate for HRA and HCAP. You can choose an existing certificate (recommended), create a self-signed certificate, or choose to not use an SSL certificate or to assign one later. Click Next.

9. Confirm your installation selections and click Install.

When Network Policy and Access Services is installed, restart your server, and you can then configure NAP.

## Configure NAP Health Policies

When NPS is installed, you still need to configure NAP to create and enforce health policies. So let's take a look at finishing up the configuration of NAP. To finish configuring NAP, perform the following steps:

1. In Server Manager, expand the Network Policy and Access Services console tree.

2. Highlight NPS (Local), and NAP is selected as the default standard configuration. Click Configure NAP.

3. When the Configure NAP Wizard begins, choose the network access server. The following connection methods are available:

   ▷ Dynamic Host Configuration Protocol (DHCP)

   ▷ IPsec with Host Registration Authority (HRA)

   ▷ IEEE 802.1X (Wired)

▶ IEEE 802.1X (Wireless)

▶ Virtual Private Network (VPN)

▶ Terminal Service Gateway (TS Gateway)

**NOTE** It is important to pay attention to the additional requirements below your choice of connection method. Each connection method requires additional steps to finish the installation of NAP. The steps depend on the connection method you choose.

In this case, you want to set up NAP using IPsec with HRA. Choosing this method invokes these necessary additional requirements, as specified by Microsoft TechNet:

To deploy NAP with IPsec and HRA, configure the following:

▶ In NPS, configure the connection request policy, the network policy, and the NAP health policy. You can configure these policies individually, using the NPS console, or you can use the New Network Access Protection Wizard.

▶ Enable the NAP IPsec enforcement client and the NAP service on NAP-capable client computers.

▶ Install HRA on the local computer or on a remote computer.

▶ Install and configure Active Directory Certificate Services (AD CS) and certificate templates.

▶ Configure Group Policy and any other settings required for your deployment.

▶ Configure the Windows Security Health Validator (WSHV) or install and configure other system health agents (SHAs) and system health validators (SHVs), depending on your NAP deployment.

If HRA is not installed on the local computer, also configure the following:

▶ Install NPS on the computer that is running HRA.

▶ Configure NPS on the remote HRA NPS server as a RADIUS proxy to forward connection requests to the local NPS server.

After configuring the additional requirements, Click Next.

4. Specify the NAP enforcement servers for HRA. If HRA is installed on this server, you can skip this step. If it is installed on another server in the domain, you need to specify which server will be used as a RADIUS client. Click Next.

5. In the next screen, grant or deny access, as appropriate. You can grant access to all users by leaving the field blank. If you want to allow/deny access to computers, utilize machine groups. If you want to allow/deny access to users,

utilize user groups. For this example, add both machine and user groups to this policy and click Next.

6. Define the NAP policy. Choose the system health validators to use with this policy. Also, check the box to allow the client system to be remediated automatically. Click Next.

> **NOTE** If the Allow Client System to be Remediated box is not selected, clients that do not meet the health policy requirements are not updated automatically and therefore are not able to gain full access to the network unless you manually update the client system.

7. On the last screen, which shows an overview of the health policy, connection request policy, and network policies you want to enforce, ensure that everything is correct and click Finish.

## Configure System Health Validator and Remediation Server Groups

Although the Network Access Protection folder exists below the Polices folder in the Network Policies and Access Services snap-in, it is actually important to talk about the System Health Validator (SHV) and Remediation Server Groups before we continue with the policy configurations because the SHV allows you to specify the settings required for NAP-capable computers, and Remediation Server Groups defines which servers will host the updates for NAP clients.

Within the SHV is the Windows Security Health Validator (WSHV) (see Figure 11.6), which contains the configuration settings and the error code configurations.

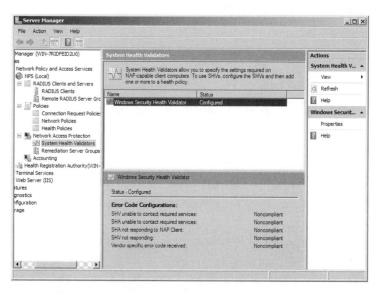

FIGURE 11.6
The WSHV, showing the error code configurations.

If you highlight WSHV and click properties in the Actions pane, you see the Configure button to set client settings. Below that are the error code configurations. You can choose to select how to resolve these error codes by choosing either compliant or noncompliant (default) for each of these possible errors:

▶ SHV unable to contact required services

▶ SHA unable to contact required services

▶ SHA not responding to NAP client

▶ SHV not responding

▶ Vendor specific vendor code received

Clicking Configure brings up a Windows Security Health Validator window that has two tabs: Windows Vista and Windows XP (see Figure 11.7)

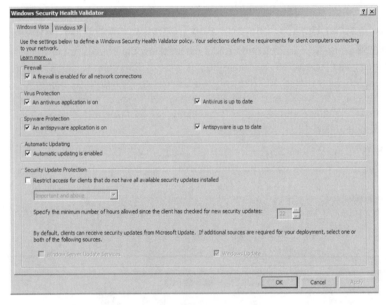

FIGURE 11.7
A properties page for Windows Vista and XP NAP-capable clients.

In this window, you define the health policy settings for the following:

▶ **Firewall:** This option indicates whether Windows Firewall is enabled for all network connections.

▶ **Virus Protection:** These options indicate whether the antivirus application is on and whether it is up to date.

▶ **Spyware Protection:** These options indicate whether the spyware application is on and whether it is up to date. (This setting is only for Windows Vista.)

▶ **Automatic Updating:** This option indicates whether automatic updating is enabled.

▶ **Security Update Protection:** You can choose security update levels (from Low to All), the minimum number of hours since the client has checked for updates, and sources for security updates.

To add remediation server groups, follow these steps:

1. Click the Remediation Server Groups folder and select Action, New.

2. Specify a group name and Click Add.

3. Choose the friendly name, IP address, or DNS name for the server and click OK twice.

You can add additional servers to the group from the properties page in the Actions pane.

## Configure Policy Properties

When you have finished setting up your network connection method, you can view and/or configure settings for the policies. In the NPS Management snap-in, expand the Policies console tree, and you see three policies configuration settings:

▶ Connection Requests Policies

▶ Network Policies

▶ Health Policies

Within each policy type, you can configure properties for the existing and new policies you set up. For instance, if you click Connection Requests Policies, you can view the NAP IPsec with HRA policy you set up. You can also see the default Windows authentication policy. Notice that the policy you created has a processing order of 2; if you have multiple network access server methods, you can set the processing order for NAP clients.

Each policy type has properties that define how NAP will behave. Let's take a look at each policy's configuration.

### Connection Requests Policies Properties

Click the NAP IPsec with HRA policy you set up and then select Action, Properties. You see three tabs here:

▶ **Overview:** On this tab, you set the policy name, policy state, and network connection method.

▶ **Conditions:** You use this tab to set the day and time restrictions for this policy.

▶ **Settings:** On this tab, you set the authentication methods, set the forwarding connection requests, specify a realm name, and specify RADIUS attributes.

## Network Policies Properties

Click the NAP IPsec with HRA compliant or noncompliant policies you set up and select Action, Properties. You see four tabs here:

▸ **Overview:** This tab shows the policy name, policy state, access permission (grant/deny), and network connection method.

▸ **Conditions:** On this tab, you configure the condition for this policy. The conditions can be based on groups, HCAP, date and time, network access, connection, RADIUS client, or gateway.

▸ **Constraints:** On this tab, you set the authentication methods, idle timeout, session timeout, called-station ID, day and time restrictions, and NAS port type.

▸ **Settings:** On this tab, you set the RADIUS attributes, NAP enforcement, and routing and remote access settings.

## Health Policies Properties

Click the NAP IPsec with HRA compliant or noncompliant policies you set up and select Action, Properties. You see a screen where you can change the policy name, set the client SHV checks, and choose the SHVs to use with this health policy.

# Plan for Security Changes and Additions in Windows Server 2008 R2

> **Scenario/Problem:** As with other portions of Windows Server 2008, R2 includes changes and additions to security. What will these changes and additions mean for how you plan and implement security in Windows Server 2008 within your organization?

**Solution:** Security is an area that continues to improve as we are constantly being challenged to stay one step ahead of unsavory characters with ill intentions. In fact, the tools, roles, and features in this chapter are all about staying ahead of the bad guys. Of course, Windows Server 2008 R2 will include some innovative and improved security enhancements.

Let's take a look at these and divide them into categories for clarity. Of course, some of the security changes that are listed may also be mentioned in other chapters, under enhancements to particular roles in Windows Server 2008.

## Changes to Security

In Windows Server 2008 R2, the changes to security will be far reaching. Let's look at each major area of change, beginning with server roles.

## Server Roles

The following is a list of security changes in server roles in Windows Server 2008 R2:

- **Active Directory Certificate Services:** Certificate Enrollment Web Service enables certificate enrollment over HTTP.

- **DNS:** Domain Name System Security Extensions (DNSSEC) allows you to sign and host DNSSEC-signed zones for added security to the DNS role.

- **Network Access Protection:** This role service can now be viewed from the System and Security item within the Control Panel.

- **Distributed File System:** Read-only domain controllers have read-only SYSVOL folders to prevent alteration of files in the folder. Read-only replicated folders will be added to prevent file additions or changes.

- **Active Directory Domain Services:** Authentication mechanism assurance will be added to control access to resources, based on whether the user logs on using certificate-based logon and the type of certificate used.

- **Web Server (IIS):** Request filtering will be added to allow you to restrict types of HTTP requests that IIS will process.

- **Networking:** Direct Access will provide remote, Internet-connected users with access to network resources, without using gateway technologies such as Terminal Services or VPNs.

> **NOTE** For more information on these new technologies, see http://technet. microsoft.com/en-us/library/dd560642.aspx.

## Authorization and Access Control

The following is a list of security changes in Authorization and Access Control in Windows Server 2008 R2.

- **User Account Control (UAC):** In Windows Server 2008 R2, UAC has reduced the number of prompts and can be configured in the Control Panel. UAC will also be enhanced for Windows 7.

- **AppLocker:** This is an upgrade from the software restriction policies. You can create rules for applications, but AppLocker does not require constant rule changes with each application update.

- **Enhanced Storage Access:** Six Group Policy settings will be added to manage Enhanced Storage devices.

- **Managed Service Accounts:** Managed Service Accounts provides automatic password management and service principal names management for applications. Managed service accounts can be managed only through PowerShell; there is no GUI interface.

> **NOTE** For more information on these new technologies, see http://technet. microsoft.com/en-us/library/dd560663.aspx.

## Identity and Authentication

A host of changes will be made to identity and authentication for Windows Server 2008, including changes to Kerberos and NTLM authentication and the addition of the following new features:

- ▶ Online identity integration

- ▶ Extensions to the Negotiate Authentication package

- ▶ PKU2U in Windows

- ▶ Smart card Plug and Play

- ▶ TLS v1.2

- ▶ Restriction of NTLM authentication

- ▶ Windows Biometric Service

> **NOTE** For more information on these new technologies, see http://technet. microsoft.com/en-us/library/dd560654.aspx.

## Security Policies and Security Policy Management

Security auditing in Windows Server 2008 R2 and Windows 7 will enable granular audit policies (which have been available since Windows 2000). In addition, these more granular policies can now be centrally managed through Group Policy.

# CHAPTER 12

# Monitor Performance and Troubleshoot

# Monitor Performance in Windows Server 2008

**Scenario/Problem:** You have installed all the roles and features you need on Windows Server 2008. Now that you have Windows Server 2008 up and running in your organization, how can you make sure that it will run at peak performance and remain reliable in your production environment?

**Solution:** Windows Server 2008 comes with several tools for monitoring performance and reliability. In fact, the main tool for accomplishing this task is the Reliability and Performance tool. This tool provides an overview of the server's performance, using performance counters, configuration information, and event trace data. This information can be turned into data collector sets to monitor specific aspects of performance. Finally, reliability reports create a visual representation of what is happening on the server.

We will look at each segment of the Reliability and Performance tool, beginning with the Resource Overview section, which provides information on server resources in real time. To start using the Reliability and Performance tool, perform the following steps:

1. In Server Manager, select Diagnostics, expand the console tree, and highlight Reliability and Performance Monitor. Immediately you get four graphs and four monitoring sections (see Figure 12.1). The four sections you can monitor in this view are CPU, Disk, Network, and Memory. Under the graphs are four sections that provide more information on how these four resources are being used on this server.

2. Expand each resource to get details on how the active processes are using these server resources:

   ▶ **CPU:** Shows the percentage of CPU usage. Expanding this resource shows Image (process), PID, Description, Threads, CPU Percentage, and Average CPU Percentage.

   ▶ **Disk:** Shows the disk activity, in kilobytes per second. Expanding this resource shows Image (process), PID, File Location, Read (B/min), Write (B/min), I/O Priority, and Response Time.

   ▶ **Network:** Measures network throughput and percentage of utilization. Expanding this resource shows Image (process), PID, IP address (or DNS Name), Send (B/min), Receive (B/min), and Total (B/min).

   ▶ **Memory:** Monitors memory faults and the percentage of physical memory in use. Expanding this resource shows Image (process), PID, Hard Faults, Commit (KB), Working Set (KB), Sharable (KB), and Private (KB) memory.

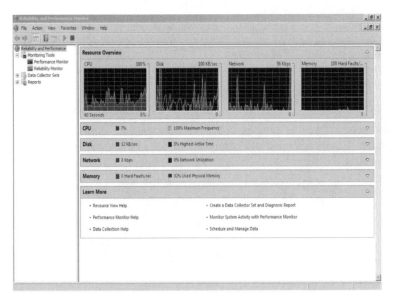

FIGURE 12.1
The Resource Overview section in the Reliability and Performance tool.

The Resource Overview section is a great place to get an immediate picture of what is going on with the server resources. You can easily see a sharp spike in any of the resources and then deal with it immediately. Sometimes the performance issues are not caused by a complete drain on resources. In such a case, you need to use more in-depth tools, as described in the following sections.

## Use the Performance Monitor and the Reliability Monitor

Under the Reliability and Performance tool is a console tree called Monitoring Tools. When you expand this tree, you see two separate monitors: one for reliability and one for performance. Let's look at how to utilize each one to monitor a server's performance data.

### Performance Monitor

Performance Monitor is a simple yet powerful tool for monitoring a server. It provides a visual method for checking performance in real time or from log files. Here's how you use it:

1. In the Monitoring Tools, highlight Performance Monitor. You see a few icons in the Monitoring window.

2. To add counters before so you can get the information you need, click the plus sign (or press Ctrl+I), and the Add Counters window appears.

**NOTE** The counters that are available for Performance Monitor vary, depending on which roles and features were added to this server. Standard counters (for example, processor, paging file) exist for all servers.

3. To add counters to this server, first choose the local machine or server name.

4. Choose what you want to monitor. In this case, add counters for the processor, so scroll to the processor and click the plus sign to the right to expand the available counters.

5. Highlight the counter(s) you want to monitor and click Add.

**NOTE** By holding down the Ctrl key and selecting counters, you can add more than one counter at a time. You can check the Show Description to provide a pane on the bottom of the Add Counters box that includes descriptions of what the counter will monitor.

6. When you have added all the counters you want to monitor, click OK. Figure 12.2 shows the Performance Monitor with added counters.

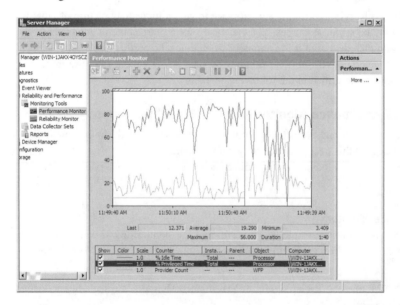

FIGURE 12.2
A view of the Performance Monitor with active counters.

Above the graph are some options (represented by icons) that you can set to customize the Performance Monitor:

▶ **View Current Activity:** This is the active graph. There is nothing to set here.

▶ **View Log Data:** Allows you to view the source of the data being monitored— from the current activity, log files, or a database.

▶ **Change Graph Type:** Allows you to change the graph type. The choices are Line, Histogram, and Report.

▶ **Add:** Allows you to add counters to the Performance Monitor.

▶ **Delete:** Allows you to remove counters from the Performance Monitor.

▶ **Highlight:** Allows you to highlight a selected counter.

▶ **Copy:** Shows all selected counters in the Performance Monitor.

▶ **Paste:** Shows all selected counters in the Performance Monitor.

▶ **Properties:** Contains five tabs:

    ▶ **General:** In this tab, you can set the display elements, report and histogram data, and graph elements.

    ▶ **Source:** In this tab, you can set the data source for the Performance Monitor. The choices are Current Activity, Log Files, and Database. This is the same setting as View Log Data.

    ▶ **Data:** Here you can add counters and change the color, scale width, and style of the graph data.

    ▶ **Graph:** You can change the graph type here. This tab also lets you set the scroll style, title, vertical axis, items to show (vertical and horizontal grid), and vertical scale.

    ▶ **Appearance:** This tab allows you to set the color, font, and border for the Performance Monitor.

▶ **Zoom:** Allows you to zoom into a section of the Performance Monitor.

▶ **Freeze/Unfreeze Display:** Stops the current counters and freezes the display with the currently collected data.

▶ **Update Data:** Allows you to update performance data after unfreezing a display.

---

**NOTE** We will talk later about creating data collector sets. For now, know that if you highlight the Performance Monitor and right-click, you see the option to create a new data collector from the performance counter you have chosen.

---

## Reliability Monitor

Reliability Monitor provides information about system stability and contains detailed information about events that affect server reliability. Reliability Monitor has a system stability chart and calculates a system stability index over the life of the system.

To view the events in the Reliability Monitor, perform the following steps:

1. In Server Manager, expand the Diagnostics console tree and then expand Reliability and Performance and Monitoring Tools. Highlight Reliability Monitor.

2. In the top half of the Reliability Monitor, you see the system stability chart (see Figure 12.3). If you highlight a particular date on the chart, you get a stability index. You can view all dates or select a date from the drop-down box in the top-right corner.

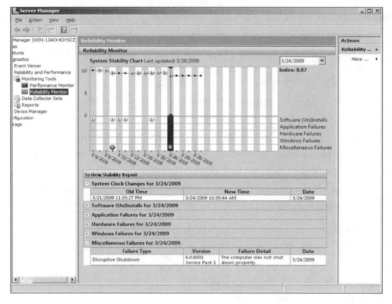

FIGURE 12.3
System stability chart with the system index within the Reliability Monitor.

Directly below the chart are informational and error alerts, which signal that an event took place within one of the five corresponding events. The system stability reports provide detailed information.

3. In the bottom half of the Reliability Monitor, notice the System Stability Report section. The reports shown here are created based on five particular events:

> **NOTE** System Clock Changes is not part of the five events, but this alert shows up whenever there is a change to the server time.

> ► **Software (Un)Installs:** When software is installed, uninstalled, or updated, the event is logged here and includes details for the event, such as software, version, activity, activity status, and date.

▶ **Application Failures:** When there is an application failure, the event is logged here. It includes details for the event, such as application, version, failure type, and date.

▶ **Hardware Failures:** When there is a hardware failure, the event is logged here. It includes details for the event, such as component type, device, failure type, and date.

▶ **Windows Failures:** When there is a Windows failure, the event is logged here. It includes details for the event, such as failure type, version, failure detail, and date.

▶ **Miscellaneous Failures:** When there is a miscellaneous failure, the event is logged here. It includes details for the event, such as failure type, version, failure detail, and date.

The information provided here is alert-type information, and there is nothing to configure. This information allows you to see how stabile your server is, based on how many events take place and the stability index. For instance, a server that is newly built and has all updates performed has a stability index rating of 10. As failures occur, that rating drops. An acute drop in this index indicates that there are serious failures that need to be addressed. The stability reports provide a means of finding the items that need to be addressed.

## Create a Data Collector Set

Data collector sets are used as a foundation for the Reliability and Performance tool. They organize multiple data collections into a single element that is used for reviewing and logging the performance of a system. There are four types of data collector sets: User-Defined, System, Event Trace Sessions, and Startup Event Trace Sessions.

To create new data collector sets, perform the following steps:

1. Highlight the type of data collector set and right-click or choose New, Data Collection Set. The Create New Data Collector Set Wizard appears.

2. Name the data collector set and choose whether to create it from a template (recommended) or to create it manually (for advanced users). Click Next.

3. Choose the template to use, from the following options (see Figure 12.4):

   ▶ **Active Directory Diagnostics:** Used for Active Directory–related data on the local system.

   ▶ **Basic:** Used for creating basic data collector sets. To use this, you must be a member for the Local Administrators group.

   ▶ **System Diagnostics:** Generates a report detailing the status of hardware resources, system response times, and processes on the local system. The report includes suggestions for streamlining operations and maximizing performance using 35 different data collectors.

▶ **System Performance:** Similar to Systems Diagnostics set, this set also generates a report detailing the status of hardware resources, system response times, and processes on the local system. The report can be used to identify possible performance issues. This set uses only 2 data collectors.

Click Next.

4. Choose the directory where you want to save this report and click Next.

5. In this last screen, choose the account under which to run this data collector set, open Properties, start the data collector set or save and close the data collector set, and click Finish.

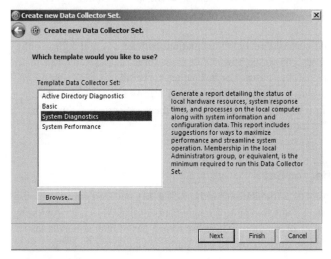

FIGURE 12.4
Choosing a template for a data collector set.

After a data collector set is created, you have to add data collectors. To add new data collectors, perform the following steps:

1. Highlight the data collector set you created and select Action, New Data Collector.

2. When the Create New Data Collector Set Wizard starts, choose the type of data collector from the following:

   ▶ Performance counter data collector

   ▶ Event trace data collector

   ▶ Configuration data collector

   ▶ Performance counter alert

   Click Next.

3. Click Add and choose the performance counter(s) you want to monitor in this collector. Click OK and click Next.

4. Finalize the creation of the data collector. Checking the box opens the properties page, where you can add additional counters and set the log type, time interval, log file name, and format. Click Finish.

## Configure Data Collector Sets

When you have finished creating a data collector set, you can perform a number of tasks on it. Let's look at some of the tasks involved in configuring data collector sets. From the Action menu you can select the following:

▶ **Start:** Causes the data collector set to begin gathering event information for this server.

▶ **Stop:** Causes the data collector set to stop gathering event information for this server.

▶ **Save Template:** Saves this data collector set as a template. This is useful for copying data collector sets to other servers.

▶ **Data Manager:** Sets the data properties for a data collector set. There are three tabs for configuration:

    ▶ **Data Manager:** Sets the following: Minimum Free Disk, Maximum Folders, Resource Policy (Delete Oldest, Delete Largest), Maximum Root Path Size, Report File Name, and Event File Name.

    ▶ **Actions:** Sets the following: View, Add, Edit, or Remove folder actions. In this tab, you can choose a condition (either age, folder size, or both). And you can choose an action for that folder (copy CAB file to directory, create CAB file, delete data files, delete CAB files, delete report).

    ▶ **Rules:** In this tab, you can import or export rule template files for the data collector set.

▶ **Latest Report:** Allows you to view the latest report for this data collector set. We discuss reports later in this chapter.

▶ **Properties:** Contains six tabs.

    ▶ **General:** In this tab, you can see the name, edit the description, add or remove keywords, and change the Run As account.

    ▶ **Directory:** In this tab, you can view or change the root directory, set a subdirectory, choose from 26 different subdirectory name formats, prefix the subdirectory with the computer name, and choose the serial number.

    ▶ **Security:** This tab provides an overview of groups and users, with permissions to this data collector set, and allows you to add/remove/adjust those permissions.

> ▶ **Schedule:** In this tab, you can create a schedule for running the data collector set. You can set the active range (beginning and expiration dates) and choose the times and days to launch the report.

▶ **Stop Condition:** In this tab, you can specify the behavior of the data collector set. You can choose to stop after an overall duration (seconds, minutes, hours, days, or weeks), choose limits such as duration or size, and choose to restart the data set when the limit is reached. Alternatively, you can choose to stop the report when all data collectors have reached their stop conditions.

▶ **Task:** In this tab, you can set a specific task to run when a data collector set stops. You can use task arguments (logs, state, user text) and set task arguments for the user text.

## Use Reliability Reports

After you create data collector sets and run the diagnostics, you need a way to view and analyze this information. The reliability reports in the Reliability and Performance tool present this collection of data in a visual report for easier management. Reliability reports are broken down into two sections: User-Defined and System. The User-Defined section is self-explanatory, based on data collector sets you create. The System section reports are based on preconfigured system data collector sets.

To view reliability reports, perform the following steps:

1. In Server Manager, select Diagnostics, expand the console tree, and highlight Reliability and Performance Monitor. Expand Reports and then expand the User-Defined console tree.

2. Click the report you created earlier, and you see a name based on the subdirectory format and serial number you chose.

3. Highlight this report, and in the main window you see the reliability report (see Figure 12.5).

> **NOTE** For the predefined system reports, you may need to return to the data collector set and choose Action, Start to begin this set. When the diagnostic test is completed, you see a report with subdirectory format and serial number in the Reliability Reports section.

The report is broken down into eight segments:

▶ **System Performance Report:** Contains the computer name, the date and time the data collector was run, and the duration of collection, in minutes.

▶ **Summary:** Contains information about the physical state of the system, including process, disk, memory, and network utilization.

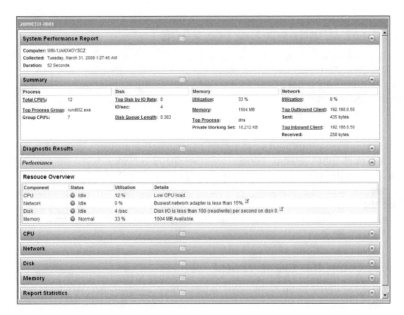

FIGURE 12.5
Overview of a user-defined report.

▶ **Diagnostic Results:** Provides a resource overview. Unlike the resource overview in real time, this snapshot view is taken during data collection.

▶ **CPU:** Provides detailed CPU usage information for processes, services, and systems.

▶ **Network:** Provides information on the network connections for this server, including TCP, interface, IP, and UDP statistics.

▶ **Disk:** Provides information on disk usage, such as hot files, disk breakdown, and physical disk statistics, including reads and writes to disks.

▶ **Memory:** Provides information on the memory of the system. This report is broken into two parts: Process (which shows memory usage on a per process basis) and Counters (where statistics are based on overall memory usage on this server).

▶ **Report Statistics:** Provides information on the computer, collection, files, and processed events.

These reports are useful in providing a detail look at a particular area of your server that may specifically need to be monitored. They also simplify the process of locating and diagnosing issues in your environment.

# Troubleshoot Windows Server 2008

**Scenario/Problem:** You have used the Reliability and Performance tool and now need to understand why a particular event took place and get information on how to correct the event.

**Solution:** Once you have monitored your server and located a problem area, you need to troubleshoot that problem. Windows Server 2008 provides some built-in tools to help you troubleshoot events that take place in your environment. We will look at two specific methods that can be used to assist in troubleshooting Windows Server 2008: the Event Viewer, which many administrators are familiar with already, and several command-line tools that can perform specific troubleshooting tasks.

## Troubleshoot Using the Event Viewer

Event Viewer is a familiar administrative tool that has been around since Windows NT. As Windows Server has improved, so has the Event Viewer, and Windows Server 2008 has made the Event Viewer better than ever by providing better filtering, better search capabilities, and an overall more manageable solution.

To use the Event Viewer to troubleshoot, do the following:

1. In Server Manager, expand the Diagnostics console tree and highlight Event Viewer. You see an Overview and Summary page of events for this server (see Figure 12.6). This is an aggregate view of all events, regardless of the source or type of event.

   This page is broken into four parts

   ▶ **Overview:** Contains information on the type of events that are logged in the Event Viewer and where they can be found.

   ▶ **Summary of Administrative Events:** Provides an overview of all administrative events on this server.

   ▶ **Recently Viewed Nodes:** Provides information about where events have recently taken place on this system.

   ▶ **Log Summary:** Provides information about the event logs, including size (current/max.), modified date, and status.

2. Expand the Event Viewer and notice these four folders:

   ▶ **Custom Views:** In older versions of Event Viewer, you could filter information to create a specific view of events in the logs. With Custom Views, you can now save those filters so that they do not need to be re-created each time. Each server role that is installed in Windows Server 2008 automatically creates this custom view.

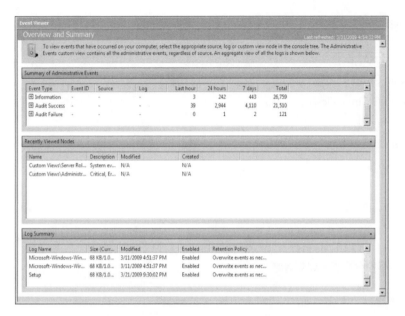

FIGURE 12.6
Overview and Summary page in Event Viewer.

> **Windows Logs:** This folder holds the familiar event log files you are used to seeing in Event Viewer. The Windows logs include Application, Security, Setup, System, and Forwarded Events.

> **Applications and Services Log:** These logs hold events that are specific to an application or a component rather than events that have systemwide effects. There are four categories for these events: Admin, Operational, Analytic, and Debug.

> **Subscriptions:** Troubleshooting an event sometimes calls for gathering information from more than one computer. With event subscriptions, you can collect copies of events from multiple remote computers. These events can then be filtered and viewed by the local server to use in troubleshooting.

## Manage Event Viewer

In earlier versions of Event Viewer, the log files provided troubleshooting information that helped you locate the source of performance issues. In Windows Server 2008, some additional options have been added to make management easier.

The top portion of the Event Viewer shows the event level, date and time, source, event ID, and task category. The bottom portion of the screen shows a detailed description of the event. It also includes a link to Microsoft's online event help, which provides more information (see Figure 12.7). From the Actions pane you can perform the following tasks for the event log:

- ▶ Open Saved Log
- ▶ Create Custom View
- ▶ Import Custom View
- ▶ Clear Log
- ▶ Filter Current Log
- ▶ Properties
- ▶ Find
- ▶ Save Events As
- ▶ Attach a Task to This Log

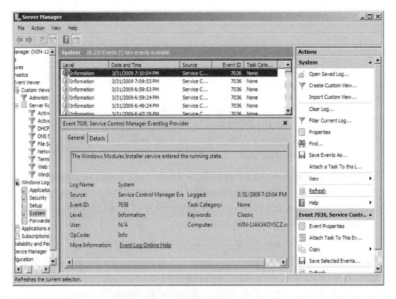

FIGURE 12.7
Detailed view of a system event in Event Viewer.

When you highlight an event, you see the following Action menu items:

- ▶ Event Properties
- ▶ Attach Task to This Event
- ▶ Save Selected Events
- ▶ Refresh

One of the newest Event Viewer features is the ability to attach a task to a log or an event. To see how this works, perform the following steps:

1. Select Action, Attach Task to This Log/Event to launch the Create a Basic Task Wizard.

2. Choose a name and description for this task and click Next.

3. On the next screen, which provides information about the log, source, and event ID, click Next.

4. Choose an action for the task to perform:

   ▶ Start a Program

   ▶ Send an E-mail

   ▶ Display a Message

   Click Next.

5. In the next screen, choose the program or script to launch, create an e-mail and choose the SMTP server, or create a title and message. Click Next.

6. On the last page, where you see the name, description, trigger, and action, click Finish.

## Create a New Subscription

To create new subscriptions, perform the following tasks:

> **NOTE** Creating a subscription requires that both the forwarding and collecting computers be configured. The Windows Remote Management (WinRM) service and the Windows Event Collector (Wecsvc) service must be running on both the forwarding and collecting computers before you create a new subscription.

1. Click Subscriptions in the console tree.

2. Select Action, Create Subscription.

3. On the subscription properties page, set the following:

   ▶ Subscription name

   ▶ Description

   ▶ Destination log

   ▶ Subscription type and source computer

   ▶ Events to collect

   ▶ User account and advanced settings

   Click OK. (After the subscription is created, you can modify these selections by going to the properties page.)

4. Repeat the process on the forwarding computers to complete this subscription.

> **NOTE** You can access the subscriptions properties page from the properties of the Windows logs in the console tree.

## Troubleshoot Using Command-Line Tools

Server 2008 provides a number of command-line tools for troubleshooting:

- ▶ **Auditpol:** Displays information and manipulates audit policies.

- ▶ **Chkdsk:** Checks the file system of a volume for errors (physical and logical).

- ▶ **Dcdiag:** Analyzes a domain controller's state at the forest or enterprise level and reports any problems.

- ▶ **Gpresult:** Displays the resultant set of policy information that can be used to identify issues with Group Policy.

- ▶ **Logman:** Creates and manages event trace session and performance logs. Provides many of the functions of the Performance Monitor, but from the command line.

- ▶ **Nltest:** Troubleshoots configurations on the OS.

- ▶ **Nslookup:** Displays information you can use to diagnose DNS infrastructure.

- ▶ **Recover:** Recovers readable information from a defective disk.

- ▶ **Repadmin:** Diagnoses Active Directory replication problems between domain controllers.

- ▶ **Sc:** Allows you to test and debug service programs.

- ▶ **Wevtutil:** Retrieves information about event logs and publishers, installs event manifests, and runs queries. You can also use it to export, archive, and clear logs.

> **NOTE** For more information on troubleshooting Windows Server 2008, see http://technet.microsoft.com/en-us/library/cc753935.aspx.

# Use the Problem Reports and Solutions

> **Problem/Scenario:** You want to proactively send errors you receive to Microsoft for further diagnosis and possibly get some resolution to your errors in a timely manner.

**Solution:** Problem Reports and Solutions, which is available in the Control Panel, is a tool that utilizes Windows Error Reporting (WER) technology to allow you to see any errors that are being reported in an easy-to-use interface. Not only can you see the errors Microsoft has made, it is much easier to get help with those annoying issues that you just cannot get to the bottom of (that is, if a resolution to the issue is available at the time). Solutions come in a variety of forms, such as the following:

▶ Workaround procedures

▶ Links to the Windows Update site

▶ Links to other websites for updated drivers or patches

▶ Knowledge Base articles

This tool allows you to set the level of consent when sending information to Microsoft. These are the options:

▶ **Allow Each User to Choose Reporting Settings:** This setting allows each user to decide if they will report errors to Microsoft. This can be set to report all errors or completely turned off to not report any errors.

▶ **Ask Each Time a Problem Occurs:** You are always be prompted before sending a report

▶ **Automatically Check for Solutions:** The minimum amount of data is automatically sent so Microsoft can see if there is an available solution. You are prompted before sending any additional data.

▶ **Automatically Check for Solutions and Send Additional Information if Needed:** The minimum amount of data is automatically sent, and any additional data that the developer needs to resolve the issue. This is unlikely to contain any personal identity information.

▶ **Send All Data:** All data concerning the error will be sent to Microsoft. This setting can be selected only with Group Policy (not from the applet in the Control Panel).

**NOTE** You can control the level of consent pertaining to user application errors. For user programs, you can either turn it on, turn it off, or allow each user to choose his or her settings.

In addition to setting your consent levels, you have the ability to block all data from a particular program from being sent. All you need to do is add that application's executable to the block list. Follow these steps to add Notepad to your block list:

1. From the Control Panel, open the Problems Reports and Solutions applet.

2. On the top left of the screen, click Change Settings. Note that you also have the following options (see Figure 12.8):

    ▶ Check for New Solutions

    ▶ See Problems to Check (disabled if there are none)

▶  View Problem History

▶  Clear Solution and Problem History

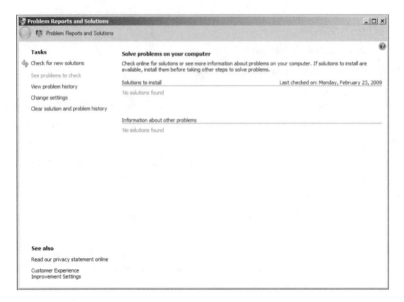

FIGURE 12.8
A look at the Problems Reports and Solutions tool.

3. Choose either Check for Solutions Automatically or Ask Me to Check if a Problem Occurs.

4. To get to the block list page, click Advanced Settings.

5. In the top portion of this page, set the consent levels for your programs and/or your Windows OS (see Figure 12.9).

6. In the lower portion of the page, add a program executable to the block list by clicking the Add button.

7. Navigate to the file you need to block—in this case, notepad.exe. You can either look through all the directories to find it, or you can utilize the search feature on the top right.

8. Highlight the file and click Open (or just double-click the file). You see the file added to the block list in the Problem Reports and Solutions tool. Click OK twice to get back to the first screen. You have successfully blocked any error information generated via Notepad from being sent to Microsoft.

**NOTE** The Problem Reports and Solutions tool can be very useful when you're managing your Windows Server 2008 infrastructure.

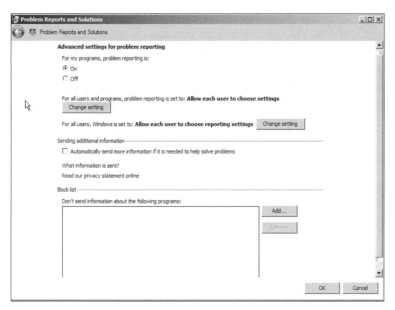

FIGURE 12.9
Set your consent levels and configure the block list.

# Monitor Performance and Troubleshoot in Windows Server 2008 R2

**Scenario/Problem:** Windows Server 2008 R2 will include many improvements and add many new features. What are the new or improved features for monitoring performance and troubleshooting in Windows Server 2008 R2?

**Solution:** Windows Server 2008 R2 will include some new performance monitoring and troubleshooting tools. Enhancements will be made to events and error reporting. These improvements include the following:

▶ Informational alerts about Windows Vista events that pertain to this server.

▶ Information about Windows Server 2008 events.

▶ Suggested procedures for diagnosing and resolving server errors.

▶ Information about how to verify that a server has been returned to a normal operating state.

New to Windows Server 2008 R2 will be the inclusion of the Best Practice Analyzer (BPA). This tool will allow you to take a baseline measurement of the server configuration and compare that baseline to industry standards for best practices for performance.

For more information on performance monitoring and specifically about new enhancements to Event Viewer troubleshooting, see http://technet.microsoft.com/en-us/library/dd299435.aspx.

# Symbols

# A

# F

# G

# T

# X

# Z

# HOW-TO

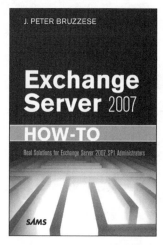

**Exchange Server 2007 How-To**
ISBN-13: 978-0-672-33048-3

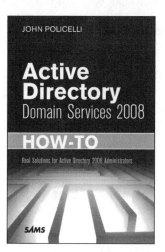

**Active Directory Domain Services
2008 How-To**
ISBN-13: 978-0-672-33045-2

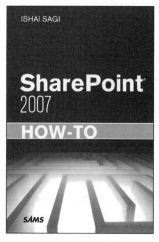

**SharePoint 2007 How-To**
ISBN-13: 978-0-672-33050-6

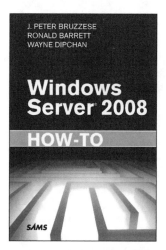

**Windows Server 2008 How-To**
ISBN-13: 978-0-672-33075-9

How-To series books are available at most retail and online bookstores. For more information or to order direct visit our online bookstore at **informit.com/store**

Online editions of all How-To series titles are available by subscription from Safari Books Online at **safari.informit.com**

# UNLEASHED

**Unleashed** takes you beyond the basics, providing an exhaustive, technically sophisticated reference for professionals who need to exploit a technology to its fullest potential. It's the best resource for practical advice from the experts, and the most in-depth coverage of the latest technologies.

**Microsoft SQL Server 2008**
ISBN-13: 978-0-672-33056-8

**Microsoft SQL Server 2008 Analysis Services**
ISBN-13: 978-0-672-33001-8

**Microsoft SQL Server 2008 Reporting Services**
ISBN-13: 978-0-672-33026-1

**Microsoft SQL Server 2008 Integration Services**
ISBN-13: 978-0-672-33032-2

---

**Active Directory 2008 Unleashed**
ISBN-13: 978-0-672-33019-3

**Microsoft Dynamics CRM 4.0**
ISBN-13: 978-0-672-32970-8

**Microsoft ISA Server 2006**
ISBN-13: 978-0-672-32919-7

**Microsoft Office Project Server 2007**
ISBN-13: 978-0-672-32921-0

**Microsoft SharePoint 2007**
ISBN-13: 978-0-672-32947-0

**Microsoft SharePoint 2007 Development**
ISBN-13: 978-0-672-32903-6

**System Center Configuration Manager (SCCM) 2007 Unleashed**
ISBN-13: 978-0-672-33023-0

**Windows Small Business Server 2008**
ISBN-13: 978-0-672-32957-9

---

Unleashed books are available at most retail and online bookstores. For more information or to order direct visit our online bookstore at **informit.com/store**

Online editions of all Unleashed titles are available by subscription from Safari Books Online at **safari.informit.com**

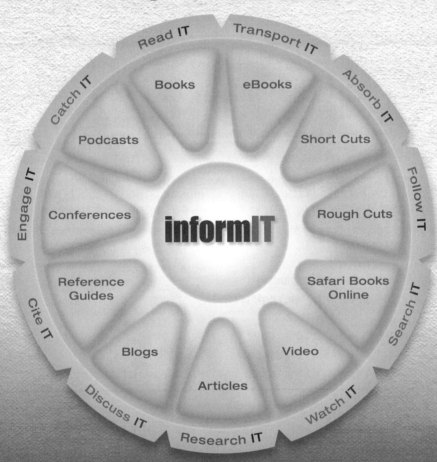

FEB 2010

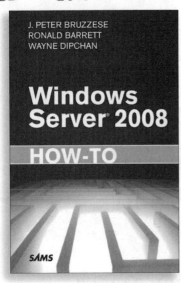

# FREE Online Edition

Your purchase of **Windows Server® 2008 How-To** includes access to a free online edition for 45 days through the Safari Books Online subscription service. Nearly every Sams book is available online through Safari Books Online, along with more than 5,000 other technical books and videos from publishers such as Addison-Wesley Professional, Cisco Press, Exam Cram, IBM Press, O'Reilly, Prentice Hall, and Que.

**SAFARI BOOKS ONLINE** allows you to search for a specific answer, cut and paste code, download chapters, and stay current with emerging technologies.

## Activate your FREE Online Edition at www.informit.com/safarifree

> **STEP 1:** Enter the coupon code: IDDIZAA.

> **STEP 2:** New Safari users, complete the brief registration form.
> Safari subscribers, just log in.

If you have difficulty registering on Safari or accessing the online edition, please e-mail customer-service@safaribooksonline.com